The
Critical
Path

Also by Brock Yates:

SUNDAY DRIVER
THE DECLINE AND FALL OF THE AMERICAN AUTO INDUSTRY
ENZO FERRARI: The Man and the Machine

The Critical Path

Inventing an Automobile and
Reinventing a Corporation

Brock Yates

Little, Brown and Company
BOSTON   NEW YORK   TORONTO   LONDON

First Edition

Library of Congress Cataloging-in-Publication Data

Yates, Brock W.
The critical path : inventing an automobile and reinventing
a corporation / Brock Yates. — 1st ed.
p.   cm.
Includes index.
ISBN 0-316-96708-4
1. Caravan van—Design and construction—History. 2. Voyager
van—Design and construction—History. 3. Chrysler Corporation.
I. Title.
TL230.5.C37Y38 1996
338.7'629222'0973—dc20   96-5856

10 9 8 7 6 5 4 3 2 1

MV-NY
Published simultaneously in Canada
by Little, Brown & Company (Canada) Limited
Printed in the United States of America

To my mother, Marguerite Yates, and
my son, Sean Reynolds, with love
and remembrance.

Contents

Introduction

Please, in the words of the late Richard Nixon, let me make one thing perfectly clear: This book was written *about* Chrysler Corporation, not *for* Chrysler Corporation. I was given the unique privilege of entering their heretofore private precincts to trace the creation of a new vehicle with no constraints whatsoever. No caveats, no prior agreements, no strictures, no demands for copy approval. In fact, the entire project was completed without any discussion of how I would write this book, other than my general verbal description to president Bob Lutz in late 1991. From the moment he agreed to the notion of my documenting the design, manufacture, and sale of his corporation's single greatest automotive project, not a word was ever uttered by anyone within the Chrysler Corporation about how I might treat the subject.

When I proposed the idea of documenting the creation of an automobile to Lutz, I had no idea which car might be on the drawing boards. Coincidentally, Chrysler's new minivan program had just begun to form up and it was obvious to Lutz and myself that this was a prime choice. After all, it was the cornerstone of the Chrysler business. It involved the greatest single gamble, $2.1 billion (later increased to $2.6 billion), in the history of the corporation. At the time Lutz approved the idea, there was no assurance of success, not only for the new vehicle, but for the company itself. Chrysler was in a state of chaos. Its longtime leader and standard-bearer, Lee Iacocca, was ending his reign under intense internal pressure, while a new and unknown entity, CEO Robert Eaton, was preparing to assume control. The new minivan had to work. A failure would simply doom the company, a fact that exerted enormous pressure on the small team that had been assembled to create it.

Like any journalist embarking into uncertain territory, I had no idea where the trail would lead me. I expected hostility and suspicion. I was prepared to be excluded from much of the process and to be escorted constantly by a public relations staffer who would monitor carefully controlled peeks inside the operation. This did not happen. While I never enjoyed total freedom to roam the factories and design spaces, I was given complete access to all meetings, large or small, that involved the minivan project at the design level. Surely there were senior sessions dealing with long-term strategies and proprietary information about corporate finance to which I was not invited, but there was no exclusion from any sessions, day-to-day, relating to the actual making of the vehicle.

If Chrysler had chosen to exclude me from the key elements of the process, the result would have been a faintly blurred and incomplete sketch of the real thing. Thankfully, this did not happen. While the book deals with a number of potential disasters, the overall conclusion — that crossfunctional teams work in modern industry — is clear.

The attitude of openness that greeted me fits a company with confidence in itself. From its leaders, the Bobs Eaton and Lutz, to its senior managers like Tom Gale and Francois Castaing (who play a significant role in the story) to the key minivan team members — Chris Theodore, Tom Edson, Dick Winter, Sham Rushwin and scores of others — the level of cooperation I received was nothing short of amazing. That I was able to operate inside the workings of the minivan platform team on a daily basis can only be confirmed by reading the following, but I truly believe the experience is unique in the annals of journalism.

I wish the idea for this book had risen full blown from my imagination without the input of others. That is hardly the case. Long-time friend and publishing executive Roger Straus III originally suggested such a book nearly a decade ago. Much has changed since then, and a series of circumstances prevented Roger and me from completing the project together. But credit for the idea is exclusively his. To my wife, Pamela, goes thanks for reviving the project following its hiatus after Roger had dropped out of the picture. It was she, following completion of my biography of carmaker Enzo Ferrari, while I was puzzling over another book project, who suggested the call to Bob Lutz which triggered this book. To those two, I owe much in the way of gratitude.

So too for Chris Theodore and Tom Edson, two key members of the minivan platform team, who spent endless hours in my company, patiently explaining the insanely complex details encompassing the creation of a contemporary automobile. They treated me without fail with courtesy and candor, even in situations that implied serious problems within their system. While they remained loyal to the company and to their mission, their honesty in evaluating situations that were less than seamlessly defined corporate policy was invaluable in the creation of this book. I remain supremely grateful for their help.

Brock Yates
Wyoming, N.Y.

The
Critical
Path

1

The Great Farewell

THE FAREWELL was an industrial-strength extravaganza. It was held in Las Vegas, of course, that Nirvana of glitz planted on Nevada's steaming desert. The setting was the immense, fourteen-thousand-seat Thomas & Mack arena, home court of the University of Las Vegas. The date was August 27, 1992. Two eminences shared the stage, one a new automobile that was a harbinger of prosperity, the other an aging tycoon whose personal dynamism had in many ways made this automobile possible.

The vehicle was the new Chrysler LH, a sensuous midsized sedan whose details had long since been leaked to the press but which was having its first official display here. The man was Lido "Lee" Iacocca, Chrysler's famed leader, who would retire at year's end. At the mandatory retirement age of sixty-five he was officially stepping down as chairman of the board and chief operating officer of one of the most famous — if not notorious — automobile companies in the world.

Lee Iacocca was not one to fade away following a brief but eloquent farewell. His retirement date had been well publicized and his successor, ex–General Motors of Europe vice president Robert Eaton, had been on board since March 1992. The "Chairman," as he was known inside the company (also as "Lee" and as "Mr. I," while his given name, "Lido," was considered pejorative and strictly taboo) had let his stand-down expand into a seemingly endless and somewhat vexatious roundelay of testimonials, banquets, factory tours, television interviews, and adoring newspaper and magazine profiles.

Twelve years after being gunned down as the president of the Ford Motor Company, after nearly a decade as the most visible and popular industrial personality in America, Iacocca was quitting the corridors of power with some reluctance.

It was incumbent on the management to usher the great man out in a celebration befitting his position. So there was this monster bash that would serve as his symbolic farewell. It was glittering show business, laden with nostalgia for the past reign and soaring optimism for the future. Celebrities, powerful and beautiful, would be everywhere, as would legions of adoring friends and associates.

The timing seemed perfect. Each year Chrysler, like its rivals at Ford and General Motors, held a series of product introductions for members of the press and their dealer bodies. They began in early summer with "long lead" previews for monthly magazine writers, then with August–September dealer gatherings, and finally with "short lead" presentations in October for the daily press and television. The August date coincided with the planned dealer presentation of Chrysler's revolutionary new LH series sedans, to be marketed as the Dodge Intrepid, the Chrysler Concord, and the Eagle Vision. Dealer previews were not quite as luxurious as in the heady days of the sixties, but they remained clubby gatherings of the rich and powerful, involving the corporate leadership and the most influential of Chrysler's over four thousand franchisees, many of whom had endured decades of feast and famine with the most unpredictable and mistake-prone of the world's major car-makers. This one would be a preview to remember.

The Iacocca farewell party was akin to the planning for D-Day compared with dealer previews of the past. The guest list was enormous, nearly eleven thousand in all, including dealers from Chrysler's three marketing entities, Chrysler-Plymouth, Dodge, and Jeep-Eagle, as well as representatives for the corporation's twenty-three international operations and twelve hundred of its most senior corporate officials. The press was specifically excluded. Four of the largest hotels in Las Vegas, Caesars Palace, the Hilton, Bally's, and the Mirage, were reserved for the throng. This was a command performance — "a forced march" — as one dealer described it. For a fee of $500 per person, the attendees were provided with a hotel room, passes to the various seminars and cocktail parties, and of course admittance to the Iacocca spectacular on Thursday evening.

Although it was easier to lure dealers to Las Vegas than to other cities, the Iacocca farewell had been a difficult ticket to sell. These were tough times in the automobile business and the expenditure of perhaps $3,000 per couple (including airfare and potential gambling losses) seemed steep to many — despite the promise of a uniquely star-studded affair. The pressure placed on dealers by the district managers (the point men who act as liaisons between individual dealers and the corporation) was enormous. In such situations the district manager can flex considerable muscle. Allotments of high-profile, in-demand cars can be manipulated as reward or punishment to individual dealers, while mundane paperwork such as warranty claims, rebates, and parts orders can somehow be expedited to dealers who cooperate in high-priority corporate campaigns. Arms were twisted, and seats were filled.

After a day of meetings and seminars, the throngs of dealers were given Thursday afternoon off to play golf, gamble, or socialize prior to being bused to the arena. The logistical nightmare of hauling eleven thousand well-heeled, occasionally well-oiled car moguls and their spouses by public transport consumed over an hour, but the show began amidst a crescendo of lights and music roughly on schedule at 5:30.

The arena was plunged into darkness and an orchestra began an overture that did battle with the chatter of the crowd. The staging was elaborate enough to leave the black-tied and begowned attendees breathless. A massive false stage had been erected on the floor of the UNLV arena, ten feet tall and roughly five hundred feet square, topped by a gigantic, glowing, five-pointed Chrysler "pentastar" logo. Hidden beneath and shielded by scrims between the arms of the star were the orchestra and three LH sedans that would rise out of the platform on hydraulic lifts. Above the arena, where the basketball scoreboard normally hung, was positioned a four-sided, twenty-by-twenty-foot video screen. One end of the cavernous room was curtained off, with a pair of podiums, one at floor level for lesser lights, the other on a riser reserved for the great man's final words. All speakers were driven onto the arena floor in mint Iacocca-vintage Chryslers.

The first entertainer, veteran impersonator Rich Little, plied the audience with his shopworn repertoire of Nixon and Reagan impressions, eliciting scattered laughter from his overworked routine. Then Tip O'Neill, the retired Speaker of the House of Representatives, eased his considerable bulk to the podium and began a windy and good-humored recollection of his relationship with Iacocca. O'Neill, the classic red-nosed Boston pol, meandered far beyond his mandated three minutes, as he reminisced how he and Iacocca had maneuvered the politically volatile issue of the 1980 Chrysler loan guarantee of $1.6 billion through Congress and how the debt was paid off in less than eight years. It was pure blather, laced with O'Neill's patented Boston brogue, but he held the throng's attention and departed to thunderous cheers as he intoned, "God bless you, Lee and Darrien" (referring to Iacocca's third wife, the flashy fifty-two-year-old — she claimed forty-two — Darrien Dallas Earle, who, with her former husband, had started the successful southern California chain of Red Onion restaurants).

Next up were the 1960-vintage McGuire sisters, who, looking amazingly well-preserved, whisked through a few numbers while insiders commented that lead singer Phyllis had enjoyed a special friendship with Iacocca for years — as well as with the late, unlamented Chicago gang lord Sam Giancana. (Despite his flashy persona and constant public attention, Iacocca was never accused of even the slightest impropriety in the gossipy popular press. The depth of his relationship with Phyllis McGuire remained totally private, as did a long and very close friendship with singer Dinah Shore.)

The program rolled on in seamless fashion with a lubricious Ricardo Montalban reprising his classic Chrysler television commercials that celebrated such elegant nonentities as "Corinthian leather," while Vic Damone crooned a tribute to Iacocca and noted that he had known the great man since starring in a Ford-sponsored NBC television show called *The Lively Ones* back in the early 1960s. Emerson Fittipaldi, the two-time World Grand Prix driving champion and Indianapolis 500 winner who worked as a performance consultant for the Jeep-Eagle division, drove in aboard a shimmering black Lamborghini Diablo and offered a few brief remarks before giving way to the Cartwright family from Cedarsburg, Wisconsin. This brightly scrubbed foursome — mother, father, and two young children — had been the subject of a popular Chrysler television commercial in which their survival in a minivan crash was graphically documented. They spoke with conviction, crediting the van's air bag and other safety components with their escape and creating the impression that it had been the singular humanity of Iacocca to which they owed their lives. Unsaid of course was the fact that during the early stages of air bag research, Iacocca was a vocal critic, arguing that the extra cost would be prohibitive.

Wayne Newton, without whom any Las Vegas affair is minor league, vamped his way through a few boilerplated show tunes before Kenny Rogers appeared, looking fit and confident, to note that he had worked years earlier as a backup singer in a Chrysler announcement show. He then tossed off his classic "Gambler" rendition before rushing to a plane that would take him to a gig in Hawaii.

To the throng in the darkened balconies that arced around the hall, the evening appeared to be zooming ahead with well-oiled precision. But backstage there was trouble. Frank Sinatra, who was scheduled to make a final surprise appearance, had arrived late and was in a surly mood. He had spent the afternoon drinking with his cronies in his Mirage Hotel suite and had neglected to rehearse the version of "My Way" with special lyrics to celebrate the departing Iacocca. Aides attempted to calm the short-fused other "Chairman" as the show oozed along out front. He was appearing as a special favor to his pal Iacocca, whom he had helped with a hopelessly amateurish television commercial in the dark days of 1979. The spot had been filmed, ad hoc, with the pair aimlessly chatting about Chrysler's future while ensconced in the corporate suite in New York's Waldorf Towers. Sinatra came across as a hesitant, blundering dolt while Iacocca offered none of the cocky, contentious "If you can find a better car, buy it" demeanor he was to develop with more experience and better direction. The official company position was that Sinatra had done the commercial as a favor, but in fact, according to insiders, he had been rewarded with some cozy stock options that generated substantial profit when Chrysler made its comeback. Sinatra also benefited from a 1984 Special Edition of the Imperial that bore his name — although the vehicle represented the worst in the outdated, Vegas-casino chrome and vinyl glitz styling that both he and Iacocca preferred.

As Sinatra simmered backstage, Chrysler president Bob Lutz drove into the arena aboard an audacious red Viper with veteran race driver, Cobra sports car creator, and old Iacocca pal Carroll Shelby. They rambled through some easy repartee before leisurely giving way to Robert Eaton, the new chairman and Iacocca's appointed successor. Eaton spoke briefly and crisply, fully aware that his time in the spotlight must be brief until Iacocca disappeared from the scene. Eaton in turn introduced Ben Bidwell, who had been a fellow executive, crony, and court jester for Iacocca at both Ford and Chrysler. He was to introduce the great man himself. Meanwhile, backstage, a percolating Sinatra began threatening to leave and return to his hotel.

Iacocca, the quintessential dream-weaver and perhaps one of the great street orators of modern times, was on his game for his final appearance. He spoke of his time at Chrysler as "five years of pure hell and five years of tall cotton" before the stock market crash of 1987 once again nearly brought Chrysler to its knees. Like his tenure as boss, his speech was a series of highs and lows, statesmanlike and measured at times, hard-edged and defiant at others. He had the crowd in his thrall. They understood that for all his chimerical visions, his daredevil sales tactics, his tough-guy muscling of executives and dealers, his failed adventures purchasing aerospace enterprises and wobbly Italian car companies, he was the last of the great car moguls, the last of a breed of men who, through their own personal charisma and audacity, could shove massive corporations in any direction they chose. The audience realized that when he stepped away from the podium the corporation would embark on a new and more measured course. The speech was perfect Iacocca, delivered with the blunt purity that was the essence of the man.

His final line, composed either by himself — as he was inclined to ad lib — or by veteran Iacocca speechwriter Mike Morrison (who had also ghostwritten his syndicated newspaper column), declared, "Chrysler won't be the same without me. It'll be better!" Then he strode into the darkness amidst cheers and a powerful explosion of music from the orchestra concealed beneath the pentastar.

He was gone. The arena went dark for a moment, then a single spotlight probed down from the ceiling, catching a blinking, clearly miffed Sinatra as he was escorted toward the pentastar centerpiece. He was handed a wireless mike and, after a second or two spent angrily scanning the crowd, started uncertainly in patent leather elevator shoes up one of the spikes of the pentastar.

Panic spread through the Chrysler operatives stationed on the floor. Sinatra was blearily wobbling upward, tightroping along with the orchestra pit yawning below. One misstep and the final act of the night would end with Sinatra executing a half-gainer into the brass section. Worse yet, TelePrompTers with the special lyrics had been stationed at the base of the giant logo, almost ten yards from the teetering singer. From where he was, he'd need binoculars to read the words. The orchestra began and the audience, sensing a grand, emotional moment, fell silent. But Sinatra faltered as the immense video screens pulsed with the scenes of Iacocca's triumphs, including his controversial, much-publicized heading of the committee to renovate the Statue of Liberty. The lyrics were keyed to the pictures, but nothing was in sync. Sinatra was waffling through "My Way," a song that he had sung perhaps ten thousand times, appearing to be too addled to remember the words of a pop classic that had become his trademark. Puzzlement engulfed the crowd as the Chrysler aides darted into the orchestra pit, preparing themselves to act as human nets should Old Blue Eyes tumble. (In the aftermath of the faux pas, a good news/bad news joke passed through Chrysler: the good news was that Sinatra could hide his own Easter eggs.)

The band played on dutifully, blaring through the entire number as Sinatra jerkily lapsed back into the original lyrics and staggered through the song. He then descended from the set without further damage to his body or his reputation.

The giant cavern went dark for a moment before a barrage of fireworks exploded, filling the place with deafening sound and rainbows of light. Out of the pentastar rotunda rose the new LH sedans as the cast of personalities surged onto the stage to join a scowling Sinatra. The affair, planned and choreographed to perfection, mercifully dribbled to a halt.

The faltering finale had seemed appropriate, even metaphorical, to many. The leader himself was now viewed by most as something less than the cocksure persona that had dominated the company for over a decade. It was time for a change and the strange behavior of Sinatra had symbolically underlined that necessity.

Regardless of his fame among the masses and the waning respect he still generated among the world's automotive community, there were many in Chrysler's management who believed that Iacocca had run out his string. It was agreed that he had saved the company in the dark year of 1979. Jimmy Carter's January 7, 1980, signature of the controversial Chrysler bailout bill provided almost $1.6 billion in federal loan guarantees to the reeling corporation. Contingent on the government funds was $2 billion in private loans from banks, financial institutions, dealer groups and suppliers, plus United Auto Worker concessions of $462.5 million. That, plus another $150 million in loans from the state of Michigan and myriad other deals, for the most part engineered by the personal persuasion of Iacocca, pulled Chrysler back from the brink of bankruptcy. By 1984 Iacocca was trumpeting record profits of $2.38 billion, thanks in part to ruthless cost cutting and a new product line, based on endless permutations of the compact K-car platform, which had been on the drawing board prior to Iacocca's arrival but was generally credited to him. This mundane four-door sedan had, through brilliant product planning, been stretched and shrunk, trimmed and retrimmed, gussied and regussied, to everything from the rakish Daytona sports coupe to an absurd limousine — reportedly produced specifically for Iacocca's pal New York rental car and tour business mogul "Billy" Fugazy.

But the true salvation of the Chrysler product line was the minivan. Introduced in late 1983 as the Dodge Caravan and the Plymouth Voyager, it was a breakthrough vehicle, a rare product that created an entire new market category for Chrysler and the automobile industry as a whole. This brilliant little box also predated Iacocca's arrival at Chrysler, but he was quick to place his imprimatur on its success and would relish the credit as it was elevated to crown-jewel status for the corporation. Thanks to the minivan and other ingenious variations spun off the K-car platform, Chrysler's profits zoomed in the mid-1980s, and by 1987 Iacocca was able to repay the government loan in its entirety, which further enhanced his reputation as a prophet of American business.

But by 1991 Iacocca's image within the well-protected and status-conscious precincts of Chrysler's Highland Park headquarters was unraveling at an alarming rate. His buying binge in the mid-1980s — American Motors, Gulfstream Aerospace, Finance America, Lamborghini, Maserati, Electrospace Systems, and four small, nearly defunct rental companies,* plus a huge buyback of Chrysler stock — had left the company in desperate shape. Its pension plan was underfunded by $2.7 billion; the American Motors acquisition, which in the long term was a wise move, had initially left Chrysler with acres of unusable factory space and had boosted its breakeven point (the point at which the company could realize a profit from vehicles sold) from 1.1 million vehicles to 1.9 million a year. Worse yet, his increasingly imperious and impetuous management style, coupled with his legendary ego, had triggered key defections from the executive suite, including his heir apparent, Gerald "Jerry" Greenwald, and longtime financial wizard Frederick Zuckerman.

At the core of the problem was the reality that Chrysler was product-poor. Iacocca's outside purchases had drained funds for replacing the frumpy K-car. Iacocca remained convinced that the little machine could be endlessly modified and altered into all manner of vehicle types. By the time it became obvious even to him that radical, aerodynamic machines like Ford's Taurus were leaving Chrysler in the dust, it was nearly too late. In 1990 profits plunged to a piddling $68 million in an increasingly soft automo-

*Iaccoca picked up Dollar, Thrifty, General, and Snappy while Ford was buying a controlling interest in industry leader Hertz and General Motors was obtaining National and Alamo. Dollar, General, and Thrifty were to be combined while Snappy was sold. In ensuing years the Big Three would use their rental fleets both to unload slow-selling models and to introduce new models in test markets.

bile market. A year later, Chrysler's losses soared disastrously, to $795 million, and in February 1991 both Standard & Poor's and Moody's Investors Service downgraded Chrysler's debt rating to junk status based on its aging products and a critical shortfall in its corporate pension fund.

In his last year, Iacocca tirelessly touted a long-term commitment to new product development of $17.3 billion to stem the criticism. The expected arrival in 1992 of the revolutionary new LH sedans would surely help. But the corporation he had saved was once again flirting with oblivion. In January 1991, the situation was so critical that Robert Lutz, the president of Chrysler, confessed to an acquaintance, "If we can stay in business for another eighteen months, when the LH and the new Jeep get to market, we *might* survive. But that is by no means certain."

Lutz made it through his eighteen-month deadline, but with few dollars to spare. He would later admit privately that during some months of 1991 there was doubt that Chrysler had sufficient funds to meet its weekly payroll. But not one dime had been diverted from the various emergency programs to develop new products — the only possible salvation for the company.

Despite the desperate circumstances, the boss maintained his stranglehold on the company. After Greenwald had departed in May 1990, the board of directors panicked. Lutz had already established a legion of fierce enemies within the hierarchy and suddenly the loss of Iacocca became a terrifying thought. To say they overreacted is an understatement. Iacocca's salary was bumped to $4.6 million with the added perk of 123,750 extra shares of common stock. Moreover, the board offered him 62,500 additional shares for each quarter he remained after December 31, 1991. The board also agreed to purchase his two sumptuous homes, one in the royal compound of all Detroit automotive kings and princes, Bloomfield Hills, and a second in Boca Raton, Florida.

At the same time the once-loved leader ordered deep and ruthless reductions in the workforce. By the time the $3 billion program of cuts was completed, over eleven thousand white-collar workers were on the street. But throughout the bloodletting Iacocca continued to live in imperial splendor. The company's new twin-engine

Gulfstream G4, the most elegant business jet in the world, served as his and his wife's personal air limousine. Everywhere he traveled bodyguards, personal aides, and public relations men followed in a retinue befitting the leader of a NATO power. In the midst of the layoffs, rising losses, and the shame of being displaced by both Honda and Toyota in domestic sales, word leaked out that Iacocca had spent almost $2 million to remodel the Waldorf Towers executive suite in New York. Union leaders were outraged, while even Iacocca's most ardent allies were left to grope for excuses. The great man seemed to be losing it.*

There were last-hour theatrics — Iacocca did not want to retire, to put it mildly — but the transition to the new administration took place without a major bloodletting. Robert Eaton, the former vice president of General Motors of Europe, was already on board since March 1992 as vice chairman and chief operating officer. A quiet, round-faced engineer from Kansas, Eaton appeared antithetical in style not only to the man he would succeed but to the one he beat out for the top job at Chrysler. That was Robert A. Lutz, a well-born man with a dazzling record that included marine aviation and a Phi Beta Kappa key from Berkeley, who had appeared to be the anointed successor to Iacocca — one step up from the president's job he had held since January 1991. Then came Eaton's shocking appointment and widespread predictions that a convulsive revolution at Highland Park was inevitable, that Eaton and Lutz, individuals with opposite management and cultural backgrounds, would engage in a bloody struggle for power as soon as Iacocca left the building. Yet considering the potential for warfare, the departure of the legendary chairman had been amazingly tranquil.

But now an entirely new game was about to begin. And the situation Chrysler faced was nothing short of desperate. Iacocca had ridden the K-car into the ground. But he and Lutz had overseen the early development of a new generation of thoroughbreds.

*On more than one occasion his lusty drinking nearly caused a public relations disaster. During the bachelor party preceding his marriage to third wife Darrien, he was accosted by a stripper who draped her ample breasts around Iacocca's neck. Amidst the laughter a photo was taken by an unidentified guest. As the photographer was easing away through the kitchen he was captured by Iacocca friend George Steinbrenner, who seized the film.

The LH sedans, already receiving the plaudits of the motoring press prior to their introduction, were to be part of the opening salvo. As radical and curvaceous as the K-cars they replaced were boxy and archaic, the LHs featured so-called cab-forward design. By moving the wheels to the outer edges of the chassis and shifting the entire passenger compartment toward the front, a large cavity for people and luggage was created, along with an aggressive, low-snouted shape that was a dramatic departure from the competition. The LHs would be second in a barrage of new products spewing out of the cash-strapped corporation. The all-new Jeep Grand Cherokee — a design legacy obtained from the American Motors acquisition — had already reached the market in late 1991. To follow in 1992 would be the firm's bull-nosed light pickup truck to be sold as the Dodge Ram. A year later would arrive other "cab forward" designs in the form of a midsized four-door to be marketed as the Dodge Stratus, the Chrysler Cirrus, and the Neon subcompact. But the capstone of the $17 billion new-product blitzkrieg would be the replacement minivan. This would be the ultimate gamble; big casino as Chrysler attempted to update a vehicle that had served as the corporate crown jewels and had, for all intents and purposes, kept Chrysler away from bankruptcy for a decade. Code-named "NS," the new minivan would be the final arbiter between success and failure. If it sold, Chrysler would survive. A bad job, and the corporation would be but a dim memory by the turn of the century.

The designation "NS" meant nothing outside a small team of engineers and marketing types within Chrysler, but its broader designation, "minivan," enjoyed worldwide recognition. Unknown two decades earlier, Chrysler's title minivan was a veritable Goliath within the automobile industry. Much envied and much copied from Tokyo to Stuttgart, the minivan was considered, properly, to be the single element that had kept Chrysler afloat during the roller-coaster ride that was the corporation's history in the 1980s. Since its introduction in late 1983, it had become the cornerstone of the Iacocca legend, a machine that he claimed (with the all-encompassing, proprietary rights of a powerful, egocentric CEO) to be his creation. That was a stretch at best, but there was no debating that his early recognition of the little box's market potential was critical to its success.

Within the hundred-odd years of the automobile business there have been but a handful of legitimate milestone vehicles — automobiles that turned and expanded the market in new directions due to their revolutionary qualities. Ford's immortal Model T was the first and perhaps the most important. Surely Ferdinand Porsche's Volkswagen Beetle was another, as was Chevrolet's cheap but powerful 1955 Bel Air and Ford's cute and similarly cheap Mustang of a decade later. Honda's first Civic, tiny, roomy, and reliable, came ten years after that, to be followed in roughly the same cycle by Chrysler's breakthrough minivan. It was a box, pure and simple, the most efficient packaging shape known to man. Its appeal to families, to housewives, to small businessmen, and to the burgeoning population of baby boomers was shocking, instantaneous, and stupefyingly profitable to a corporation comfortably and complacently entrenched as America's third automaker.

At the time of Iacocca's farewell extravaganza, Chrysler was nearing its four-millionth minivan sold. By comparison, that number was nearly one-half of the *total* vehicles — cars, sport-utilities, and light trucks — sold by Chrysler over the past decade. Literally every major rival in the business, including General Motors, Ford, Toyota, Nissan, and Mazda, had tried their own variations of the Chrysler machine and all had fallen wide of the mark. Chrysler dominated half the minivan market, despite the incessant challenges.

Eaton and Lutz's gamble — their bid for Chrysler's survival — was to create, from a clean sheet of paper, the "NS," a minivan that stepped boldly past all competitors and imitators and maintained Chrysler's dominance of the minivan market. It had to succeed. There was no room for error. Pressure was increasing by the day. Ford was once again on the attack, with a new van due in 1994, a full year before Chrysler's would reach the public. General Motors and Toyota, both of which had botched their early attempts to produce a serious threat, were unlikely to repeat their mistakes as they readied upgraded models for introduction in the mid-1990s. No one in the Chrysler hierarchy retained illusions that their market share was inviolate. Buffing and cleaning the crown jewels would not suffice. Mining, cutting, polishing, and elegantly mounting an entirely new set was the only possible alternative.

Friday morning, as bleary-eyed dealers and executives crowded Las Vegas's McCarran Airport on their way home from Iacocca's farewell bash, a small cadre of men and women were back in Auburn Hills, heads down, wielding technological picks and shovels in that pivotal mission. Only three years to go, $2.1 billion to marshal. There was no time for rest and no room for error.

2

Building the Box

BELLY UP to any upscale bar in Detroit and you're likely to encounter at least one industry insider who will lament that had he not been cursed with cretinous, tunnel-visioned bosses, *he* would be renowned as the father of the minivan. Feed him a few drinks and he will pledge to provide written documentation of his prescience. He might even be telling the truth: The notion of a tiny, garage-sized personal van had been noodled around by perhaps hundreds of Detroit designers and engineering types since the early 1950s, but little or nothing materialized from their visions.

When Chrysler's first minivan exploded into the marketplace as a 1984 model, there was universal acknowledgment — much of it grudging — that Chrysler's minivan, marketed as the Dodge Caravan and the Plymouth Voyager, was a stroke of genius. Some even claim it was the first truly original vehicle to be produced in Detroit since the Ford Model T.

While the public perceived Chrysler minivans as all-new and embraced them with unexpected ardor, they were far from unvarnished originals. For decades car companies had circled the concept with near misses, machines that rivaled the Caravans and Voyagers in size and purpose but missed the mark because of design deficiencies mandated by budgetary constraints, marketing myopia, or a combination of both. Despite the incessant crowing that issues from the automobile industry about "all-new" or "original" cars, most such claims are egregious bragging. Automobiles are seldom created from blank sheets of paper. They are the result of steady, incremental development, metamorphosed from exist-

ing designs employing mechanical components already in the corporate inventory. The aged trick of updating basic platforms (the
same chassis, engines, suspensions, gearboxes, wheelbases, tracks,
etc.) by "reskinning" or "perfuming the pig" with fresh sheet metal
is a cheap and effective marketing tactic. Of course, car-makers do
sometimes begin from the ground up — as in the recent cases of
Chrysler's LH sedans, Ford's sales-leading Taurus and Sables, and
the minivans — but such a process involves wagering billions in attempting to divine the future tastes of the public. Evolution is still
safer than revolution, especially in Detroit. European and Japanese
manufacturers have traditionally been more inclined to sell the
same models for cycles of four to six years before introducing totally new versions, while the domestics played the "all-new" game
with basic vehicles that were sometimes as much as twenty years
old. American manufacturers began to follow suit in the 1980s,
having discovered that consumers were increasingly skeptical
about their sheet-metal masquerades.

Thirty years ago, during the boom decade of the sixties, the Big
Three treated the annual restyling game as a quasi-religion. Year
after year the same automobiles appeared in showrooms; tarted-up
clones essentially unchanged since their creation. The market was
strong and competition, save for a scattering of imports, was
nonexistent. Why gamble on new models when the public was gob-
bling up the same old iron? After all, hadn't General Motors tried
to break fresh ground with the Corvair, only to be pilloried by
Ralph Nader, the American Trial Lawyers, and the U.S. Congress?
Prudence being the obvious alternative, the industry turned in-
ward, contenting itself with the mundanities of annual restyling
promotions.

In this atmosphere of isolation and paranoia any notions of a
minivan were confined to perhaps a few long-forgotten designers,
although rough drafts of the concept were already plying the American roads. The zany Volkswagen Microbus, which appeared in
1949, and the Corvair Greenbriar, introduced eleven years later,
were prototypes of the new concept. Both were rear-engined, underpowered, and cursed with swing-axle rear suspension systems
that made them unstable and unpredictable. The Microbus was to

become a favorite among sixties flower children and California surfers, while the Greenbriar disappeared in a wave of anti-Corvair publicity and poor sales before the decade ended.

Ford and Chrysler trailed into the marketplace in the mid-1960s with the Ford Econoline and Dodge E-100 vans that were designed for the small commercial delivery market. Both were front-engine, rear-drive machines, meaning that any advantage in additional interior room was nullified by the intrusion of the engine bay between the front seats and the driveshaft running below the length of the cabin. It is therefore not surprising that the utility of these small boxes escaped the leaders of the industry, although Detroit did begin producing full-sized, front-engine, rear-drive delivery vans in the late 1960s.

Following the lead of customizers, the Big Three began equipping them with lavish passenger interiors, large V8s, and the same power options available on luxury sedans. The big vans had wide appeal, both as commercial transporters and as elaborate touring machines, but because of their great size and relative inefficiency they were unsatisfactory substitutes for workaday sedans and the still-popular station wagons.

The obvious opportunity lay in creating a van with more power and better handling than the VW but with less bulk. Such a concept was casually explored in design studios around Detroit, but it took the audacity of a few men and the quirkiness of a notorious auto mogul to bring it to market.

Of all the various studies that were being considered for a so-called minivan in the late 1960s, perhaps the one that had the greatest potential for a breakthrough was created not at Chrysler Corporation but in the crosstown engineering and styling spaces of the Ford Motor Company. One of the company's most creative thinkers, designer Don DeLaRossa, had penciled a version of the VW and Corvair that utilized a critical variation: front-wheel drive. A veteran stylist, DeLaRossa started his career following World War II as an apprentice at Buick before moving to Ford, where in the early 1960s he worked on the creation of the megahit Mustang. When Ford acquired the noted Italian coachbuilding firm Carrozzeria Ghia a decade later, DeLaRossa commuted between Turin and Dearborn, gaining in the process an awareness of the Europeans' penchant for efficient packaging and small, efficient vehicles. He therefore identified front-wheel drive as the essential ingredient for maximizing interior space without the handling penalties accrued by hanging the engine and transmission off the back of the chassis like a caboose, as had been done with the Microbus and the Greenbriar.

The late 1960s was a period of heightened concern within the industry for enhanced fuel efficiency and reduced engine pollution. As a result, standard station wagons had become smaller and lower, which in turn reduced their cargo and passenger capacity. It seemed logical to DeLaRossa and several of his associates in the Ford design studio that the concept of a small van with front-wheel drive might replace the wagon and open a whole new market. Gene Bordinat, Ford's chief designer and DeLaRossa's boss, identified the concept as a viable suburban transport module: a functionally sized box that could be employed for family hauling and shopping errands more efficiently than the conventional station wagon. But despite Bordinat's and DeLaRossa's enthusiasm, their concept — internally dubbed "Mini/max" — was buried by the company's distraction with muscular, gadget-laden sedans like the LTD, the Torino, and the Thunderbird. The American mass market, it was believed, remained mesmerized by the flash and chromy panache of big cars and, save for a tiny claque of progressives in the Ford hierarchy, the "Mini/max" seemed as silly and irrelevant as the handful of Datsuns and Toyota sedans that were beginning to trickle into southern California.

Lee Iacocca retained an iron grip on Ford at the time, operating as the powerful regent within the notoriously Balkanized organization of Henry Ford II, the profligate, spoiled, willful, and capricious grandson of the great automotive pioneer. Iacocca had risen to power in the singularly political atmosphere at Ford thanks to his skills as a salesman and the stunning success of the 1964 Mustang sports coupe. This machine, an artful patchwork of bits and pieces scavenged from Robert McNamara's Bauhaus Ford Falcon economy car, propelled Iacocca to the chair at the right hand of the Emperor Henry. With him rose Harold "Hal" Sperlich, a restless, ascerbic, but brilliant product planner who — perhaps more than any other individual — had done the nuts-and-bolts design work on the Mustang. Sperlich had been raised in the small city of Saginaw, Michigan, the son of a plumber with a proud ancestry of German artisans and craftsmen. Like many young men who grew up in pre–World War II Michigan, Sperlich considered little but a career in the automobile industry, and following his graduation from that great fountainhead of auto executives, the University of Michigan at Ann Arbor, hooked on with Ford.

Audacious from the start, with an innate sense of proper design and engineering, Sperlich had talents that were spotted by Iacocca as he and a group of young lions moved up at the Ford Division in the early 1960s. Their job was to revive it from the slumber created by the reign of Robert McNamara (who went on to apply his empty technocratic vision on an international scale as secretary of defense under Kennedy and Johnson). The team's masterpiece was the Mustang, which launched Iacocca, Sperlich, division manager Don Frey, and stylists Joe Oros and Gene Bordinat on a fast track within the company.

Unable to suffer fools and lacking the Machiavellian political skills of Iacocca, Sperlich made powerful enemies within the financial and marketing departments. Despite the triumph of the Mustang, both groups were rooted in empirical thinking, suspicious of the kind of creativity and daring needed to bring new products to market. "Henry Ford was a slave to these people," recalls Sperlich. "He believed as they did: that you could only expand existing markets, not create new ones. Ford Motor Company could only take a bigger slice of an existing pie, but could never create a bigger pie, according to them." It was this brand of ossified thinking — which permeated the entire Detroit industry — that was to ultimately drive Sperlich out of Dearborn.

But thanks to Iacocca's patronage, he continued to wield considerable influence until 1970. At that point Henry Ford, increasingly irritated by Sperlich's outspoken tactics, vetoed Iacocca's plan to promote him to head the company's European operation. Despite this vote of no-confidence, Sperlich was unrepentant in his conviction that revolutionary changes were necessary in the way American automobiles were designed and built if they were to remain competitive. A steady downsizing trend, triggered by the Volkswagen and exploited in full by the Japanese, was expanding. Consumers were seeking smaller, better built, more fuel-efficient automobiles, while pressures for increased levels of safety and radically lower levels of pollution were intensifying in Washington and among the opinion leaders of the nation. These harbingers of a major upheaval were for the most part ignored in the Detroit executive suites. Progressives like Sperlich were dismissed as Chicken Littles who failed to understand that American's fascination with big horsepower, glitz, and gadgetry enjoyed a Mt. Rushmore–like permanency.

But the automotive world was tilting on its axis. A majority of the major European manufacturers were moving toward front-wheel-drive systems, which allowed the entire drivetrain, i.e., engine, transmission, and differential, to be packaged with the front wheels, thereby increasing passenger compartment space *and* reducing weight (by eliminating the driveshaft, which connected the rear wheels to the front-mounted engine). As the decade of the 1970s opened, Volkswagen, Fiat, Renault, Citroën and British Motors Corporation — which had produced the breakthrough Austin Mini and the Morris Mini Minor — were hard at work on new front-wheel-drive designs. Even more ominous (although completely disregarded in Detroit) was tiny Honda's upstart Civic. This brilliant, three-door hatchback was a near perfect refinement of the Mini Minor. Coming as it did from a motorcycle manufacturer that had been in the car business less than ten years, the Civic was reviled by the Big Three as too small and cramped for American tastes. That is, until it and other Japanese products had captured *half* the bellwether California market by the mid-1970s.

Adding to Sperlich's frustration was Ford's response to the so-called import invasion. It had come in the form of the eminently ordinary Pinto, a smallish coupe with a conventional rear-drive layout and a lumpy, low-output four-cylinder engine. General Motors, equally myopic, came to market with its rear-drive Vega. It would join the Pinto among the most poorly conceived vehicles ever to be produced by major auto manufacturers.

Increasingly isolated from the mainstream marketers at Ford by his advocacy for front-wheel drive (the cost of developing new engines and combination transmission-differentials called "trans-axles" being the primary objection), Sperlich and his group began laying down the designs for the Fairmont, a conventional midsized sedan, while engaging part-time in advanced design exercises. One such long-range project was the subcompact front-wheel-drive Fiesta sedan that was to be produced in Spain prior to Sperlich's departure from Ford. Sperlich had also been an enthusiastic advocate of the moribund DeLaRossa/Bordinat Mini/max idea.

The 1973 Yom Kippur war triggered the OPEC fuel crisis and a fevered distraction in Detroit for more efficient, high-mileage automobiles. Within months every executive in the Big Three was touting front-wheel-drive sedans as the savior of the industry. Suddenly the Mini/max made sense and Sperlich commissioned a series of market studies on the viability of such a machine. The expert who carried out Sperlich's order was a quirky researcher from the Polish neighborhoods of Detroit named Norman Krandall. It was said that Krandall found a kind of perverse pleasure in shooting down — with hard numbers — the conventional thinking of the corporate sales and marketing experts. This time Krandall amazed even himself. His first set of data indicated a potential new market for the Mini/max of 800,000 units a year! Skeptical, he did a second study. The same result. This astounding figure would not, according to his findings, cannibalize sales from existing Ford products but embodied an entirely *new* market — one that promised to be twice the size of the much-celebrated first-year Mustang production figures and was vastly more profitable because of a potential sticker price of over $10,000. If Krandall was initially reluctant to accept the existence of such a vast untapped market, he was a Pollyanna compared to the company's finance and marketing staffs, who might as well have been presented with a formula for perpetual motion or the discovery of the Lost Chord. Krandall's revelations were summarily dismissed.

Unrepentant, Sperlich constructed a prototype in secret. Code-named "Wolf," the little van was powered by a Honda Civic engine and transaxle simply because no such components were available inside Ford. While imperfect and underpowered, the little machine showed potential, and budgeting plans ($600 million) were formulated. Iacocca later claimed that he approached Soichiro Honda, the founder and patriarch of the fast-rising car manufacturer, to purchase 300,000 engine/transaxle units but was turned down. It didn't matter; the entire concept was rejected by the senior management at Ford. But exactly how and why the Mini/max was killed remains a mystery — especially as it relates to Lee Iacocca's role.

In his autobiography, Iacocca claims that he was an early advocate of the Ford Mini/max and places the blame for its demise squarely on Henry Ford II. But David Halberstam, whose insightful 1986 book, *The Reckoning*, traces the rise of Nissan and the fall of Ford during the prior two decades, indicates that in fact Krandall's findings got little support from either Iacocca or any other member of Ford's senior management. Iacocca wrote that Henry II rejected the idea by grousing that the company did not indulge in "experiments." But the reality remains that apart from Krandall and Sperlich, who was about to be fired, and Bordinat's design team, who were often dismissed as airheaded *artistes*, this singular opportunity was discredited and ultimately ignored by virtually every influential occupant in the Dearborn Glass House.

This dereliction of vision at Ford, which might be described as one of the most costly mistakes in the history of the automobile industry, was almost repeated by their rival. Chrysler Corporation, that traditionally star-crossed, chronically cash-poor, and at best marginal member of the Big Three, had been in the large van business since the early 1970s. Their bulky, front-engine, rear-drive Dodge Ram series had led the industry in the expansion from stark commercial vehicles into family cruisers with plush interiors, carlike stereo systems, and luxury-level power options. By the middle 1970s, a small cadre of Truck Division designers and engineers became convinced, like their discredited Ford counterparts, about the potential for a new compact van with carlike manners that could be housed in a normal garage. A leader of this group was G. Glenn Gardner, the chief of product planning for the Dodge Truck Division. Gardner had assembled a small team of engineers and designers with the notion of creating what they referred to as a "super van." Like the defunct Ford project, it was to be powered by a compact front-drive power unit. To compete with the Japanese, Chrysler had rushed to market in 1976 with its tiny front-drive Dodge Omnis and Plymouth Horizons, but their 65 hp four-cylinder engines were simply too feeble to propel Gardner's notion of a "super van." By the mid-1970s it was becoming increasingly evident to even the most hidebound Chrysler executive that the corporation lacked the financial muscle to compete head-to-head, model-to-model, with Ford and General Motors. An all-purpose, generic automobile was needed to save the company: midsized and economical to build, operate, and maintain; a machine that could be adapted to a variety of body styles without major investment. The vehicle, code-named "K-car," was intended as a last-hour, all-or-nothing chance to keep Chrysler from going the way of Nash, Studebaker, Hudson, Willys, Packard, and Kaiser-Frazer — all of them major car-makers that had been driven from the market since the end of World War II.

The tiny cadre of "super van" advocates, led by Gardner, his boss, Dodge Truck Group vice president Gordon Cherry, fellow product planner Bruce Benedict, stylist Dick McAdam, and advanced engineering specialist Leo Walsh, believed that the K-car drivetrain could form a cheap and practical basis for their little van. They were to be joined by other progressives in the company, including a pair of young, fresh-faced designers named Tom Gale and John Herlitz, who would create the internal packaging and ergonomics. This was, in all but name, a "team" concept: a small crew of men from various disciplines working toward a tightly focused goal. Such efforts were not unknown in the industry. All of the Big Three had employed the team tactic on various occasions; Gardner had worked in similar circumstances when the Valiant compact sedan had been developed in the late 1950s. However, the notion of converting an entire company away from the traditional vertical management system into a maze of cross-functional teams remained as foreign as the elimination of whitewall tires and chrome bumpers.

The sales and marketing staffs of both the Dodge and Chrysler/Plymouth car divisions hooted down the idea of the "super van," as their counterparts at Ford had done, claiming that a compact van would eat into the sales of their station wagons and their full-sized passenger vans. Moreover, they argued that the corporation needed a small pickup truck to compete with the rising tide of Japanese models as well as with GM and Ford, who were already in the market with downsized brands. If any money was to be allotted to new products, it should be spent on a compact pickup, not a radical, front-drive, midget-sized van appealing to an uncertain market.

But Gardner's "super van" enthusiasts refused to relent. Working with modest funds scavenged from other projects, they created a series of plywood mock-ups in the Truck Group's Highland Park engineering spaces. The low floor of these simple boxes, thanks to the absence of an intruding driveshaft, meant easy entry and exit and the ability to fit in any garage. Moreover, they offered cavernous carrying capacity for their size, while being drivable by women, who found the larger vans too cumbersome to maneuver and park.

While Detroit traditionally designed its vehicles from the outside in — i.e., creating an external shape and then packaging the passengers and drivetrain in the leftover space — Gardner and Bruce Benedict, the program manager on the vehicle, defied convention by first establishing rigid interior dimensions and then wrapping them in a boxlike structure. They decided on an interior height of four feet with a width of five feet — including a full four feet between the rear wheels in order to accommodate what had become an industry storage benchmark: a 4×8-foot sheet of plywood. The minivan would utilize the K-car's 2.2- and 2.6-liter four-cylinder overhead camshaft powerplants — a reluctant choice at best, considering their tepid maximum 104 horsepower output. K-car suspension bits and other components would also be adapted to save tooling costs.

One major dilemma demanded a solution. Research offered no clear course of action regarding the mundane question of doors. How many would there be and how would they be configured? Initial plans included conventional four-door, station wagon–like openings, but were rejected when research indicated that customers wanted at least 30-inch (the width of a standard house door) openings on the sides. Several women expressed wariness of a left-side door that might expose small children to passing traffic. Numerous variations were tried: twin, hinged doors on both sides and at the back, a single, hinged door on the right, and one sliding door on the right. But a single solution remained unresolved, even after the polling firm of Rogers National Research found that potential customers wanted carlike handling and road manners, as opposed to the harsher, truck-based behavior of the bigger vans. The buyers asked for flexible seating, with room for as many as seven passengers. Walk-through from the front pair of bucket seats was given high priority, as was the easy removal of the rear seat, which ought to provide three-person-wide capacity. A flat floor for storage was deemed critical, as was a powerful V6 engine. The last requirement was the source of alarm, because it was known that Chrysler had no such powerplant in its inventory, with no prospect in sight for at least five years.

Again, ironically, Henry Ford II came to Chrysler's rescue. After killing any opportunity for Ford to capture this nascent market, he unconsciously tossed his smaller, struggling rival another bone. Growing more moody and dissolute by the day, Ford summoned Iacocca in late 1976 and demanded that he eliminate Sperlich. Ford had tired of his impertinent challenges and his open disrespect for the gray-faced apparatchiks who formed the company's senior management. "You have an hour and a half to fire him," pronounced Henry, noting that it was 3:30 in the afternoon. Iacocca could no longer cover for his protégé and, passing the buck, assigned surrogate William I. "Bill" Bourke to pull the trigger on Sperlich's dazzling twenty-year career.

The man who had been responsible for so many product innovations at Ford did not remain on the job market for long. In early 1977 he was hired at Chrysler as the corporate vice president of product planning and design. Sperlich instantly immersed himself in the development of a series of vehicles intended to revive the smallest and weakest member of America's vaunted automotive triumvirate. Haunted by poor quality and oversized, overweight automobiles, Chrysler's single hope lay in the K-car. There was little in the way of surplus cash to devote to radical schemes like the "super van." But within weeks after arriving at Chrysler's Highland Park headquarters, Sperlich became aware of the project and offered it his support. Gardner's group was rewarded with a sufficient budget to convert a small former White Truck engineering building on Grand River Boulevard for further development. A series of full-scale clay models in various configurations were fabricated. One was a radical, shovel-nosed version, the second a pure box. The third was an amalgam of the two and quite similar to the version that would become the basic model, code-named "T-115." More models, in clay and plywood, were created, along with a seating buck to evaluate interior spaces. Three small public clinics were held in Denver, San Diego, and Atlanta. A fair percentage of the respondents judged the vans to be ugly, but the overall results, based on the interior room and function of the machines, was positive. While the issue of the door configuration still defied a clear solution, the design group arbitrarily decided to end the debate by mandating a four-door layout; two conventional front passenger doors, a large, right-side sliding door, and a gaping rear lift-gate. No one was totally convinced that this was the perfect setup, but the internal arguing was ended and preliminary planning moved forward.

The project still remained bogged down in the corporate back-waters. The sales and marketing types continued to ridicule the idea. Gardner & Co. seemed doomed. Then Henry Ford II struck again, once more unwittingly giving succor to his struggling crosstown rivals. Less than two years after dumping Sperlich, he fired Lee Iacocca. Five months later, after the dust had settled from this surprising boardroom assassination, Iacocca followed his old associate into the fifth-floor executive suite at Chrysler.

His exodus triggered a steady flow of talented Ford managers to follow him within the next few years, men who would become players in Iacocca's "new" Chrysler Corporation. Financial wizard Jerry Greenwald, Ben Bidwell, Paul Bergmoser, Gar Laux, and Ford's most ardent minivan advocate, Don DeLaRossa, all made the crosstown transfer, prompting industry insiders to begin calling Chrysler "Little Ford." The last and most important expatriate was Robert Lutz, who had been with Ford for twelve years, where he had risen to executive vice president of truck operations and a member of the board of directors.

According to official Chrysler hagiography, Iacocca is said to have arrived at Highland Park, discovered the nascent super van, and instantly became its enthusiastic supporter. But the story is more complex and hardly as visionary. While the project had expanded under Sperlich's umbrella to a point where Gardner's staff was operating at both the Grand River location and in a cramped corner of the advanced engineering section on the main floor of the K. T. Keller executive building in Highland Park, it remained a stepchild in corporate planning. Iacocca agreed with his senior staff that Chrysler simply could not afford such a new vehicle, with all available resources (about $700 million) in the cash-strapped company being devoted to the K-car sedans. Sperlich argued that the K-car drivetrain (engine and transaxle) could easily be adapted to the super van, but he made little headway.

In a last-hour attempt to save money, Gardner and his staff experimented with rear-drive versions employing the twenty-year-old Chrysler slant-6 engine, but found that the intrusion of the bulky powerplant into the passenger compartment defeated the basic purpose of the expansive interior. Worse yet, pressure continued to build among the senior staff to meet the threat of the new Japanese mini–pickup trucks with a small truck of their own. The T-115 seemed dead.

Gardner & Co. pluckily continued their research, which revealed that both retired people and families with teenage children were seeking vehicles with increased passenger and cargo space, plus maneuverability in traffic and parkability in normal garages. "We produced a report that indicated a potential market of one million units a year," recalls Gardner. "The sales and marketing guys nearly laughed us out of the meeting. Iacocca questioned our data and vetoed the project, agreeing that the company needed a small truck instead of a minivan. Gordon Cherry, who was solidly behind the T-115, and I went out for a few drinks after the meeting and felt totally defeated."

Then Sperlich made a pivotal move. On a Friday in late 1979 he called Gardner to his office and produced a manila folder. Inside was the red-covered report that contained the Ford market research that Norman Krandall had conducted on its defunct Mini/max. It confirmed the possibility of a new, 800,000-unit vehicle market. "Sperlich had never even mentioned the Ford project to us up to that point," says Gardner. The Krandall folder was studied and recorded, then returned to Sperlich the following Monday and never seen again. Thirty days later a fresh market research study containing the data from *both* Ford and Chrysler was presented to Iacocca. Faced with overwhelming data, much of which he had already seen at Ford, Iacocca turned around. Slowly, steadily, he was drawn into the camp of supporters of what was now referred to as the "minivan."

As forceful a leader as he was, Iacocca got no free ride to produce the T-115. Both Ford with its Ranger and General Motors with its S-10 were moving into the small pickup market, and conventional wisdom demanded that Chrysler follow suit. "He took tremendous heat," says Gardner.

It may have been Chrysler's comparatively modest size (Sperlich recalls how minuscule the corporation's management seemed to him after arriving from leviathan Ford — although DeLaRossa was stunned to discover that the design staff was bloated to over seven hundred men, many of them redundant) and weakened financial position that played to the minivan team's advantage. Iacocca realized that Chrysler had neither the hardware nor the funds to wage a multifront war against the imports and his own local rivals with a compact pickup truck. He was becoming convinced that Chrysler was simply out of its weight class and had no choice but to probe into niche markets unoccupied by its major competitors. With each passing day the T-115 — with its ease of production by employing the K-car drivetrain — not only seemed feasible but critical to the survival of the company. Sanguine that the highly tuned Detroit intelligence network offered no indication that any other car-maker, domestic or imported, was considering a similar vehicle, Iacocca finally brushed aside all management opposition and injected an additional $500 million into the loan package he was seeking from the government and the unions to restructure Chrysler. The program was approved with a modest projected annual volume of 155,000 units. "But there was one problem," recalls Gardner. "Iacocca left out the need for an additional $131 million in manufacturing costs, which bumped the actual budget for the T-115 to $631 million. Somehow at the last hour he found the extra funds and managed to get them included in the federal loan package."

A small group of engineers and designers, numbering no more than one hundred, completed the plans for the minivan, and the aged Windsor, Ontario, plant was converted to manufacture what was to be called the Dodge Caravan and the Plymouth Voyager. They were in fact identical vehicles, differing only in paint and trim and embodying a decade-old marketing strategy called "nameplate engineering."

Massive hurdles still remained as Chrysler geared up for an autumn 1982 introduction of the T-115. Naysayers in the company, including many on the design team, worried that the K-car four-cylinder powerplants, paired with either a four-speed manual or three-speed automatic, offered anemic performance at best. The marketers fretted over the entire concept, expressing doubts that American consumers would be attracted to what they considered a gussied-up truck. John Naughton, an ex-Ford man brought to Chrysler by Iacocca, pushed hard to call the T-115s "Magic Vans" and developed a promotion campaign around magician Doug Henning to market the vehicles. It was mercifully killed. One public relations staffer was given the assignment to woo the female market, offering special advance previews to editors of major women's magazines and arranging for noted home entertainment and decor guru Martha Stewart to use a Caravan as her official company vehicle.

Then came the recession of 1982 and the entire T-115 project was delayed — first for six months and then for an entire year as sales slumped and Iacocca's government loan kitty reached alarmingly meager levels. "This may have been a blessing in disguise," says Gardner. "With the economy weak and car sales off, you have to wonder if consumers would have taken the chance to buy an entirely new type of vehicle like the minivan. By the time the economy perked up a year later and we introduced the vehicle in the fall of 1983, they were in a much better mood."

The first production version of the T-115 rolled off the Windsor, Ontario, assembly line in September 1983, with considerable press coverage *and* a glitch that the more superstitious witnesses construed as an evil omen. The chairman, riding a wave of public adulation based on his new television commercials and his soaring reputation as the savior of Chrysler, was to drive the first minivan off the line. All went well, with flashbulbs popping and television cameras rolling, until Iacocca attempted to leave the van. Somewhere deep in the innards of the machine a circuit snapped and the electric door locks refused to release. As public relations staffers and senior management types gaped in horror, the great man struggled to get free, yanking frantically at the door handles and rapping for help on the window glass. Finally several workers rushed forward and unlocked the door.

The initial reviews were positive. *Car and Driver*, the largest and most outspoken of the mainstream automobile magazines noted, "The T-115, known as the Dodge Caravan and the Plymouth Voyager, is no woozy frolic in the outlands of automotive design. Rather, it is a sparkling example of the kind of thinking that will power Detroit out of its rut and may very well serve to accelerate Chrysler's drive back into the big time. As a box on wheels, the T-115 is that good."

The "box" offered a near-perfect cargo space. Its easy entry, smooth handling, and excellent visibility made it an instant hit with women in particular. Some potential customers complained about the lack of power issuing from the two underwhelming four-cylinder engines (one built by Chrysler and a second from Mitsubishi), but the expansive utility of the vehicle seemed to compensate for the lack of performance, at least until a V6 could be sourced, either from within the company or from Mitsubishi, the Japanese manufacturing colossus with whom Chrysler had a joint-venture agreement to manufacture and sell compact cars.

Sales started slowly. In the final months of 1983 only 9,109 minivans were sold, causing some in the company to second-guess the wisdom of the entire project. *Ward's Auto World*, a Detroit-based journal of the industry, grumped, "Chrysler's product planners are nearly euphoric about its potential because it's a logical solution to solve several problems simultaneously. But logical vehicles have failed in the past, or their sales were limited to eccentrics. Most minivans either have faded away or metamorphosed into larger vehicles."

Not quite. The box was about to become a breakthrough vehicle that then–vice chairman Jerry Greenwald crowed, "will be at least as revolutionary as the Mustang was in the 1960s." He was right. Sales exploded to beyond 200,000 units in 1984, then past 250,000 the following year. By 1988, over 450,000 minivans, now with an optional Mitsubishi V6, were being sold annually, in both short- and long-wheelbase versions and in a myriad of option packages.

The corporation was blessed by timing. General Motors and Ford, as well as the major Japanese manufacturers, had glutted the compact pickup market with front-engine, rear-drive designs that were unsuitable for adaptation to a minivan format. "This gave us a five-year open field," recalls Gardner. "Nobody in the industry could respond quickly enough to overcome our advantage."

Caught off guard by the phenomenon, GM, Ford, Toyota, and Nissan all rushed to market with competitive vehicles, but corporate pride prevented them from shamelessly copying the Chrysler package. In adhering to the self-destructive "not invented here" syndrome, each compromised the elemental, boxlike, front-drive design of the T-115 and missed the mark. GM and Ford insisted on rear-drive setups, which lacked the low step-in and easy entry of the Chrysler. Ford erred further with a radically drooped snout on its Aerostar that earned it the "Dustbuster" label, a faux pas that GM additionally enhanced with its 1990 Chevrolet Lumina APV, Pontiac Trans Sport, and Oldsmobile Silhouette, all of which offered grandly streamlined noses that appeared to belong on monorail locomotives. Toyota's Previa deposited its underpowered four-cylinder engine exactly midship — a gesture of corporate hubris and a technological tour de force, but in reality a noisy intrusion into the passenger compartment. As rival after rival failed to dent the T-115's dominance, Chrysler management types marveled at their good fortune. "If only one of them had the balls to swallow their pride and just copy what we were doing, we wouldn't have had a ten-year free ride," mused Dave Bostwick, Chrysler's head of research, who possessed hard data to prove that the T-115 was a dead-solid-perfect hit on what the public desired. Over the first decade of the T-115, 3,773,385 units were sold. Unthreatened, the corporation controlled 50 percent of the booming market segment.

By 1987, Mitsubishi, in which Chrysler had obtained a 25 percent share of joint-venture car manufacture centered around the new Diamond Star Motors in Normal, Illinois (with Gardner appointed as its general manager), was providing V6 engines for both the regular T-115 and a long-wheelbase "maxi." The Chrysler minis dominated the new market, easily maintaining its 50 percent share of sales and banking profits by the balesful (roughly $6,000 gross per vehicle). But Sperlich and others understood that the corporation was once again resting on its product laurels and ignoring a growing need for new vehicles. The basic K-car was nearly a decade old. Any advantage it enjoyed had long since passed. Chrysler's entry in the full-sized pickup segment, which was growing by the year, was hopelessly outdated against newer Ford and Chevrolet entrants.

Sperlich was pressing hard for new products, ever the intense, unrelenting point man for progress. But his longtime boss and patron now seemed more distracted by the aggrandizement of the Iacocca image than the long-term stability of the company he had saved. At the very hour that Lee Iacocca's new Chrysler Corporation seemed to bask in the brightest glow of its renaissance, it was poised for yet another plunge toward oblivion.

This time the competition was ready. They had gotten the message that the minivan was here to stay as an integral component of the domestic automotive market. It would be impossible for Chrysler to end-run GM, Ford, and the imports again with a surprise of the magnitude of the T-115. The corporation would have to make a frontal assault against known defenses. The new minivan would therefore be evolutionary, not revolutionary, and would have to embody features already well known to the buying public and to the enemy: capacious interior room, front-wheel drive, easy access and egress, efficient utilization of space, adequate power, safety features, and enhanced comfort and reliability. As massive change was once again about to descend on this most volatile of the major automotive manufacturers, the single constant in the mix was the knowledge that in order to maintain leadership in the critical minivan market segment nothing less than an absolute world-class vehicle would suffice.

3

Bulldoze the Walls

EVEN AS the K-cars and the minivan brought fat profits to Chrysler in the mid-1980s, the situation there was far from tranquil. Quality continued to be marginal. Each year Chrysler's products ranked at or near the bottom in the widely respected J. D. Power surveys of quality and customer satisfaction. Rivalries between the various divisions — Dodge and Chrysler/Plymouth in particular — bordered on the openly hostile. And the whole way of making cars remained a hidebound, bureaucratic nightmare. Each division had overlapping and totally redundant styling, marketing, engineering, and sales operations, each known as a "chimney" in this aging smokestack industry. One member of the corporation's product planning office described it as "a system diabolically designed to make grown men behave like small children." The traditional and inefficient management "chimneys" were constructed with a brick and mortar that had hardened to stone over the decades.

Under this archaic modus operandi — which permeated the entire domestic industry — automobiles were designed, manufactured, and marketed by a series of independent duchies within the corporations. A new vehicle would generally be mandated by the executive sales and marketing staffs. The design group would then create the basic styling package and pass it over the transom to the engineers to cram the mechanical components into the preordained dimensions. The blueprints, as they were, would then be handed to the manufacturing group, who were left with the often baffling puzzle of how to mass-produce a complex machine into which they had had little or no input. Financial control remained in the vise grip of top management, which maintained veto power over the entire process and could (and often did) demand major changes up to the moment the first production models rolled off the assembly lines.

The chimney system was a nightmare in terms of cost and efficiency, but no one in Detroit had either the power or the vision to change it. Internal rivalries were rampant and Iacocca's public pronouncements about the "new" Chrysler Corporation were dismissed as so much blarney inside the offices and factories that made up the chimneys.

Rather than facing these problems at home, Chrysler went on a spending spree in the mid-1980s. All of Detroit was in an acquisitive mood. Fat with cash, General Motors' chairman Roger Smith embarked on his infamous alliance with H. Ross Perot while buying crazily into the fields of computers and robotics. The purchase of small custom automakers became fashionable, and GM snatched up Lotus cars in England and a controlling interest in Sweden's Saab. Ford countered by buying smallish Aston Martin and — for what finally totaled a whopping $4-plus billion — the enfeebled but legendary luxury car-maker Jaguar. Initially Iacocca's interest lay in Italy, where he swallowed up Lamborghini and Maserati, a pair of tiny manufacturers of high-performance sports cars. The Maserati purchase resulted in a convertible based on the K-car platform called the Chrysler TC (after the name "Lido" was considered), which both sold and performed poorly. The car represented perhaps a low point in Iacocca's alliances with Italian car builders, but he persisted by arranging with giant Fiat to distribute Alfa Romeo sports sedans in the United States.

Still fascinated with the notion of diversification that gripped many Fortune 500 boardrooms at that time, the chairman next purchased Gulfstream Aviation, the upscale executive-jet manufacturer, for $242 million. This not only put Chrysler in the aircraft business, but provided Iacocca with the most elegant personal business jet in Detroit.

Yet the ultimate prize was another automobile company of sufficient size to expand Chrysler's market share and, in a personal sense, to satisfy Iacocca's intense urge to steal sales from arch-enemy Ford. The target had been identified as early as 1986: strug-gling, French-dominated American Motors, a company that, despite a weak automotive product line and a minuscule 2 percent of the domestic market, possessed a jewel that Iacocca viewed as a profit-maker with vast potential: It was an American icon called the Jeep.

American Motors had been a star-crossed entity since its forma-tion in 1954 from the ruins of Detroit's Hudson Motor Car Com-pany and the Nash Motor Company of Kenosha, Wisconsin. Always overmatched against the power of the Big Three, AMC attempted to increase its market share in 1970 by obtaining the nearly-defunct Kaiser Willys Sales Corporation (itself a last-ditch amal-gam in 1954 of the aged Toledo, Ohio, firm of Willys-Overland, the remnants of Studebaker and Packard, and postwar Kaiser-Frazer Corporation of Willow Run, Michigan). Among the plethora of products offered under the AMC Rambler label, ranging from sporty Marlins and Javelins to lumpy Gremlins and Hornets, not a single product was capable of gaining anything but a brief, novelty-like advantage against the deluge of vehicles pouring forth from the likes of General Motors and Ford. Chronically underfunded and cursed with a weak dealer network, American Motors struggled through the seventies until, in 1979, when the venerable French automaker, Régie Nationale des Usines Renault, obtained an initial share of the company. A year later that share was increased to a majority interest. By all logical definitions, American Motors was French. The government-owned French conglomerate attempted to use its new American outpost as a marketing tool to sell a series of heavily French-flavored cars like the Alliance (nicknamed "Ap-pliance" by the trade press) and the Encore, without notable suc-cess. Renault had dabbled with American sales since the early 1950s but, displaying typical French chauvinism, was reluctant to tailor its products to American driving needs.

The only valuable item in the AMC/Renault inventory was the Jeep, which had maintained steady sales despite its antiquated Toledo factory complex and a singularly churlish United Auto Workers local. In 1984, an updated Jeep Cherokee and the Jeep

Wagoneer were introduced by AMC/Renault, along with the Encore and Alliance compact sedans. Those vehicles, coupled with a joint venture with the Chinese government to build Cherokees in Beijing, produced the first small AMC profit since 1979. But the relief was temporary. The following year brought serious labor troubles at both the Kenosha and Toledo plants — with UAW sabotage of new Cherokees at the latter factory souring relations to the point of breakage. Parent Renault announced losses of $1 billion and openly discussed closing the nearly ninety-year-old factory complex.

Pressure from Paris was building to get the AMC house in order. The Socialist Mitterrand government was facing national elections with state-owned Renault hemorrhaging cash and having lost the number-one sales position that it had held in Europe from 1980 to 1983. The only bright spots in its colonial possession were the solid-selling Jeep line and a state-of-the-art factory being completed in Bramalea, Ontario, where an Americanized version of the Renault 25 sedan called the Premier was to be manufactured. Preliminary planning was also under way for a highly advanced redesign of the Cherokee, code-named "ZJ."

With French workers being laid off at home, rumors began to circulate through the incestuous Detroit auto world of a possible buyout. The story was fueled by an arrangement between Chrysler and AMC for Chrysler to assemble "M-body" vehicles (Chrysler Fifth Avenue, Dodge Diplomat, and Plymouth Gran Fury) at the AMC Kenosha plant. But Iacocca's larger target was threefold: the new 2.2-million-square-foot Bramalea factory, the company's 1,472-member dealer body, and far and away most important, the legendary Jeep name and product lineup.

"Legendary" was an understatement. According to market research produced by Chrysler, "Jeep" was a household word, second only to "Coca-Cola" as the most recognized brand name in the world. Since its introduction in 1940 as a small U.S. Army General Purpose (or "GP" or "Jeep") vehicle, the little four-wheel-drive, go-anywhere machine had become an American archetype. Over 660,000 had been produced during the war by Willys-Overland and Ford (after the original designer and contractor, American

Bantam, could not keep up with production). Following the end of hostilities in 1945, thousands of the sturdy four-wheel-drive machines with the 65 hp four-cylinder engines were sold as surplus. Willys-Overland immediately sought to exploit the market by building slightly more civilized peacetime versions. The company added a station wagon model in 1946 and an open roadster version called the Jeepster in 1948. Willys then attempted to reenter the passenger car business in 1952, with disastrous results. It, like other secondary players in the business, was simply overwhelmed by the resurgent Big Three. Two years later it was absorbed by famed wartime industrialist Henry J. Kaiser. The father of the Liberty and Victory cargo ships, Kaiser had teamed with former Graham-Paige executive Joseph Frazer in 1947 to begin manufacturing Kaiser-Frazer automobiles at the former Ford-built Willow Run aircraft plant, west of Detroit. He was to find the Big Three considerably more formidable than Admiral Doenitz's U-boats and was forced into the alliance with slumping Willys-Overland. His new company, called Kaiser-Willys, was never a factor in the marketplace, although the Jeep line continued to sell steadily, even after it was finally absorbed into the desperate little circle of embattled automakers called American Motors in 1970. Once again the ubiquitous Jeep, an oddball machine that so many companies failed to understand (with more to follow), was passed along to new owners as an unwanted stepchild.

In 1974 the Jeep Cherokee, a boxy but slightly smaller version of the leviathan Wagoneer, was introduced and became a solid seller. Three years later a four-door version came to market while the Wagoneer was dolled up with luxury options and aimed at the upscale suburban and country gentry market. Heavy, cumbersome, and crudely built, the Grand Wagoneer rose to cult status among America's most affluent car buyers. Unopposed in the marketplace until the Range Rover arrived in 1987, this old ark possessed the highest demographic profile of any vehicle sold in America. Customers boasted an average household income of over $90,000 a year. American Motors officials liked to brag that a substantial percentage of Grand Wagoneer buyers paid cash. AMC executive Joe Cappy mused that each year his dealers would be unfazed when informed that once again the Grand Wagoneer would be unchanged save for perhaps a new paint color or the addition of a minor accessory. They would simply order more, based on the constant demand. Better yet, gross profit on each Grand Wagoneer sold was $9,000! The seemingly unassailable market position of the fat-cat Wagoneer, plus the solid sales of the Cherokee and its various permutations (Comanche Pickup, Jeep Wrangler, etc.) were the central attractions of the AMC buyout for Iacocca, despite strong sentiments within Chrysler that such a purchase was insanity.

Excluding a tight coterie of allies, Iacocca enjoyed minimal support from his senior management regarding the AMC purchase. Even Chrysler president Hal Sperlich opposed the move, convinced that environmental pressures, the government, and the cost of fuel would kill large cars and large engines. Still Iacocca drove ahead, bulldozing any opposition, including his old ally Sperlich. By March 1987 a deal was hammered out following ten weeks of intense negotiations. The total price would be $1.6 billion, and involved one of the most complicated deals in big business history. Three powerhouse banking firms were in the game: Salomon Brothers representing Chrysler, Lazard handling the Renault interests, and Shearson Lehman negotiating for American Motors. Out of the deal Iacocca received the Jeep name and the newly opened plant in Bramalea, Ontario, valued at $400 million with a capacity of 200,000 vehicles per year, plus a neighboring facility at Brampton with an 80,000-vehicle capacity. The transaction involved *two* full planeloads of documents — in English and French — flown to the Federal Trade Commission in Washington to counteract any potential government antitrust action.

Overall the purchase was celebrated by Wall Street, which affirmed that the extra manufacturing capacity, AMC's dealer body, and the Jeep lineup composed a bargain. What the financial types chose to ignore was Chrysler's aging K-car-based products that badly needed major reinvestment and the corporation's bloated management and outdated manufacturing philosophies. Also glossed over was the suspicion that the French had "cooked the books" and questions of how the two corporate cultures — one smug and laden with tradition, the other half-French, half-American and totally disheartened — would be melded into an effective team.

While Wall Street celebrated the AMC buyout, unrest was rampant within the Chrysler dealer body. Letters were sent to Iacocca from various dealer organizations expressing concern about the lack of any new and original products and the continued lackluster showing of Chrysler vehicles in various public surveys and media evaluations. *Consumer Reports* and other car-testing organizations constantly pilloried Chrysler for shabby quality while the prestigious J. D. Power Quality Survey and Customer Satisfaction Index consistently ranked Chrysler at or near the bottom. Even the minivan, cherished by a loyal owner body now numbering nearly one million, was at best marginal in terms of squeaks, rattles, and reliability. With nothing more than rehashes of the K-car and a few regussied AMC rejects on the horizon, the dealers were becoming openly restless.

Then a second, unignorable, wake-up call to Chrysler came from archrival Honda. A story appeared in late 1987 in the trade paper *Automotive News* outlining Honda's aggressive plans to displace Chrysler as the number-three automaker in the nation. The article, quoting both Honda president Tadishi Kume and American boss Soichiro Irimajiri, exuded Honda's well-known pugnacity and confidence. They predicted that, operating from its new base in Marysville, Ohio, Honda would by 1990 outsell Chrysler domestically *and*, as an added insult, begin exporting Accords back to the homeland. This would put lie to the aged shibboleth that American workers were incapable of building cars with quality levels equal to their Japanese counterparts.

By all measurements, Honda was a miraculous success story. While dozens of car companies in the United States and Europe were crumbling during the immediate post-war years, Soichiro Honda, a rebellious ex–motorcycle and car racer, built a manufacturing empire, first with world-class motorcycles, then with efficient, jewel-like economy cars. Honda had been in the car business less than thirty years, yet had risen to a plane with Mercedes-Benz and Toyota in terms of engineering creativity and product quality. (Honda had just replaced Mercedes-Benz as number one on the J. D. Power Customer Satisfaction Index.)

By the mid-1980s, the miracle of Japanese industry — their *kan-ban* "just in time" supplier network, their lifetime workforces, their linkage with powerful banking and government institutions, their obsession with quality and engineering, etc. — had been endlessly documented. Attempts had been made to integrate some of the more effective Japanese procedures into the American system, especially in terms of supplier scheduling and assembly-line methodology, but many Detroiters discounted their systems as too different, too homogeneous, and "too Eastern" for much of them to be effectively transferred to the American Midwest.

Honda's challenge laid the future bare for Chrysler. Either they would enliven their product line and improve the quality of their cars, or Honda's bold predictions would come true.

Iacocca's first response was predictable — he commissioned a study. The noted consulting firm Bain & Co., which had successfully reorganized Procter & Gamble, was hired to examine Chrysler's dilemma. They responded with a recommendation of re-aligning the company by brands, in much the same fashion that already existed. The chimney system was not threatened. "It was the same old system," recalls one Chrysler insider. "Lee fired them without implementing any of their plan, but he knew what the dealers were talking about."

So did a small but growing group of senior management and a group of young junior engineers and financial types who formed something called the "Youth Advisory Committee." This was one of dozens of such organizations within the Big Three, which generated occasional reports that were instantly relegated to company archives. But as the heat of late summer 1987 simmered across the flatlands of southern Michigan, this heretofore ignored group was poised to shake the corporation almost to the grave of Walter P. Chrysler.

The most recent Youth Advisory Committee's report had mentioned Honda again and again as the paradigm of a company masterfully exploiting the needs of younger consumers. In the wake of the *Automotive News* story on Honda, Lutz and Sperlich heard about the report, as did Chrysler chairman Jerry Greenwald, and a directive was issued instructing corporate public relations director A. C. "Bud" Liebler and vice president of program management Ron Boltz to cochair a study by the Youth Advisory Committee to determine what was at the core of Honda's success. "Know thine enemy," groused Lutz. The committee was given firm instructions that no punches were to be pulled and that vivid contrasts between Chrysler and Honda were to be drawn.

Jim Finck, a skinny engineer with a mournful mustache and shaggy hair, was selected as the twelve-member Honda study team leader, with a slight, bright-eyed Japanese-American woman named Reiko McKendry on board as the only member who could speak and read Japanese. The selection of McKendry was laden with irony. The protégée of chief financial officer Robert S. Miller Jr. — known universally as "Steve" — McKendry was a University of Wisconsin MBA who, by her very presence, typified the insularity of the American automobile industry. Not only was she a woman in a predominantly male environment, but McKendry represented but a handful of individuals in the entire corporation fluent in Japanese. While Chrysler had maintained a working relationship with Mitsubishi since the late 1970s and operated the joint-venture Diamond Star Motors in Illinois, all business was carried out in English. As Iacocca railed about "a level playing field," no effort was put forth by his executive staff to learn more than a few words of the language of a nation that threatened to overwhelm them. Also serving as key players on the team — all of whom were under thirty years of age — were Phil Jansen, a production specialist, Bill Wrobel from sales, and Gloria Lara, a financial analyst. Tim Emmitt, a dapper young MBA from the University of Chicago who had transferred from GM only six months earlier, was taken on board after his boss had refused the assignment. "He *gave* it to me," recalls Emmitt. "Frankly, I figured I had nothing to lose." Operating with a blend of youthful confidence and chutzpah, the team plunged into their assignment with what might be described — especially to the mossbacked establishment — as revolutionary zeal.

"It was amazing," remembers Finck. "After starting the study we quickly discovered that nobody at Chrysler was talking to anybody else. Suddenly a bunch of people in the company were threatened. One vice president heard about the study and hauled his representative off the project. In our initial meetings fourteen so-called chimneys were represented — get that, *fourteen independent* operations within the company — engineering, design, manufacturing, marketing, sales, finance, you name it, that *never* had any contact with each other below management level! What we all knew going in but were afraid to admit was that Chrysler was building *terrible* automobiles. Aside from the minivans, our product line was not only shabby, but our customers didn't know one brand from another. Take the LeBaron for example: Originally it was an expensive custom-built sedan, then a front-wheel-drive K-car coupe and even a convertible. In 1987 *five* different models carried the LeBaron label. We changed our nameplates to a point where the customer not only didn't know the difference, but didn't care."

For three months the team met daily, weekdays and weekends. Typically they were in session by seven o'clock in the morning at their Highland Park office, while numerous trips were made to Honda's Ohio base of operations. Finck's small home in suburban Detroit became the setting for late-night sessions, punctuated by what became known as "mystery meals" — potluck donations from members, ranging from Chinese takeout to homemade tuna casseroles. By mid-November, the first of the three-phase reports was ready for distribution, both to upper management through a series of meetings and a video, complete with the standard selection of bar graphs and pie charts. The executive committee would be presented the final report in a truncated version a month later.

The first phase was given to a group of senior vice presidents in Conference Room A at the Highland Park fifth-floor executive level. "We frankly didn't know whether or not we were going to be fired," Finck recalls. "The team had long since decided that what we had found out had to be discussed whether the powers-that-be liked it or not." With a second phase of the study and a summary due before the end of 1987, Finck and his team were careful not to unload all their ammunition at the first session.

The plan was to begin slowly, to break the news to the corporate establishment of what the team had quickly determined: that Honda was about to blow the doors off Chrysler. Finck opened with a short history of Honda, noting that it was barely forty years old, having first dominated the Japanese (and worldwide) motorcycle industry before producing its first miniature S500 and N600 motorcycle-based cars in 1963. A sea change came in 1972/73 with the monumental Civic, the first great modern subcompact, then with the larger and even more successful Accord three years later. Finck made it clear that Honda was deadly serious in its oft-stated intent to sell one million vehicles in the United States by 1991 and thereby relegate Chrysler to fourth place as a domestic producer.

Reiko McKendry followed by declaring that Honda's structure was based on decentralization. "Honda believes that centralization leads to bureaucracy and bureaucracy stifles creativity," she said, knowing that the statement was aimed directly at the ingrained bureaucratic duchies that infested Chrysler. Honda's average employee age was thirty-two years — ten years junior to Chrysler's. "Honda encourages its employees to believe that nothing is impossible and that risk-taking will involve mistakes, which are expected and forgiven," she said. That was yet another blow at the seamless, no-fail, pass-the-buck philosophy that permeated Chrysler as well as all of domestic industry.

"Honda's structure was divided into three independent entities; Honda Motor Co. (sales), Honda Research and Development (product design), and Honda Engineering (manufacturing). They were based on what they called a 'paperweight' organization, which was," she said, "like the traditional wide and flat Japanese paperweight which, metaphorically, spread creativity and responsibility in a broad, flat plane across the company." Honda was an engineering-based operation, amplified by McKendry's observation that twenty of its thirty-five-member board of directors had engineering degrees, while only twelve of Chrysler's thirty-six board members were similarly qualified. Like Finck, McKendry harped on the single, transcendental theme of the Honda business ethic — the customer was king and had to be served by teams of aggressive, youthful, often rebellious experts in engineering and manufacturing.

Phil Jansen, like Finck a tall, lean engineer in his twenties who looked slightly uncomfortable in his role as a corporate Cassandra, stated that Honda made major model changes every four years or so, literally twice as quickly as Chrysler. Significant alterations in their models — including new engines — often came every two or more years. Honda offered seventeen different powerplants within its smaller model lineup, as opposed to Chrysler's sometimes limited and archaic invention of three basic engines (a four, a V6, and an aged V8).* Their system, involving 276 independent outside suppliers, all of whom were involved in the product-planning process, had helped double production capacity from one to two million units since 1981 and heresy or no, Jansen stated that Honda's goal of selling one million vehicles in the American market by 1991 was more than possible.†

Bill Wrobel added to the dismal picture by noting that in the past year Chrysler had lost 1.1 percent in market share while Honda gained nearly 2 percent. Honda led all manner of surveys, including J. D. Power, in terms of owner loyalty, quality of service, and reliability, even surpassing icon Mercedes-Benz in most categories.

Gloria Lara capped the disheartening news by reporting that Honda was enjoying 8 percent faster growth worldwide than Chrysler and that its expenditures in research and development were nearly double. Long-term growth through product development resulting in modest but steady returns to its shareholders was a Honda priority, as opposed to Chrysler's penchant for quick, temporary boosts in profits and stock prices. "Honda will tolerate lower short-term profits and lower dividend yield in order to gain a higher long-range price-earnings ratio," said Lara before Finck quietly summarized the six main points of the Honda philosophy:

1. Customer satisfaction is paramount.
2. The team approach maximizes the talents of its entire staff.
3. Its autonomous research and development arm is the key to engineering creativity and excellence.
4. Honda's sales are expected to grow despite potentially diversionary short-term cycles in the market.

---

*Chrysler was also sourcing V6 engines from Mitsubishi, and a turbo diesel truck powerplant from Cummins Corp.
†Honda was short of the mark. Sales of its Honda and Acura Divisions totaled 803,367 units in 1991.

5. Profits must be reinvested despite the needs of shareholders.
6. Honda competes to *win* in everything it does.

"Overall, they took the report pretty well," says Finck. "There was
some grumbling about comparing apples to oranges, but both Lutz
and Sperlich encouraged us to carry on, regardless of what the reaction might be." While the two men were heading in divergent directions within the company, both were similarly inclined to rattle
the establishment, to doubt the conventional wisdom of the day
and to constantly seek better products.

Phase two of the Honda study came as the team gained both
nerve and cohesiveness. "It was amazing," recalls Tim Emmitt. "In
the beginning there was a certain suspicion among all of us, coming as we did from different, separate departments. But the more
we worked together, the more the team became efficient. It was the
same message we ended up trying to transmit in the study."

By the time the team was ready to present the second phase of
the study, Chrysler's fortunes had worsened. The thunderous October 1987 crash of the stock market that saw the Dow Jones drop
over 500 points signaled what was sure to be reduced car sales in
the immediate future. Closer to home, Iacocca was still smarting
from a federal grand jury indictment of the corporation for odome-
ter tampering. The case involved a cabal of Midwest-based underlings spinning back odometers on used vehicles and selling them as
new. Iacocca responded with mass firings and was forced to apolo-
gize publicly.

But the problem went deeper. The sag in the car market revealed
tremendous vulnerabilities on the part of the corporation. Its primary product line was composed of artlessly regussied K-cars:
squared-up, chrome-lavished arks, most with puny four-cylinder
engines that smacked of the early 1970s. A new sedan, called the
LH, was on the design boards, and AMC's ingenious new Cherokee
ZJ lurked in the wings, mired in corporate in-fighting. Short term,
the company was at least two design cycles out of phase with the
industry leaders. While the American Motors acquisition brought
an infusion of new life and new designs into the business, its aged

factories in Kenosha and Toledo meant only added overhead and overcapacity in a soft market. Word was passed that Iacocca was planning to close the crumbling Kenosha complex in direct contradiction of a pledge he had made to the United Auto Workers local. He was also under the gun to shutter Chrysler's ancient Jefferson Avenue plant in Detroit's eastern inner city. Such a move was sure to trigger a public war of words with Detroit's powerful and profane mayor Coleman Young, who had allied himself with Chrysler during the 1979 bailout.

The study team understood full well that carping about the wonders of archrival Honda, which was gliding gracefully from one market triumph to the next, would surely irritate already damaged corporate egos. But they pledged to proceed, regardless of the potential damage to their individual career paths. The second phase was more tempered, dealing with Honda's emphasis on people and independent thinking. The Japanese phrase *"wai gaya,"* roughly translated "the sound of people talking" was noted as an example of the incessant exchange of opinion and information that transfused Honda's engineering staff. Again, the priority on youth was emphasized, as was the elemental goal of customer satisfaction. In all, it was a palatable meal digested easily by the senior staff.

"I knew we were making headway," recalls Finck. "During the second-phase report Bob Lutz put out his cigar. When Bob Lutz stopped smoking, you knew you had his attention." Bud Liebler sent a memo to Finck noting that "Phase II was a blockbuster — provocative, insightful, fascinating and, in some ways, frightening."

Word reached the team that Iacocca himself had heard of their project and wanted to be on hand as the final report was rendered. Finck and his cohorts realized they were handling dynamite. The final phase, including their conclusions, contained the stuff of revolution, akin to Leon Trotsky preaching to the Romanovs. But by then the entire group had become convinced that Chrysler was so off the track for continued success that an all-out, bombs-away assault had to be made on the hierarchy, including His Highness. A preview of the final draft, to be presented on February 1, 1988, to the top management at a private session set for the Bloomfield Hills Country Club, was given to Jerry Greenwald in his Highland Park office. Reiko McKendry, the diminutive Japanese-American, hit Greenwald head on, hammering him with data that verified the presumption that the so-called Honda way of building automobiles was the wave of the future. Moreover, her numbers, based on Chrysler employee polling, confirmed that the corporation's posturing about quality and product excellence was a sham. "Greenwald began to twitch in his chair," says Finck. "We began to wonder if we'd gone too far; suddenly the prospect of being fired became a reality." Turning back was impossible. The last blow would have to be struck.

The gathering took place as planned at the Bloomfield Hills Country Club, with Lutz hobbling in on crutches, the penalty for his traditional head-on skiing style. The entire executive committee was present, including Iacocca, who was known to have a low tolerance level for long-winded brainstorming sessions. The team had been told to hold their presentation to less than two hours or else endure the wrath of the Chairman. Bidwell, the only one of the seniors with a sense of irony, tried to relax the youngsters by announcing, "There's a gallows set up on the eighteenth hole. Let's hope we don't have to use it."

Based on what they were about to hear, a mass lynching was possible. Never in the history of the automobile business had a group of management elite been subjected to such candor by a collection of impudent juniors. Jim Finck, no doubt thinking about Bidwell's good-natured threat, launched the presentation with the results of their survey — involving 270 randomly selected Chrysler employees — conducted by the team in early January. The results were shocking. For all of Iacocca's public and internal posturing about the "new Chrysler Corporation's" commitment to quality, *only 10 percent* of those polled believed it was an important priority to management. The winner by a wide margin? *Short-term profit.* Forty-one percent of those polled believed it to be the number-one goal of the company management, with market share coming home a distant second at 16 percent. Another 12 percent mentioned cost reduction, with quality (10 percent) and company image (9 percent) finishing deep in the ruck. A second battery of data followed, perhaps even more shocking: *30 percent* of the employees polled believed quality should be the top priority, with customer satisfaction and product innovation second and third on their list. Long-term profit came in a distant fourth, with merely 12 percent of the vote. Clearly, the employees and the management were diametrically opposed in terms of both the perceptions and the realities of Chrysler's goals. Finck observed that it was the study team's findings that finance alone governed Chrysler's product decisions while at Honda the independent, risk-taking, mistake-prone, always daring, always competitive, always creative project teams were in charge.

So far Iacocca seemed to be taking his medicine, although neither he nor any of his board was ready for feisty Reiko McKendry. Here was this Japanese-American junior management *kid*, barely tall enough to peer over the podium, lecturing the American King of Automobiles and his middle-aged, all-male, megabuck court. "The team is convinced that too strong a focus on profit derives the wrong results in the long term," she said evenly. "It is one thing *to say* we are customer driven, another thing *to be* customer driven," she noted spikily.

McKendry pressed on. She boldly contrasted the way Honda and Chrysler created new products. Honda's teams worked toward a common objective, yet were autonomous, cross-functional, and always accountable. Chrysler on the other hand had four different power structures — engineering, finance, manufacturing, and marketing — working on the same project, but each with different objectives.

Lutz's cigar was unsmoked. Bidwell's normal cheery expression had darkened. Eyes darted toward the chairman. How was he taking this lecture, no, this dressing down, from a Japanese-American woman whose annual salary wouldn't taxi his Gulfstream jet down Detroit Metro's runway? Iacocca often used the pejorative "Jap" in private conversations and some in the room wondered whether the great man's temper might boil over and cancel the entire proceeding with a mass firing of the upstart team.

But he sat, riveted by the disclosures. McKendry noted that new products coming from the joint Mitsubishi/Chrysler Diamond Star Motors based in Illinois were being delayed an estimated fourteen months because of Chrysler management lethargy, paper-shuffling, and meddling. "We believe Chrysler is politically divided by functional areas and that this division begins at the top," said McKendry, leveling her gaze at the Chairman. She saved her biggest blast for the end. Noting that Honda offices contained no walls or dividing partitions, McKendry said in low, determined tones, "We believe that a bulldozer should be brought up to the fifth floor of the Keller building and physically knock down the walls." *A bulldozer! Knock down the walls on Mahogany Row?*

Another woman, Linda Rumschlag, followed McKendry and continued the attack. "Honda believes in its people," she said, noting that its decentralized organization, delegation of responsibility, encouragement of risk-taking and training seemed light years ahead of Chrysler's structured, compartmentalized, aging organization. Rumschlag injected, almost as a footnote, that the promotion rate for Chrysler engineers was much lower than that for financial employees — just the opposite of Honda. "Youthfulness is a state of mind," she said, adding that enthusiasm, fresh ideas, and vitality can thrive regardless of age.

Phil Jansen then stepped up, charging that Chrysler's research and development was underfunded and often bootlegged from other companies. It had no center focus. The team recommended an autonomous R&D organization, and Jansen added that the company's founder, Walter P. Chrysler, was a firm believer in advanced engineering and long-range research. At present, he said, Chrysler's strategic planning was reactive to funding, confused, and redundant. In 1987 no less than *six* long-term plans had been published and product changes were taking more time, not less than in the past. He noted with irony that the new LH sedans planned for a 1993 launch were supposed to embody "expressive style," "capable function," a low cowl height (35.7 inches), and independent rear suspension. But, asked Jansen, "what are the customer's *needs?*" Did they know or care about "capable function" — whatever that meant? Gaining confidence toward what was obviously a fascinated and receptive audience, Jansen asked, "Do we need four distinct taillight designs on our upcoming 1991 minivan [a reskin of the aging T-115]?" Does this satisfy the customer's needs? Does the customer care? Jansen ended his report by repeating the central theme: Honda stresses customer benefit while Chrysler's multiple, contradictory messages and product lineup leave the buyer wary and confused.

It was about over, this guerrilla assault on the royal palace. Finck's summary was simple, unemotional, and to the point: The Honda philosophy centered on four elemental themes: (1) It trusts its people, (2) it believes in the team concept, (3) its long-term focus is on customer satisfaction, and (4) it values *product excellence* and *innovation* above all other business considerations.

The image of McKendry's Caterpillar diesel crashing down the hushed hallways of their palatial fifth-floor quarters dancing in their heads, the executives shook hands with the team, complimented them on their efforts, and headed for their nearby homes in the sumptuous corporate enclave of Bloomfield Hills.

The following day the team gave their presentation to a second group of upper-level executives, then were invited to a private lunch with Iacocca. To their surprise, the chairman said he liked what they had said. He pledged that their report would not be stuffed away in a musty archive and forgotten. After he signed autographs for the group, they departed, expressing amazement at the impact they had made. "We never expected that much attention," says Finck, now a senior engineer on the minivan platform team. "We had no power, but we were able to act as a catalyst for masses of ideas that seemed to be spreading through Chrysler about the changes that were needed." The team gave their presentation five more times to standing-room-only audiences within the corporation. They had suddenly become the hottest ticket in Highland Park. Two hundred copies of the report, marked confidential, were printed. A videotape was recorded by the team for further internal distribution. Still, they did not receive universal rave reviews. "Some managers were really upset," Finck recalls. "A few refused to let their workers see it. We were accused of being disloyal, of being young punks who didn't understand the realities of business."

But they had well and truly touched a nerve. By pinpointing the vast contrasts between what was then the most progressive automaker in the world and their own fusty, overblown, isolated, and smug company with plummeting sales and profits, the Honda study team had uttered the unspeakable. Never before in the history of the American automobile industry had the mice bitten the corporate lions. And more important, never before had the lions even noticed the mice existed, much less had any influence over the corporate ecosystem.

On February 12, 1988, the team's dozen members signed a memo to Iacocca amplifying the crucial need for Chrysler to establish a corporate philosophy. "A philosophy is not a collection of words that leaves the interpretation up to the reader; a philosophy that is clear has only one objective. Honda has chosen to make complete satisfaction of its customers its objective." The memo concluded with a list of eight "action steps" that were to serve as a tocsin for the company:

1. Establish a corporate philosophy for the twenty-first century. It must be accomplished through senior management teamwork and be totally clear and understandable for all employees.
2. Establish corporate priorities through the efforts of cross-functional teams that are consistent with the corporate philosophy.
3. Directly involve executives to work as a team to refine corporate strategy priorities.
4. Communicate the philosophy and strategic priorities to all employees.
5. Support the philosophy and priorities with senior management's actions as well as words.
6. Develop a cross-functional team to determine if the skills of the workforce are appropriate to accomplish the stated priorities.
7. Recognize and reward teamwork efforts that achieve the corporate priorities.
8. Repeat steps four through seven consistently.

Iacocca liked what he read, although considerable time would pass before he would accept Honda's concept of totally integrated, cross-functional teams. He did, however, sanction a series of internal surveys and studies, all of which seemed to confirm what the team had claimed: that Chrysler's mission was murky and confused to its employees. Somehow the Honda team had triggered a release of frustrations. In the ensuing polls came an outpouring of bitterness and open hostility that shocked the most jaded of senior management. One employee wrote: "Several years ago Mr. Iacocca challenged us with our slogan, 'We don't want to be the biggest, just the best.' That sounds great, but . . . again . . . our words are hollow. Every time we find some additional profit we look to reduce the content of our products without reducing price." Another charged, "We are being asked to make bricks without straw." "The company has fostered an environment where product people (people who actually come in physical contact with the automobile) have a very limited job potential for the future. In other words, the further you can remove yourself from coming in contact with an automobile in the workday, the better off you'll be," said an engineer. "Does Iacocca think making his $20 million a year and continually asking the rest of us to sacrifice is going to work forever?" asked a middle-management executive.

A skilled tradesman at a Chrysler assembly plant wrote: "It is disheartening to come from a quality lecture and find a production foreman knowingly running bad parts because he has to have numbers [i.e., to meet production quota]." "We are passing [producing] junk," charged another. An engineer who would later be assigned a key role in the new minivan program, Tom Edson, dared to put his name to paper when he wrote: "Chrysler needs to emphasize long term viability, not short-term profits. Cost and timing are driving decisions, not quality. Meeting profit targets and missing quality targets will kill the cash cow," he wrote. "We are slowly diminishing our capability to design and develop automobiles due to our depreciated technical staff, facilities and technical equipment. There is no leadership in technology and," he noted, "morale in the engineering ranks is low." He summarized his concerns with a direct statement to Iacocca: "If I was CEO for one minute I would change the bonus formula to 60 percent quality, 40 percent market share." Other engineers and technical experts launched similar broadsides at management and survived. In fact, many like Edson were installed in key positions as the corporate culture slowly re-vamped itself. "We have developed too much bureaucracy in the system . . . put in place too many controls. We spend more time be-ing a watchdog over the system than getting things through the system."

And so it went, page after page, volume upon volume of over fourteen thousand employee surveys pouring in from every shop, department, and factory in the Chrysler empire. The complaints, many of them petty and self-involved denouncements of corporate wage scales, promotion practices, health benefits, working condi-tions, and so on, were to be expected. But the overriding theme that alarmed the executive committee was the same identified by the Honda study: The employees *knew the secret:* that for all the rhetoric and chest-pounding by the chairman, Chrysler possessed no viable corporate philosophy or any concurrent long-range strat-egy that would involve, much less inspire, the entire workforce.

More studies confirmed the problem. One discovered that 30 percent of the employees polled claimed there was virtually no teamwork within their own departments, while 52 percent believed it to be nonexistent between other departments. Sixty-five percent admitted they had no idea where Chrysler was headed, with a like number charging that management failed to keep them informed of any strategies — if in fact any existed. Fully 60 percent said that management was insulated from the workforce and unwilling to accept any suggestions on how to improve products. A shocking 69 percent were convinced that their immediate supervisor's decisions would inevitably be changed or vetoed by some faceless entity above him.

Iacocca was stunned, as were the executive committee members. He told his six hundred top managers that "We've been listening. We've been taking notes. We learned a lot about ourselves. Some of it we like. Some of it we don't. The part we like, we're going to keep. The part we don't, we're going to change. And I mean right away." Such pronouncements for reform were standard boilerplate rhetoric in the automobile industry. For decades men like Iacocca — Ford and GM men as well as Chrysler — had periodi-cally found religion. They pledged better management and better automobiles (especially smaller, more efficient, higher-quality products), only to lapse back into the same old habits. Would this be different? "It sounded good at the time, but we'd heard so much of it all before," said a veteran Chrysler engineer.

But Iacocca meant business. He convened a series of senior management sessions at the elegant Kohler, Wisconsin, resort and conference center. Executives gathered, forty at a time, for what were called "truth weeks." Here the same weaknesses — lack of a corporate philosophy and long-range strategy, the absence of cross-functional administration, feeble research and development funding, and a low priority for engineering — were openly and often savagely articulated.

Change at Chrysler had an ardent advocate in Bob Lutz, who had championed the Honda study. And, oddly, the controversial purchase of AMC had brought inside the company the seeds of a new order — a crew of executives who had not grown up within the culture of Chrysler and who had different skills and styles of management.

In 1986, Lutz had made the switch from Ford to Chrysler. He was a tough-minded product expert with a strong European orientation and rigid Germanic opinions about what good automobiles were all about. Lutz came aboard as executive vice president in charge of trucks, international operations, and Chrysler's component suppliers, but it was clear to industry watchers that this towering, talented, occasionally arrogant ex–Ford, BMW, and General Motors executive would hardly content himself with such a sideline role in the corporate fortunes. Like Sperlich, Lutz wore his strong, outspoken opinions on his sleeve and an early clash between the two men was expected. But Bob Lutz was only one of several aggressive executives who would challenge the old Chrysler hierarchy not only from Ford but from the ruins of American Motors. Unlike many auto management types, who were, in terms of passion for their product, interchangeable with the men who ran plumbing fixture empires or discount furniture chains, Bob Lutz loved automobiles . . . not to mention motorcycles, helicopters (which he flew expertly), and airplanes. He was an accomplished fast driver, collected vintage racing cars and was a student of motor racing history.

Joe Cappy, who had served as AMC's president and CEO during its final hours — and who was openly angered by the French capitulation — was retained as group vice president of the newly formed Jeep-Eagle Division, which was formed from the remnants of his old company. Cappy headed a nucleus of about a dozen top AMC executives and engineers who were to play major roles in Chrysler's future. John Tierney, who acted as chief financial officer at AMC, became chairman of Chrysler Financial Corporation, while Tom Foley, head of corporate planning for the French, assumed similar duties at Chrysler. Most of the native French staff either returned home or left the business entirely, with one major exception. Francois Castaing, a slight, hawk-nosed former racing engineer on Renault's Formula One team, had served as group vice president for product and quality and was furious at what he considered a Renault betrayal just as AMC was on the verge of a comeback. Castaing chose to remain in the United States as the vice president of Jeep truck and engineering — a job that involved the development of the new, advanced ZJ and placed him in a direct line of fire from the entrenched Product Planning Group headed by Hal Sperlich and his allies. Joining Castaing was veteran engineer John Nemeth, AMC's product development chief, who became director of engineering at Chrysler.

Also coming aboard was Chris Theodore, a cocky young engineer who had been in charge of engine engineering at AMC and was a close friend and associate of Castaing's.

Thrusting men like Castaing and Theodore into the midst of Chrysler caused convulsions that are still being felt today. Recalls one of the AMC transfers, "You've got to remember that in those days Chrysler was fat with cash. They were coming off three or four good years in the mid-1980s and were resting on their laurels with the minivan and the Dodge Dakota midsized pickup — both of which enjoyed exclusivity in the market. On the other hand we came from a totally different culture that on the surface seemed defunct and discredited. After all, it was them who were buying us. What was not understood at the time was that we were already operating with cross-functional teams, if for no other reason that we didn't have enough money or personnel to do otherwise. But compared to the complex, structured chimneys that were spread throughout Chrysler, our little operation seemed at the time to border on insignificant."

Few people outside Detroit understood the rigid cultural boundaries that separated the giants of the industry. There were distinct differences in the look and manner of the management; GM men (*very* few women) were inevitably Waspish and perfectly groomed, while Ford's staff were more ethnically diverse, more garrulous, and flashily dressed. Chrysler people seemed to be leaden engineering types in Perma Press shirts featuring plastic pocket protectors packed with mechanical pencils. The distinctions were often transgenerational, with families proudly claiming that grandfathers, fathers, and sons had worked for the same corporation. Across the spectrum of the workforce, from the United Auto Worker bluecollars, to tailored executives, massive prosperity had been produced by such loyalties. From the sandy shores of Lake Huron to the chilly, remote reaches of the Upper Peninsula stood thousands of second homes as testimony to the lavish retirements allotted to the loyalists. Each weekend, northbound Interstate 75 would be packed with masses of motor homes, snowmobiles, trailer boats, dirt bikes, sports cars, and elegant sedans, all driven by the beneficiaries of eighty years of corporate largess. Michigan claimed the largest registration of private boats in the world, thanks to the prosperity of the automobile business. The men and women of Chrysler, General Motors, Ford, and even the remnants of American Motors bore their loyalties with pride.

Based on these ingrained allegiances, it would take years for the outriders and refugees from AMC to be integrated into Chrysler. But slowly the reality of the alliance sunk in to all who sought longterm futures with the organization. Initially the point of contact between the two companies would be the four-door Jeep that was intended to replace the aging Grand Cherokee. AMC's ZJ prototype, with its refined unit-body construction, seemed to be the logical design for development. But the Chrysler Product Planning staff, led by Sperlich, had intended to create the new sport-utility vehicle from its existing Dakota pickup platform and fought the notion of adopting the ZJ. The wrangling would delay the Grand

Cherokee's debut by more than a year and would grease the skids for the loss of several talented Chrysler loyalists who resisted the AMC incursion.

By late 1987 the dispute between Iacocca and Sperlich had deteriorated into public sparring. New men with new ideas — Lutz and Castaing primary among them — were displacing Sperlich and longtime Chrysler chief engineer Jack Withrow as the corporate product gurus. Each group had its own agenda: Sperlich's a logical but aggressive expansion of the current Chrysler lineup from its highly successful K-car base, while the interlopers centered on a revolutionary restructuring of both the products and the way they were being designed and built. In early 1988, Hal Sperlich, one of the most innovative product planners in the history of the industry, walked out. Withrow would soon follow. It was on the surface a polite departure, accompanied by the obligatory promotion-cum-demotion and lavish flattery passed around by all parties for public consumption. Sperlich spoke of "personal freedom after thirty years in harness" and inferences of his chronic back trouble were published. But the source of pain was Lee Iacocca, whom Sperlich grew to revile because of his increasingly imperious executive style and his lavish expenditures on properties outside Chrysler's core business. The arrival of American Motors' dissidents was the last straw and Sperlich departed, his job inherited in part by archrival Lutz and Iacocca pal Ben Bidwell. Sperlich was to later reflect, "Lee Iacocca became Henry Ford, the very man he hated most."

Despite the loss of key executives like Sperlich and Withrow, there is no question that the cultural revolution caused by the American Motors purchase generated enormous long-term benefits and, in retrospect, may have been the single most important element in Chrysler's most recent revival. But initially the small band from their defunct Southfield headquarters was treated more like refugees from a defeated nation than colleagues from a rival automobile company. And with good reason. Chrysler — Iacocca's "new" Chrysler Corporation — seemed to be riding high. How, questioned the establishment, could a collection of losers from a fringe car-maker offer anything to mighty Chrysler?

A great deal, as it turned out. Castaing, Nemeth, and Theodore brought with them plans for the ZJ Jeep that was vastly superior to anything Chrysler had on its drawing boards. It was built on a unit body, wherein the body and frame were fabricated as a single, rigid element as opposed to the aged, traditional method of mounting a body structure on an independent pair of frame rails. The ZJ, as envisioned by the tiny American Motors engineering group, was by all standards of design an excellent effort, despite internal sniping from within the Chrysler staff.

But the impact of the American Motors outcasts far transcended any single portfolio of vehicle plans they might have brought with them from Southfield. The arrival of this band, for the most part evidencing little or no initial loyalty to a company they regarded more as conquerors than employers, injected an atmosphere of skepticism and doubt into an organization that, despite a roller-coaster ride in the marketplace, had never engaged, until the Honda study, in serious self-evaluation of how and why it was do-ing business. It was the AMC dissidents whose experience showed effective alternatives to Chrysler's chimneys.

But in the end, after all the meetings were adjourned, the video-tapes rewound, the reports read and filed, and the manifestoes cel-ebrated, one simple, critical mission remained: To survive, Chrysler Corporation had to begin building world-class automobiles, in-cluding the best minivan that had ever been built.

4

The Chimneys Collapse

AS AMERICA'S industrial machine clanked and groaned through the 1980s, Japan's seamless, perfectly tuned, fully computerized perpetual-motion miracle seemed certain to consign it to the scrap heap. The bestseller lists became infested with treatises about the causes and cures. Men like Tom Peters, Peter Drucker, Michael E. Porter, and John Naisbitt enjoyed instant celebrity status as they savaged the nation's good gray moguls and divined solutions to stem what appeared to be the total destruction of the nation's manufacturing sector. Many of their observations relating to efficiency, labor management, motivation, finance, and planning were spot-on, and had their various formulas for change been embraced, it is possible that much of the agony could have been avoided. So too if the Detroit executives had, thirty years prior, listened to the teachings of their countryman, W. Edwards Deming, whose fundamentals of statistical quality control had been treated like divine commandments by the men running Toyota, Nissan, and Mitsubishi Heavy Industries.

But it is seldom in the nature of Americans to act with judicious foresight. Prescience is not our long suit. We are more inclined to drive head-on, full speed toward disaster, slamming on the brakes only at the last possible second. Our predilection is toward revolution, not evolution, and a certain Darwinian code of survival of the fittest remains a centerpiece of our business ethic. In American business, failure breeds revolution, contrary to success breeding evolution. In the case of Chrysler, the need for change was obvious as the corporation grew fat with cash in the early 1980s, but the management remained asleep at the throttle. Then was the appropriate moment for contemplative study of the Japanese threat and how to counter it. With the corporate ship on a steady course, measured, incremental steering adjustments might have been made to streamline and downsize the entire process by which their automobiles were designed and manufactured. But Iacocca, bursting with hubris, chose an opposite track, unloading billions for aerospace, defense, and financial operations unrelated to his core business. This squandering of capital and the upheavals it triggered in the Highland Park executive suite led to the tectonic shift in how the corporation did business and — most important — to its survival. Revolution, not evolution. No logical, carefully devised plan here; no clever formula that could be illustrated on four-color graphs or spreadsheets, but rather a noisy, smash-the-furniture riot that somehow, fortuitously, thankfully, almost accidentally, saved Iacocca's "new" but now *very* old Chrysler Corporation.

The single most important act in this improbable revival was the purchase of American Motors. The infusion of new executive blood, plus the financial crisis the purchase triggered, indirectly forged a double-edged sword of Damocles that hung over the management. This in turn prompted the marginally seditious Honda study and additional corporate frontal lobe massaging in the form of other internal studies and reevaluations. Iacocca also approved funding of the Liberty Project, an outrider "skunkworks" engineering and design group assigned to create — much as GM was doing with Saturn — a revolution in manufacturing that would lead to a new domestically produced compact.

A kind of hands-on, automotive think tank, Liberty ultimately helped develop what would be marketed as the Diamond Star–produced Eagle Summit, Plymouth Colt Vista, and the Mitsubishi Expo microvans. Liberty's other projects would include the alternately fueled Patriot racing car, but many traditionalists in the company derided Liberty as a "sandbox" where airheaded visionaries were permitted to play. Other more progressive types understood that most Japanese companies had similar operations and valued them greatly.

But it was clear that no matter what orderly procedures, sophisticated academic strategies, mathematically sound formulae or intricate organizational reforms might be instituted, Chrysler's salvation lay in the hands of the men (and a precious few women) who could tell good automobiles from bad and knew how to build them. Iacocca was scheduled to retire at the end of 1992. His position as one of the three or four most influential figures in the history of the industry was assured. But he had lost the handle on how to save Chrysler as he had done a decade earlier. His expected successor, Jerry Greenwald, had left in May 1990, opening the path to the CEO's chair. His departure was not viewed as a disaster by people who understood Chrysler's product weakness. For all his financial acumen, Greenwald was hopelessly ignorant about automobiles.*

But aggressive new men were rising up, fortuitously as it turned out, to fill the void at the top. They were nuts-and-bolts types whose passion was great automobiles, not great profit-and-loss statements. Leading the pack was Lutz, bumptious, imperious, Swiss born, American educated, and boiling with enthusiasm to create world-class cars. With him came Francois Castaing, soon to be elevated to vice president of engineering. Like Lutz, he had been reared in the European tradition of fast, nimble, taut machinery that put to shame the hated "Detroit Iron" that the Big Three had been foisting on the public for years.

Castaing and Lutz were kindred souls. Fluent in several languages, they could converse both in French and English. Both were very fast behind the wheel. Both were comfortable in the European school of hyper-speed autobahn and auto-route travel. They understood mechanical excellence and demanded standards far above those of the off-the-rack Detroit executives. Although Castaing had no direct role in the Honda study, he had been discussing the Japanese company's management style with AMC associates since 1984. His experience with Renault's Formula One racing program,

---

*Many top executives, like Jerry Greenwald, knew next to nothing about the vehicles they built. Once Greenwald was picked up by a corporate operative at a California airport and driven to his hotel in a Chrysler Fifth Avenue. Greenwald did not know how to operate the air-conditioning controls, although they had been essentially unchanged on Chrysler products for nearly twenty years.

wherein a small group of like-minded individuals, with a single goal, marshaled millions of French francs into a world-championship motor-sports program, had convinced him of the merits of a cross-functional team. He understood Chrysler's desperate need for reformation. Not only had he operated within a similar concept at Renault and — in a *defacto* sense — at cash-strapped American Motors, but he knew that Ford's successful Taurus sedan had been developed prior to its 1985 introduction on a modified team basis. General Motors had experimented with teams, as had Chrysler with Gardner's back-door development of the T-115 minivan. Following that triumph, Gardner had led a similar-sized team in the development of the Dakota pickup, yet another niche-selling triumph for the corporation. But now seemed the time to stop dabbling with the concept and to get serious; to demolish once and for all the dreaded, hated, and counterproductive "chimneys" and to shove Chrysler into the modern industrial world.

Joining Castaing and Lutz in their drive toward platform teams was Chrysler's slight, soft-spoken vice president for design, Tom Gale. A designer notably unlike the prima donnas and poseurs who once populated the industry, Michigan-born Gale possessed none of the multilingual elan of Lutz and Castaing. But his instinct for automobile esthetics was positively aristocratic. His most recent styling triumphs were the lovely, tightly rendered Diamond Star coupes, introduced in 1988 as the Plymouth Laser, Mitsubishi Eclipse, and Eagle Talon (sold through the Jeep-Eagle dealer network). It was Gale who became the third member of the triumvirate, with Lutz and Castaing, and who would exert the most intense pressure for massive change within Chrysler. Soon other like-minded men and women would join them, but as the old guard slowly stepped aside or were driven out of Highland Park, it would be this trio — a Midatlantic man, a Frenchman, and a native Michigander — who were to trigger the great revolution within the corporation.

Throughout the crisis years of 1988–1991, a single mission preoccupied the corporate planners. The new LH sedan was to be the $1.6 billion centerpiece successor to the K-car. Early planning began in the mid-1980s and there was no debating that the car would be front-wheel drive. Iacocca had pledged that Chrysler would operate exclusively in that configuration. Tom Gale's design team had created a swoopy preliminary shape, to be known as "cab forward," by mounting the wheels at the outer corners of the chassis. The passenger compartment could then be moved forward, maximizing internal room. Initially the design called for a so-called east-west engine layout — i.e., the powerplant was to be mounted crosswise in the engine bay, thereby shortening the hood while gaining foot room. The advance chassis group had almost completed its preliminary planning by late spring 1988 when Francois Castaing, now under the patronage of Lutz, made his first decisive move. Having been instrumental in the design of the AMC (now Eagle) Premier, which carried its V6 engine "north-south" — i.e., in the conventional longitudinal position — Castaing lobbied hard for the LH to be so altered. He formed a small group of engineers into what was called an "Iron Eagle" team and, in thirty days, converted a prototype Premier two-door coupe (called the X59 Allure; never produced) to carry the 3.3-liter LH V6 engine in the "north-south" configuration. The prototype was shown to senior management in one of the road test garages at Highland Park, where it was favorably received. "Iron Eagle" prompted the LH engine position to be changed, ostensibly to reduce dreaded "NVH," which was industry argot for the much-hated, but hard to eliminate, triple bugaboos of "noise, vibration, and harshness." "Castaing also claimed the north-south layout would improve crash-worthiness and improve the turning radius, but some engineers on the project suspected the reason lay in the fact that the Renault/AMC/Eagle Premier had a north-south layout. That was Castaing's car at AMC," says a former Chrysler engineer who left the company in 1991 to become an automotive journalist. "To us, there was French ego involved. There were so many American Motors engineers on the LH project that we began to wonder who bought who."

This attitude was typical of the turmoil within the engineering ranks and the executive suites, as men (and a few women) maneuvered for position. Assignments and titles were changed almost by the week. "It was constant; a pillar-to-post situation that had everybody in limbo," recalls the ex-engineer.

Even Ben Bidwell, the longtime Iacocca friend and ally from the Ford days, was confused. During a five-year span between 1986 and 1991, the veteran executive held five different major management positions, each with such august titles as executive vice president, vice chairman, president, co-president and chairman. Greenwald had been assigned to three totally different executive posts within the same time frame, as Iacocca moved his players on the board in a mad game of corporate chess.

Slowly, agonizingly, the corporation was groping its way toward a total reorganization based on what were to be called platform teams. If the Honda study and the extensive senior management evaluation sessions at the Kohler, Wisconsin, Conference Center had revealed any truths, it was that the ancient "chimney system," with its vertical isolated empires of specific function, was utterly obsolete. Lutz and Castaing, as well as Tom Gale and a few other progressives in upper management, believed that a series of project teams involving cross-pollination of design, engineering, finance, marketing, supply, and so on were the wave of the future and had to be implemented immediately. A small spin-off team was created to design and build the expensive, limited-production Viper sports car, but the establishment within the company discounted this as a big-boys toy and an irrelevance to the major mission.

Contrary to conventional history, Iacocca initially hated the idea of reorganizing on the basis of platform teams. "He talked about splitting Chrysler into four individual companies," says Chris Theodore, "but he wouldn't accept the idea of breaking down the old system. What he was suggesting were four smaller versions of what we already had. That didn't make any sense at all."

By late 1988, Castaing, with Lutz's ardent sponsorship, had been elevated to succeed the departed Jack Withrow, vice president of engineering. This gave him a proper power base to make his first serious move toward forming a platform team. Castaing drove to the Diamond Star plant in Normal, Illinois, to meet with Glenn Gardner, who held the title of president, but was in reality idling in place as a cadre of Mitsubishi production experts actually ran the factory. Gardner was an obvious choice. Ten years earlier his tiny team had, in the midst of an oppressive bureaucracy, created the first minivan and later the Dakota pickup. Now, having watched the lean and mean Japanese method of building cars in Illinois, he alone seemed to possess the overview necessary to handle the formation of a team to complete the LH program.

"I first heard the phrase 'platform team' discussed in mid-'88," recalls Tom Edson, a career engineer who was destined to become a linchpin in the NS minivan project. His wife, Maureen, was employed in the Chrysler Corporate Strategy office and through her he understood that planning new products was a lugubrious process: a molasses-slow passage through shoals of committees, task forces, polls, and studies. "We were 'perfuming the pig,' doing what we called 'fluff and buff' jobs on current products, while the LH — which a lot of people in the industry said stood for 'last hope' — and the new Jeep were bogged down in committees." "It was hopeless paper-shuffling in endless rounds of dog-and-pony acts," says another engineer. "The strategy was simple: If you had to give a status report, you simply told management what you *thought* they wanted to hear, then prayed you would be moved to another assignment before the issue either got fixed or the real truth came out."

It was this sort of reality that caused Castaing to give Gardner the LH assignment. The policy shift was intended not only to increase efficiency and to end the archaic chimney system (and what Lutz had described as "a bunch of PT boat captains trying to run a battleship") but to create a system of accountability within a tightly run team with a single, specific goal. By the time Gardner took charge, the LH project was nearly three years old, having lain dormant due, in the main, to what the departed Hal Sperlich describes as "Lee having lost focus."

Gardner's so-called new car platform was sold internally as a trial balloon. Iacocca consented, reluctantly, although he continued to toy with his four-independent-division concept and, worse yet, insisted on exercising his mogul-style veto power. "People were afraid of him," recalls a former Chrysler engineer. "He was such an imposing presence that people went out of their way to avoid him, in part because of fear and in part because the word had passed through the company that as far as automobiles went, he had lost it. Quite simply, he had terrible taste." During early 1987 the design group had been hard at work creating an interior treatment for the 1988-model C-body Dodge Dynasty and Chrysler New Yorker that was European in theme with muted fabrics, bucket front seats, and functional instrumentation. The designers delayed until the last hour before showing it to the Chairman, in hopes that he would accept the more contemporary treatment based, if not on taste, at least on expediency. Not so. Iacocca was furious, rejecting the styling out of hand and demanding that his beloved fake wood and tufted velour trappings be fitted — at substantial extra cost.

Gardner's smallish band of engineers, designers, product planners, and manufacturing and finance types was set up, not within the corporate compound at Highland Park, but rather a dozen miles north up Interstate 75 in a dingy industrial park on Featherstone Road in Auburn Hills. They worked within a long field goal kick of the immense Silverdome and only yards away from where surveyors were beginning to stake out the contours for Iacocca's vast billion-dollar Chrysler Technical Center. Working adjacent to the sandbox gang from the Liberty group, who were also housed in the Featherstone Road clutter of buildings, the team set to work to sort out the preliminary schematics and layouts that formed the basis for the vehicle that was, in theory at least, to form the opening salvo in Chrysler's new company-saving edition of vehicles.

While it would seem that the LH team was doomed to labor in isolation, everyone in the corporation worked in a similar state of seclusion and policy darkness. The chimney system, which permitted each major activity to operate independently, was separated not only philosophically but geographically. The manufacturing staff responsible for actually forging, stamping, bolting, and welding the vehicles into salable entities, were headquartered at Mound Road and Outer Drive, three miles east of Highland Park. The engineering group was housed in an outbuilding of the aged K. T. Keller complex at Highland Park while the design, sales, and finance arms operated from the new Walter P. Chrysler Building a long walk or short drive across a broad manicured entry boulevard. "Setting up a meeting with more than one other group to discuss product planning was like organizing a summer vacation trip to Europe for your family," quipped one veteran.

Legions of committees were in place to counteract the confusion and redundancy. Like GM and Ford, Chrysler attempted to save money by commonizing parts throughout its product line. All Chrysler radios, air-conditioning units, ignition switches, keys, etc. were employed throughout the line. The same was true at GM and Ford, where dome lights, door latches, transmissions, and radios were spread throughout the product lineup to save costs. But this practice often produced badly compromised vehicles. By requiring off-the-rack components — as opposed to specially designed versions — the tasks of making the pieces fit efficiently on the assembly line often suffered as well. The result was costlier, badly built automobiles.

The most absurd-sounding group was the "common holes" committee, which convened periodically with the mission to standardize, where possible, various apertures in bodies and frames — bolt holes, rivet holes, holes for instruments, holes for door handles, antennae, headlights, bumper brackets, in order to save costs. Because of redundancy and bad planning, Chrysler employed over *fifty thousand* different fasteners — nuts and bolts, cotter pins, tie-wraps, rivets, cable, snaps. Many in the company knew cost could be reduced by half with sensible commonization practices. But with each chimney operating independently, the overlap of repetition could never be corrected, despite incessant corporate directives to cut costs. A joke passed through the company during one of the periodic cost-cutting campaigns: Change "Jeep" to "Jep," thereby saving millions in letter *e*'s. Many of the more serious attempts were as futile.

Richard "Dick" Dauch, who preceded Castaing as corporate vice president of manufacturing, was an executive of the old school who in many ways epitomized Chrysler's traditional way of doing business. A tough-talking, up-through-the-ranks line boss, Dauch ruled "by intimidation," according to several engineers who worked with him. Like most veterans in the industry, assembly-line speed was essential to Dauch and it was generally maintained that minor glitches would be corrected following final assembly or by the dealers rather than slow the pace. This was true throughout the entire American automobile industry, where all manner of flawed components — electric motors, transmission components, gears, sheet-metal stampings, trim items, paintwork — would sail through the system in the name of assembly-line speed. The logic: The component *might* work despite its poor quality, and if not, it would be corrected by the dealers under warranty. Dauch and Lutz hated each other. Not only did their muscle-bound personalities conflict, but so did their manufacturing philosophies. Dauch understood the current system and felt it should be maintained, with incremental adjustments. Lutz, ever the revolutionary, advocated massive changes with more worker empowerment as articulated in the Honda study.

In the meantime the men in the trenches saw only modest changes as the warfare in the executive suites intensified. Rich Schaum, a former American Motors engine specialist, was one of thousands within the corporation who worked in medieval conditions compared with their Japanese and European rivals. "We had 104 dynamometers in the engine department at Highland Park. Some of them dated back to before World War II," he recalls. "Dynamometer Bay number 29 had a plaque stating that Walter P. Chrysler had dedicated it in 1939! It was so old that it used vacuum tubes that we could only source in Russia!" Schaum and his associates worked in frustration as the archaic Chrysler system consumed five years to design and produce a new engine — almost twice as long as their overseas rivals.

During the turmoil, the corporation had been laboring to produce an updated version of the T-115 minivan code-named "AS." This would involve a total reskinning of the original platform and was to be introduced in the fall of 1990 as a "totally new" Dodge Caravan and Plymouth Voyager. Designer Tom Gale had created a neatly styled update of both the interior and exterior. It remained generically related to the little box that captured the market in 1984, yet offered hundreds of subtle improvements. But the internal warfare remained intense. The interior design group had concentrated heavily on aesthetics, while the engineers worked to create efficient "reach zones," i.e., areas within arm's reach that made the instruments, radio controls, and so forth easily accessible to the driver. But the chimney system, which mandated that these improvements be implemented by the designers and engineers with minimal consultation, caused enormous turmoil. "It was aesthetics versus ergonomics. The design group and engineering group were two armed camps," says Tom Edson.

More big-time trouble in the form of Lee Iacocca was on the way. It had always been the prerogative of automobile bosses to imperiously mandate detail changes on automobile designs, no matter how late in the program. Such was the case with the AS, which possessed a so-called character line (a styling trick to break up a flat expanse of sheet metal, both for aesthetics and added rigidity) on the right rear quarter. It displeased the Chairman. Moreover, he hated the radius curves of the window glass on the left rear quarter of the AS. He demanded changes, although Gale and other executives angrily argued that millions had been spent on the aperture stamping dies necessary to punch out the body panels in mass production. Iacocca would have none of it. The change was dictated at an extra cost of *$100 million.* "Gale went nuts," remembers Edson. "He fumed that for one hundred million extra bucks during the original design process he could have created a smoother look which would have made the AS much better able to compete with Ford's more aerodynamic Windstar during the year prior to arrival of the totally new NS." Such was the profligate power of the old American auto mogul.

Worse yet, Iacocca rushed ahead to be the first to market with an old hydraulically controlled automatic transmission that had been in the works since 1987. During the same period every major manufacturer, domestic and overseas, had been at work on similar units, intended to replace the three-speed automatics that had dominated the industry for years. Chrysler's version, known internally as the "A-604" and in the sales brochures as "Ultra Drive" was a superb design — on paper. But when it arrived in the market on the updated AS minivan models, a plethora of tiny weak points caused thousand of breakdowns. Iacocca's gamble to beat the competition had the potential of branding the company with the mark of Cain.

Within weeks of introduction in late 1990, new minivans were being towed into dealerships across the country with failed transmissions. The word was passing through the industry — and, more

ominously, through the network of mechanics, gas station operators, car dealers, auctioneers, wholesalers, journalists, safety experts, and disgruntled minivan owners — that the A-604 was a
disaster. News reached Highland Park that *Consumer Reports*, the
influential, nonprofit publication that was believed inside the company to be notoriously anti-Chrysler (its chief automotive tester
was a former Chrysler engineer), was about to publish a major de-
nunciation of the transmission. A meeting of the Chrysler Executive Council, chaired by Iacocca, was called and Chris Theodore,
then heading a group known as the "Current Platform Power
Team" was summoned to help solve the problem.

No one in the room was exactly leaping out of his chair to vol-
unteer. The A-604 was a labyrinth of flaws. No single Achilles' heel
was evident, but rather a series of interconnected mechanical and
electronic glitches that caused terminal failure — often within the
first thousand miles of operation. Finally Iacocca tired of the wrangling and buck-passing. "I'm going to take a piss. When I come
back, somebody's going to have the assignment," he growled.
While the Chairman was relieving himself, Lutz gave Theodore the
dubious honor. In a headlong, no-sleep marathon, he and a small
team managed to transform the A-604 into a workable unit and
thereby help Chrysler dodge what might have been a fatal bullet.
But he would pay a price. Ugly letters and memos, some anony-
mous, were delivered to Lutz and Iacocca, denouncing Theodore as
a toady, an AMC interloper, and an opportunist who was using his
friendship with Castaing to climb over the bodies of old company
loyalists. The internal fury generated by Theodore's appointment
only amplified the rift that existed between the Chrysler establishment and the AMC newcomers. Logically, it would have seemed
that Theodore's repair of the potentially disastrous transmission
flaw would have been the cause for widespread celebration, but his
allegedly blighted background more than offset any credit accruing
to him from the traditionalists. "One letter to Iacocca called me 'a
beard-pulling little jerk who ought to be fired.' That kind of stuff
being said to the Chairman really hurt," he recalled.

But thanks to Theodore's little team — and the arrival of the
Gulf War, which drove the issue off the front pages — the poten-

tially disastrous A-604 was transformed from a leper's curse into a noncontroversial four-speed automatic. But once again this brush with disaster pinpointed how the old way of doing business was totally obsolete in a world of intensified competition and elevated consumer awareness. Even at that, certain design flaws persisted. Because of poor design, minivan owners in the Rocky Mountain states experienced chronic fuel pump failure at about twelve thousand miles. Yet the design was unchanged for the nearly fifteen-year life of the T-115, in the main because it was cheaper to service the warranty calls from the smaller customer base than it was to invest in a redesign of the fuel pump location and layout.

Slowly, reluctantly, the lethargic "new Chrysler Corporation" changed direction. The rapid, light-footed movement of Gardner's LH platform team from problem to problem, accompanied by impressive savings of funds, persuaded Iacocca that there was value in the new concept being worked out on Featherstone Road. He had little choice but to seek new solutions. By the end of 1990 his company was once again on the verge of oblivion. Sales of his stable of outdated, boxy K-car derivatives were slumping in a recession-blitzed market. The corporate market share had dipped below 10 percent. He had sapped the coffers with the $1.1 billion investment in the immense Auburn Hills Chrysler Technical Center, which was now being called "Iacocca's mausoleum." It did in fact become such a major financial burden that the corporation was forced to turn it over to a consortium of major lending institutions, and to arrange a long-term lease for the property. Additional funding was also needed to complete the LH program and to finalize production of the long-delayed Jeep Grand Cherokee. Interest payments on $1.1 billion in high-interest (12.4 percent) corporate bonds totaled $130 million a year. Unfunded pension liability hovered near $4 billion. While Iacocca railed publicly against the Japanese, the government, and the economy as the source of his company's troubles, most of the blame could be traced to the fifth floor of the K. T. Keller Building in Highland Park, where inefficient, outdated policies made worse by profligate spending were driving Chrysler toward bankruptcy.

Much has been written about the genius of Chrysler's platform team concept, and, because it was created during the final hours of

Iacocca's watch, it has been included in his lengthy honor role of achievements. Attempts by scholars, business writers, and industry analysts to systematize the teams' creation and to bring a modicum of logic to the process demanded giant leaps of faith. Truth be known, Chrysler did not reorganize itself by careful self-analysis and the implementation of arcane business school philosophies. The platform teams rose out of chaos and the acts of desperate men. Ironically, if Iacocca made a contribution, it was unwitting. His purchase of American Motors — justified for other reasons — perhaps provided the essential triggering mechanism. The ensuing clash of cultures was a godsend. With the arrival of men like Castaing and Theodore, the entire, ingrained Chrysler way of doing business was thrown out of synch. Turmoil led to reevaluation, which in turn led to genuine progress. "Hell, we already were a platform team at AMC," muses Theodore. "We didn't have enough people or money to operate otherwise. When we got to Chrysler we saw unbelievable waste and inefficiency. Because of our size at AMC we had to operate with tiny groups, which were forced to make major decisions. The design guys, the manufacturing and financial guys — everybody — had to work together. There was no other way. At Chrysler we faced endless committee meetings, reports, and studies prior to any decisions being made. It was only natural that Francois would try to implement the smaller, more flexible units that had worked for him." Slowly, agonizingly, the refugees, in concert with the revolutionaries inside Chrysler, cracked the old system.

The department known as Current Platform Engineering was split into two units; the small-car team (known as PL, which would ultimately come to market as the Neon), headed by Bob Marcel, and the minivan team with AMC veteran John Nemeth in charge. These two groups would function with Gardner's large car LH group as "teams" — each with fully integrated staffs covering all missions within the car-making operation. Ultimately a fourth platform group encompassing Jeep/Truck would be formed. But Castaing made further modifications on the customary Detroit organizational model. Unlike Ford and General Motors, Chrysler was destined to operate without an advanced engineering group — the so-called corporate think tanks assigned to create long-range technology in terms of new engines, transmissions, manufacturing techniques, and so forth. Rather than support another layer of bureaucracy, which often operated at cross purposes with lower-echelon engineering groups within the company, Castaing, with Lutz's sanction, gave each of the four platform teams special assignments relating to advanced product planning. Gardner's large-car team was assigned the job of developing the corporation's computer design functions. Nemeth's minivan team was to develop new powertrains, e.g., engines, transmissions, and differentials, while Marcel's small-car group were to create advanced electronics, engine controllers for lower emissions and enhanced performance. Along with lightweight body structures using materials like aluminum and plastics in place of steel. The Jeep/Truck team was assigned to research alternate fuels and other environmental problems while concentrating on the creation of vehicles in the booming sport/utility and pickup market segments.

The transition was hardly smooth. "You talk about internal strife," recalls one Chrysler loyalist. "This was war!" The traditionalists, already furious about the incursions of the AMC interlopers, now watched their entire corporate structure being torn asunder. Suddenly specialists were forced to become generalists. "Look at it this way," says Bernie Swanson, a laconic engineer who headed the small design group on the minivan platform team responsible for suspensions, "in the old culture you might have a guy who was *the* shock absorber expert in the company. Nobody knew more about shock absorbers than he did. He had his own little protected bailiwick. You wanted to know about shock absorbers, you talked to him. Now, under the new platform team principle, everybody had to know about shock absorbers — and spring rates and suspension geometry and everything else relating to suspensions. The guy working under the old system was suddenly forced to become a broad-gauge expert. They lost their protective cover."

Sham Rushwin, a no-nonsense, up-through-the-ranks former hourly laborer who would ultimately manage the manufacturing process of the new minivan, recalls, "Under the old system you could ramrod things through; bulldoze 'em past people with brute force because you knew more about the subject than they did. But now, with the teams, everybody was theoretically an expert on everything. That wasn't quite the case, but at least they knew enough so that there weren't any secrets."

As the old replaced the new, there were mass defections. Some bright young engineers, after receiving company-paid master's degrees and being designated as management trainees, decided that the corporation was doomed. "We jumped ship," says one. "I figured that Chrysler just could not survive the internal strife and the losses it was absorbing in the market. Obviously I was wrong." More vocal antiteam employees were shoved aside, either given early retirement or shunted into backwater jobs. Castaing and Lutz, along with Tom Gale and other progressives in top positions, moved quickly to reestablish order in the ranks. In all, seven thousand engineers in the corporation were reassigned within the teams and four "Godfathers" were designated to oversee the operations. Castaing, as vice president of engineering, was to supervise Jeep/Truck, while Ron Boltz looked after the $1.3 billion PL small-car team. Tom Stallcamp, the corporation's purchasing chief, was to monitor Gardner's large-car LH operation while Tom Gale, the soft-spoken design chief, was assigned to oversee Nemeth's mini-van team.

It had long been acknowledged that a replacement of the T-115 would be necessary. While the 1990 AS reskinning would serve the corporate needs for a few years, Chrysler's management understood by the late 1980s that the T-115 platform was becoming intolerably long in the tooth. The minivan was too critical a component of the corporate product mix to be incrementally updated. Unlike the origination of the T-115 a decade earlier, which had arrived, through a series of propitious gambles and unconventional marketing concepts, a new version had long been accepted as a future project. There were no pivotal meetings or epiphanies, no flashes of brilliance from a single executive, that could be credited to the emergence of the new vehicle program. It was assumed by everyone, from Iacocca on down, that the T-115/AS platform would be obsolete by the mid-1990s and that the corporation would have to invest billions for a replacement. It was not whether Nemeth's little team would create the rough outlines of the new minivan; it was how they would create it and how much it would cost that embodied their challenge.

Nemeth was nearing retirement and would soon give way to Chris Theodore, whose star was rising after correcting the A-604 transmission fiasco. Both men, along with Gale, understood the magnitude of their assignments. The executive staff was wrangling over the final dollar amount of the project, with budgets ranging between $1.7 and $2.5 billion for the new minivan. But one thing was obvious: This would be the single largest and most important investment ever made by Chrysler, at least since the K-car gamble and perhaps since the corporation's formation in 1925. The minivan was the crown jewel, the single product that enjoyed an exclusive franchise in the car business. It was the source of one-half (some analysts claimed two-thirds) of Chrysler's profits. Failure to create a product that would maintain a nearly 50 percent share of the booming minivan market in the face of intensified competition from Ford, GM, and the imports, might be a fatal blow to the company. There would be no government bailouts, no wildly charismatic character like Iacocca to restore public confidence, and no surprise secret weapon like the first T-115 minivan. This time Nemeth and his tiny group from various disciplines in the business would, in the words of Theodore, "require John to get an enormous project accomplished with meager resources and to take unbelievable risks."

While pinpointing the exact moment at which the new minivan became a reality, at least on paper, is impossible, a key meeting of the Product Planning Committee chaired by Lutz was pivotal to the program. On April 22, 1991, that group, headed by Nemeth and product planner Dick Winter, received approval to proceed with the basic concept for the new minivan. They outlined the size of the vehicle, its "hard points," i.e., dimensions like wheelbase, height, width, and seat locations, and planned powertrain options. Numerous other planning sessions would be held, with incremental approvals by senior management, but this was a critical session at which a decision was reached to design and manufacture the complete, up-from-the-ground replacement minivan to maintain Chrysler's stranglehold on this key market segment into the twenty-first century. It would involve a "replacement strategy" for the T-115/AS, as opposed to the creation of an all-new market as had occurred in 1984. During the meeting, Nemeth and his team outlined plans for the vehicle's design as well as broad-brushing where and how it would be assembled and general concepts of pricing and sales philosophies.

As the little team was forming up, General Motors' Saturn project was preparing to roll out cars from its new Tennessee plant in a project that had swallowed $5 billion and was predicted by industry analysts never to generate a profit. Meanwhile Ford had committed a similar figure to its so-called Mondeo "world car" small-car concept and was deep into a minivan program (after several false starts) known only as Win-88. The corporate intelligence network was, as usual, operating at full strength. There being no secrets within the Big Three, Theodore knew that this time Ford would not be as wide off the mark as it had been with its Aerostar "doorstop." Thanks to a source within Ford that was mysteriously passing information through a General Motors pipeline ("I was getting Win-88 information *from GM* still on *Ford stationery*," he muses), Theodore and his associates understood that the new Ford effort would be deadly serious competition.

"We were going to work on a fifty-foot trapeze," said Rich Schaum. "And without a net."

5

The Varsity Takes the Field

NINETEEN NINETY had arrived in Michigan with its customary wintry gloom. Storm warnings were again flying over Highland Park. The corporation's dismal cycle of slumps, which seemed to come at ten-year intervals, was again repeating itself: outdated car models, a sagging market share, feeble finances, a lame duck leader, and the perception — by the public and financial markets — of a perpetual weak sister in the automobile business.

But somewhere deep in the bunkered corporation lay a glimmer of hope. The new breed, the outcasts, the refugees, the revolutionaries who had been silenced and rebuffed for so many years, were beginning to flex some muscle. Nemeth's tiny planning group — the advance party of his platform team — had gathered in what they called their "war room" — a vacant styling studio in the Walter P. Chrysler Building in Highland Park. Work began simply enough on a U-shaped sprawl of three large conference tables. With Nemeth were men like financial expert Frank Sanders, whose assignment was to establish a firm budget for a new minivan codenamed "NS."* Also included in the group was ace product planner Dick Winter, an engineer whose most recent project, the Diamond Star coupes — Eagle Talon, Plymouth Laser, Mitsubishi Eclipse,

---

*In retrospect, none of the team could recall exactly what the "NS" designation stood for, other than to note that all minivan platforms were labeled "S" within the engineering department's coding system. (Small cars were "P," midsized were "J," large cars were "L" for no apparent, logical reason.) The then-current minivan (1991–1994 model) was called "AS"; the small-volume European export version available during the same time frame was known as "ES" (presumably for "European S") while the new export minivan, to be constructed at the Graz, Austria, facility, was to be called "GS" ("Graz S" perhaps?).

were winning awards from the automotive press. Herm Greif, a veteran quality control and vehicle evaluation expert, was also present, as were engineers Bob Feldmaier, recently transferred from Gardner's LH group, and Tom Edson, who was to become a pivotal member of the minivan team. Bruce Donaldson, an engineer whose specialty was the expensive and labor-intensive area of manufacturing, came aboard to contribute his expertise on that critical subject.

Like literally dozens of his associates in middle-management engineering posts within the Detroit automobile industry, Edson sported a de rigueur résumé: engineering degree from the University of Michigan, a master's from rival Michigan State, and additional training at the Chrysler Institute — the so-called charm school for young executive prospects. His corporate career developed within the now-divided chimney system. He floated around in various engineering departments, and worked at the proving grounds on suspensions before becoming what he referred to as a "door guy." "Anything you wanted to know about Chrysler doors, you asked me," he would later muse.

But beneath the layers of Edson's vertical training lurked a generalist of the type being sought for the platform teams. Daring thinkers and even those — God forbid — who were prepared to gamble and *lose* were being recruited. Edson's overtly critical comments written during Chrysler's self-examination period had no doubt impacted his assignment as management began to seek out the progressives in their midst. "In the old days it was 'process first, people second,'" said Edson. "When the teams formed up that all changed."

The decision to embark on the creation of a totally new minivan arose in the dark days at the end of the 1980s, as Honda surpassed Chrysler in domestic sales and it became clear even to Iacocca that only a total commitment to new vehicles of the highest quality could save the corporation. "Perfuming the pig" no longer worked. Iacocca, Eaton, Lutz, Castaing, Gale — the entire top management of Chrysler — agreed that in order to survive Chrysler would have to continue to dominate the minivan field. And in order to maintain that dominance, they had to conquer it afresh.

The first group of minivan planners numbered no more than twenty. Their goal was clear, as laid down in a jointly written mission statement that they would not tamper with for the life of the project: "The new minivan team is dedicated to design, build and deliver a product — second to none — that will ensure Chrysler *global minivan dominance* into the 21st century."

Initial planning sessions centered on the Ford Motor Company concept called a "Red Book," a compendium of engineering and design plans that set general parameters for the cost, size, weight, power, and so forth of the vehicle. From this developed what engineers called "the architecture" of the new minivan.

It was accepted doctrine that no serious deviation would be made from the concept of the original T-115: front-wheel drive, flat floor, generous interior space, and two wheelbases — long and short — to appeal to the broadest range of customers. Two interior dimensions were considered critical: the capability for "walk-through" from the front seats to the back and capacity for a 4×8 sheet of plywood with the rear seats folded down. Others were more subtle, such as keeping the exterior height under seventy inches, so that the minivan fit into conventional garages and car washes. More interior room, with added storage capacity, was considered essential, as were better rear seats that could be removed more easily, and improved integrated child seats, which Chrysler had pioneered in the current AS. Extra glass area to improve visibility was also on the wish list, as were such carlike safety features as dual air bags, ABS brakes, and 5 mph bumpers. While minivans would still be classified as "trucks" by the government, Nemeth and Co. understood that the key to success was to make the NS as "carlike" as possible. "No matter what the government said, minivan buyers believed they were buying a version of a passenger car, not a truck, and they wanted 'carlike' features," recalls a member of the team. Added to the requirements was Lutz's desire for a "BUX" ("built up for export") version that would further his goal to make Chrysler a player on the worldwide automotive scene.

Examples of the competition were purchased and driven in long and hard comparison tests. Suspicions confirmed: GM's swoopy-nosed APVs got low marks for frontal visibility — considered a key element, especially with women drivers. Mazda's MPV and Ford Aerostar, both front-engine, rear-drive layouts, lost points because of their increased height caused by the intrusion of the driveshaft through the passenger area. Toyota's wildly styled, midengined Previa was an engineering tour de force with its pancake four-cylinder engine but was deficient in terms of performance and NVH.

Meanwhile, Ford intelligence sources indicated that a pair of major challenges were on track in Dearborn. A joint venture with Nissan to produce a small, high-quality van roughly sized like Chrysler's short-wheelbase model (the Mercury Villager and Nissan Quest) would be followed by the Win-88 (to be sold as the Windstar) based on its Taurus platform and aimed at Chrysler's long-wheelbase, upscale market. If all went according to plan, the Win-88 would reach the public over a year ahead of the team's nascent NS. Clearly, no time could be wasted.

The focus of the team's minivan architecture was the so-called H-point, the place where the hip joint of the 95th percentile driver is located. Once this was decided upon, the total vehicle architecture moved outward, from that single, critical point. Working from the H-point, the designers would establish what were called "hard points," i.e., exact positions in terms of wheelbase, suspension pickup points, firewall and engine location, fuel tank position, instrument panel placement, and so on. The H-point had to be sufficiently low to permit easy entry and egress, yet high enough to offer the visibility and "command of the road" sensation that made minivans appealing to women and small-stature males. If the H-point was too high, the vehicle became tall and gawky, with handling, aerodynamics, and access adversely affected. Too low, and the vehicle became too carlike and sacrificed interior room and driver visibility. Moreover, there were realities that far transcended any customer considerations: manufacturing and design esoterica like limitations on overall height of the vehicle. If the minivan was more than seventy-two inches tall, rail car transportation would be limited to two decks rather than three. That would add $25 per vehicle to the transportation cost — a fatal flaw in such a price-sensitive market.

Haunted by the corporation's reputation for shoddy quality, the team carved in stone an edict that the NS would feature a "one millimeter body," i.e., a body structure that would not vary in dimension more than one millimeter (.0394 of an inch) at any one of forty-eight key points on the vehicle. This would entail building a world-class body shell, wherein door gaps, trim fit, window flushness, wind noise, and so forth would embody precision rivaling the best from a company that had traditionally built vehicles with tolerances as much as three and four times one millimeter. In order to attain the stringent new limit, lengthy discussion was initiated with the outside suppliers who would provide the body stamping dies and tools, the robot welders, the framing jigs, and other accessories necessary to fabricate the steel "box" that formed the elemental structure of the NS. The NS team also included all "closure panels" — doors, lift-gate, and hood — in the "one millimeter" limit.

The team briefly considered, then rejected, a "north-south" engine arrangement of the type Castaing had designed for the LH (too great an intrusion on interior space) and a full-frame design, i.e., with a separate frame and body (some potential benefits in weight and cost, but penalties in NVH). Independent rear suspension was planned, but as the project moved ahead, the starkly simple leaf spring, with origins dating back to the chariot, won by default as the most functional and cost effective. (The team was to resist this layout on principal until very late in the program based purely on the notion that *something* had to be better. Nothing was.)

Like Gardner's group fifteen years earlier, the team wrestled with door configuration. Swinging? Sliding? Narrow? Wide? Left side? Right side? The design studio jigged up a current AS model with a large LH rear door mounted in place of the sliding right side panel door. It was not acceptable. Pending customer research by marketing expert Dave Bostwick, it appeared that an update of the original setup created for the T-115 was the optimum choice, although a comparable left-side counterpart remained an option.

If there was an opportunity for a marketing breakthrough — a new element in minivan functionalism — it would be a left-side sliding door. Early research indicated the considerable appeal of such an option, although some women customers had expressed reservations about an opening for children on the "traffic side" of the vehicle. More than that, there were serious engineering drawbacks. A major goal for the new minivan was a radical reduction in

NVH and an overall increase in structural stiffness. A gaping aperture on the left side of the shell posed a serious threat to overall strength. To counteract such a weakness might require additional bracing (accompanied by added cost and weight) elsewhere in the body. Also, where to place the gasoline filler cap, which was traditionally located on the left-rear quarter panel? How could this be accessed if the sliding door was open? (It would be solved with a lockout that prevents the door being opened when the filler cap is also open.)

Right, left, or both, it was agreed that the sliding track upon which the door operated demanded a radical redesign. The T-115 track consisted of an ugly gash along the right rear flank of the vehicle. Worse yet, the internal mounting system produced an obtrusive headliner bulge immediately above and behind the passenger seat that prevented rearward adjustment to increase foot room for taller drivers. The Chrysler designers shamelessly mimicked Toyota's Previa, which had its track neatly concealed beneath the rear quarter window, making it practically invisible to the unpracticed eye. This not only made the rear quarter panel clean-lined and esthetically pleasing, but additional work by the engineers eliminated the headliner lump, thereby increasing interior aesthetics and headroom.

Intelligence filtering from Ford indicated that the Win-88 would not have a sliding left-side door. It had been tried only a few times, on smallish Japanese vans intended primarily for the home island market, and some in Chrysler doubted it was worth the risk in terms of cost and structural integrity. Others believed the gamble was worthwhile, if for no other reason than to probe into new areas of customer convenience where it appeared the major competition was not venturing. In the end, the left-side sliding door would be included in the architecture, but only as an option. Bob Lutz, always in the vanguard of change, was an ardent supporter of the addition. "When was the last time you saw a three-door sedan?" he repeatedly questioned during early planning meetings.

In the engineering spaces of Highland Park's antiquated complex, Rich Schaum's Powertrain Team was manifesting another aspect of Castaing's cross-functional concept. While Nemeth and Co.

were laying down the basics of the NS, Schaum's group was developing a new generation of engines that would power a variety of products planned within the next five years, including the minivan. Already in the final testing stages was a new, lightweight V6 that, in three displacements (3.3, 3.5, and 3.8 liters) and various levels of performance, would power the LH sedans and in certain applications, the AS and NS minivans. Also in the works was a highly advanced four-cylinder for the new PL (Neon) compact and the midsized JAs (Cirrus and Stratus), which would form the core engine for the NS minivan. The engine would operate under a simple edict from Lutz: Make it as strong and silent and smooth as any four-cylinder from Europe and Japan and once and for all time, end the indictment that Detroit was incapable of designing and building world-class small-displacement engines. The new 4-valve fours, in a single-overhead camshaft 2-liter form for the PL and a high-tech, high-output 2.4 liter with twin overhead camshaft and twin balance shafts for the JA and NS, were to be up and running by July 1991 — giving Schaum's team less than twelve months to create all-new powerplants — or *four years less* than was the customary corporate time frame.

As Schaum's little team labored against their rigid deadline, Sanders and the rest of Nemeth's group continued to hash out the details of the NS — not the least of which was the total cost of the program. Despite its declining financial condition, the Chrysler board realized that its only salvation was a $17.3 billion crash program to develop new products to replace the fusty, discredited K-cars.* It was an expensive, audacious, hubris-laden scheme, because no one, from Iacocca on down, had a clear idea where the funding would come from, much less if Chrysler would be in business five years hence.

As the Chairman publicly touted his product programs and postured bravely about the corporation's future, he was quietly hawking the sale of Chrysler to Fiat and his archenemy Ford. Both companies, with serious financial burdens of their own, declined to bite on what they appeared to be permanently damaged goods.

---

*A sum, factory insiders mused, that was greater than the *total* profits generated by the corporation during its first six decades in business.

Lutz, whose singular knowledge of product gave him enormous leverage in vehicle planning, liked what he saw of the NS team's initial concepts. They had laid down a vehicle that was to weigh between 3,500 pounds for its cheap, short-wheelbase model and 4,800 pounds for its expensive, long-wheelbase model. It would offer 0–60 mph acceleration in the eleven- to twelve-second range. Gas mileage would span from 21 to 28 mpg, depending on the model. Aerodynamics, now critical to fuel economy, would provide a slippery, carlike .35 cd (co-efficient of drag).

The team proposed a launch of the vehicle in January 1995, with production planned at between 560,000 and 630,000 units a year from three assembly plants: the current unused St. Louis South and the Windsor, Ontario, complex that was producing all minivans, plus the new Graz, Austria, factory if an export model was approved.

The major priorities, as outlined by Nemeth's group, included seating comfort, cargo storage space, improved climate control, driver visibility, easy entry/exit, handling, and maneuverability as well as better braking response. Weaknesses in the current minivan that had to be corrected were its endemic buzz, rattles, and squeaks, oppressive wind noise, poorly fabricated doors, locks, latches, and body hardware, a feeble climate control system, and ergonomically incorrect seats and seat belt systems.

The core problem centered on money. To achieve their goals, the team estimated that the NS would cost $2.25 billion to design and manufacture. Under such a plan it would remain on the market until 2006 with cosmetic updates. Sanders's proposed target was a gross profit of $6,000 per vehicle, meaning a 34 percent margin on revenues, prior to any sales incentives.

Too expensive, said Lutz and the board. To stay within the long-range plan, a funding total of $1.7 billion was their upper limit. "You've got one-point-seven; that's all that's left," he told the team. For such a modest figure (but still more than Chrysler had ever expended for a single model), draconian cuts would have to be made. All-wheel drive would be eliminated. Perhaps a single wheelbase vehicle would have to be manufactured, thereby ending Chrysler's clear advantage in the marketplace with its long and short chassis offerings. Engine options would have to be reduced, as would a mass of new ideas like the sliding left-side door, a five-speed manual transmission, a security alarm system, zone-controlled air conditioning, electronic memory front seats, and perhaps Schaum's zoomy new 2.4-liter four-cylinder engine. The team also said that $1.7 billion would eliminate any two-tone color schemes as well as antichip paint, reduced fit and finish, and a variety of advanced robotics and wire-welding processes planned for the assembly plants.

Worse yet, Sanders estimated that production capacity might have to be slashed to 523,000 units annually, which threatened to reduce Chrysler's share of the booming minivan market from 50 percent to 35 percent.

A lengthy debate ensued over what was to be known as "the new coat, old coat strategy." In order to cut costs, some team members argued that both the old and the new minivans ought to stay in production, much as was being done — quite successfully — with the older Jeep Cherokee and the new Grand Cherokee. Significant savings could be realized by not having to produce duplicate tooling and assembly lines at both the St. Louis and Windsor factories. The plan called for St. Louis to build the NS for the upscale market while Windsor continued indefinitely with the cheaper T-115. This issue was to remain unresolved for some time to come.

As planning for the NS gained momentum through the summer of 1990, the corporation was on the verge of yet another seesaw ride between hope and despair, of tightroping between prosperity and oblivion. The usual turmoil roiled up and down on Mahogany Row. Greenwald had departed that spring, seemingly leaving the path to the chairmanship open for Lutz when Iacocca retired in December 1992. But it was not to be. As the president began to — as one insider put it — "build his own company within the company," Iacocca was preparing to shoot him out of the saddle. There is no doubt that he was privy to Lutz's increasingly sharp criticism of his stewardship and surely took umbrage. Moreover, there was a growing sentiment among Iaccoca's retinue that Lutz was a loose cannon.

His open warfare with Dick Dauch led to the veteran production chief's angry departure. During the same time Lutz's marriage came apart and he entered into a protracted divorce action with his second wife, Heide, that kept the readers of Detroit's two major newspapers entertained until the divorce was finalized in November 1992. He managed to survive a crash landing of his helicopter but was not so lucky when he was arrested for a 100-plus-mph blast up I-75 in a company-owned Lamborghini Diablo. Unimpressed by the stature of his offender, the arresting officer hauled Lutz off to the station house, where he had to be rescued by one of Chrysler's senior security staff. These events, plus his increasingly outspoken campaign in behalf of altering the corporate culture — no matter how constructive — made him serious enemies in Highland Park and seemed to doom his ascendancy to the top job.

At the same time Chrysler's business fortunes continued to tailspin. Massive layoffs spread through the white-collar workforce, while ratings from Standard & Poor's and Moody's plunged to the junk bond level. Losses for 1991 were projected to push toward the billion-dollar mark (in actuality *only* $795 million) as Iacocca carped about the Japanese import invasion while demanding sufficient quotas (read tariffs) to create what he called a "level playing field."

As a modest counterbalance to all the bad news, Chrysler opened its new Jefferson North assembly plant, where the revised Grand Cherokee was to be built. It was to mark the last (possibly forever) major automobile facility to be erected within the city limits of Detroit. Another positive sign was the impending completion of the massive Chrysler Technology Center in the northern suburb of Auburn Hills which would — almost by accident — be perfectly formatted to accommodate platform teams and Chrysler's switch to cross-functional management. Better yet, Glenn Gardner's engineering team knew that they had a winner on their hands as the prototype LH sedans circulated the company's proving grounds in Chelsea, Michigan, and at Wickenburg, Arizona, with surprising style and grace.

The little minivan team had soldiered on through this confusion, trying to hammer out the initial architecture of a vehicle that they had to accept was underfunded by perhaps several hundred million dollars. A series of consumer clinics had been held during the late summer and fall of 1990, marshaled by marketing expert Dave

Bostwick. In his late thirties, with the build and manner of a retired Big Ten middle linebacker, Bostwick's lineage in the car business involved his father, a career General Motors photographer, and a brother who was a Pontiac dealer. Regardless of his family's ties to GM, Bostwick was a committed Chrysler loyalist who set out to learn exactly what strengths and weaknesses the current minivans possessed among their owner body. Working for what was now known internally as the "minivan platform team" after it had replaced the old "Red Book" format, Bostwick set out to organize a number of focus groups involving Chrysler minivan owners. They were selected at random from lists provided by R. L. Polk, a firm specializing in compiling automotive registration data.

"We knew going in that our minivans were not 'lifestyle' purchases," he says. "In other words, they didn't appeal to specific demographic segments of the market like luxury cars or sporty cars, but rather to a large cross-section ranging from young families to retired people to housewives to small business men. We also knew they were committed buyers. Eighty-five percent said they intended to purchase another minivan — although not necessarily one of ours."

Working with Jeffrey Keefe, the San Francisco polling firm, Bostwick organized four focus groups in September 1990 in Boston, Orlando, Minneapolis, and San Diego. The format was the same for each, a one-day session in a large hotel conference room, involving twenty to thirty current owners, questioned on three basic areas: the reasons for buying a minivan in the first place, what they wanted in future models, and what Chrysler should avoid changing. On display was the 1991 Dodge Caravan SE minivan and several interior styling layouts, including the mock-up of a left-side sliding door prepared by interior design chief John Herlitz and his team. "We learned a lot," recalls Bostwick. "It was apparent that function was radically more important to them than to owners of other types of vehicles. Price was not a total factor and we were told that Chrysler had the best concept in minivans but not the best quality. Good package, bad quality, was the message. Out of the discussions seven basic requirements seemed to surface. The customers wanted two wheelbases, long and short, in addition to better quality, improved seats, functional doors, advanced safety, and contemporary but not far-out styling. They seemed to like the notion of a sliding left-side door, with 70 percent claiming they would spend an extra $500 for such an option. Another thing we learned —" says Bostwick, "minivan owners loved to talk about their vehicles. More than any other owner group we'd ever polled. They wouldn't shut up. We ended up with thirty-two hours of taped comments."

Bostwick and his researchers set out again a month later, this time to Oakbrook, Illinois, where they staged what the industry calls "ride and drive." Four vehicles (called "properties" in the business) were present: a Plymouth Voyager SE, a Mazda MPV, a Chevrolet Lumina APV, and a Toyota Previa. All were fresh, low-mileage vehicles that eight separate focus groups — again minivan owners — used to journey around suburban Chicago. The results were clear and not unexpected: The Chevrolet accrued low marks because of its weird, droop-nose styling and its poor frontal visibility. The Previa was faulted for its engine noise and the intrusion of its midship engine compartment into the passenger area. The Mazda and the Voyager were the winners, although the group disliked the MPV's rear-drive layout and complained about the Plymouth's wind noise and questionable quality of hardware (door handles, switches).

While Bostwick and his research team were poring over the reams of data and editing the videotapes from the sessions, Tom Gale's exterior design team, headed by veteran stylists Ernie Barrie and Dave McKinnon, was completing the first clay mock-ups of the new NS. Seeking a more streamlined look and better aerodynamics, they lowered the H-point two inches. It didn't work. "Our design guys are sometimes keyed to emotion. Aesthetics versus function, that sort of thing," says Bostwick. "The Previa was bought on emotion because of its zoomy styling and unconventional engine location, but it wasn't enough. It lacked function. But some of the designers loved it, based purely on their own emotional response." Bostwick recalls a sharp exchange with one of the designers, who had observed that the Previa might outsell the Chrysler ASs if they had sufficient production capacity — and if the Japanese weren't on the defensive over Iacocca's accusations that they were dumping minivans into the American market. "Maybe we need new designers," Bostwick had snapped in response. He was in turn reminded that his corporate researchers had warned repeatedly that the public would reject the so-called cab-forward design that was about to make the new Chrysler LH sedans a major hit in the marketplace. Such debates reminded industry observers of what famed screenwriter William Goldman had observed about the motion picture business: "Nobody knows *anything*." Based on the erratic rollercoaster fortunes that had formed the history of the automobile industry, his comment was as applicable to Detroit as it was to Hollywood.

In retrospect, some members of the team may have been simply going through the motions, proceeding with plans — a sort of wish list — while resigned to the reality that whatever they did they would be vetoed by the financial people. "That was the way it always happened," recalls Bostwick. "The design guys could lay down a really great concept, only to have it chopped to pieces by the number-crunchers. But this time that wasn't going to happen."

Bostwick's December 1990 report on his findings to 115 key team members centered on five central themes. It was apparent that potential customers were primarily concerned about safety, quality, carlike handling, comfort, and a fair price. Also of prime importance were at least four large, useful doors (with a fifth optional), excellent visibility, seat height, easily removable rear seats (a weakness on the current models), and "pass-through" capability from the front seats to the rear. Interestingly, Bostwick told his associates that styling was not among the top ten reasons for a minivan purchase. It was important, however, according to the data, that Chrysler offer *both* V6 and in-line four-cylinder engines. In all, the team seemed to be on the right track with its two-tier (long and short, expensive and cheap, multioption) marketing plan. "We were winning by default," said Bostwick. "The arrogance of our competitors was keeping us number one. Presuming that somebody wouldn't eat crow and simply copy what we were doing, we had a shot at holding our leadership in the market."

Based on the inputs from the focus groups, the designers commenced building four full-sized fiberglass styling bucks or "forms" while Herlitz's group worked up a variety of interior layouts. Gale's Highland Park team, led by Barrie and McKinnon, put together three of the models, while out west Neil Walling had his Pacifica Studio team creating a fourth version. Located in a small Carlsbad industrial park north of San Diego, Pacifica was a distant Chrysler outpost considered to be better keyed to the bellwether California car market. Pacifica's renderings were always more *outré* than those arising from the drawing boards of Detroit, but that enhanced their value to contemporary and creative minds like Gale's and Herlitz's.

The early months of 1991 were consumed by detailed team planning as the designers completed their four different styling themes. Two of them, called "Silver Bullet" and "Response," were by Barrie and McKinnon's staff. Both were roughly the same size (with 116-inch wheelbases) as the model currently on the market but the "Silver Bullet" featured a radically sloped windshield and a one-inch-lower H-point. The "Reach 2000" offered more conservative styling, but with driver seating positioned well forward in comparison to other concepts. Neil Walling's Pacifica crew created a scaled-down version with a modest 110-inch wheelbase and featuring a flowing nose treatment reminiscent of the new Dodge Intrepid LH sedan. At the same time Herlitz's interior designers were working with outside suppliers like seat-maker Atoma to develop an optimum passenger compartment. "In years past we did the design work then passed it on to the suppliers to figure out how to build it. This time they did most of the design work, saving time and money while giving them the opportunity to create a product best keyed to their manufacturing capability," he says. This would offer as much as 70 percent cost savings in the design and development of outside-supplied components, although some industry critics argued that such a strategy gave Chrysler's major suppliers too much control over core technology and left the corporation vulnerable to business cycles beyond its control. But Tom Stallcamp, who was now Chrysler's vice president for procurement and supply, had developed a program called SCORE (supplier cost reduction effort). He maintained that competition among the corporation's twelve hundred production suppliers (down from thirty-two hundred) radically cut costs while generating extra profits for the outsiders. (Ninety percent of the corporate buys were sourced from 150 so-called "first tier" suppliers that manufactured such volume components as steel, tires, glass, paint, plastic interior parts, etc.) Herlitz's relationship with seat-maker Atoma was a prime example of the overriding Stallcamp policy.

Bostwick next organized what was called "the S-Body Package Directive Quantitative Static Clinic" in the San Jose, California, Convention Center in early May. Three hundred minivan owners were again invited to evaluate the four new styling exercises, plus a collection of current Chrysler minivans and the competition from GM, Ford, Mazda, and Toyota. This time the invitees were not told which company was hosting the affair in order to minimize prejudice. (A chronic danger of such focus groups is that the guests will naturally favor the hosting company out of a vague sense of obligation.) Bostwick injected a new element to enhance his data-gathering. He handed out 150 grid-pad computers developed by ADR, a Detroit software manufacturer. First used in earlier PL (Neon) clinics, the grid-pad offered "interactive polling" of an automotive product. Carrying the five-pound unit on a small harness, the focus group participants toured each vehicle in a set pattern, answering a series of questions (like, dislike, yes, no) while regarding the vehicles on display, which would be digested and processed by a computer for quick analysis. A vast array of questions was posed relating to engines and transmissions, long and short wheelbases, interior layout, and, most important, the styling of the four mock-ups. The Pacifica enjoyed the most favorable response in terms of pure aesthetics, but was judged to be too small. The challenge for Gale & Co. was to integrate the most pleasing elements of Walling's design into a larger package (actually two packages — long wheelbase and short — which the focus groups were explicit in demanding).

The upshot of the joint effort — Bostwick's research plus the design team's multiple plans and the inputs of the suppliers (who would ultimately produce *70 percent* of the NS's component parts) — would be referred to as a "consensus package." It would be an amalgam of all four styling bucks, built on established themes of two wheelbases specified by the focus groups. The H-point would remain exactly like the current AS. The windshield rake, which Tom Gale determined to be critical in terms of visibility, appearance, wind noise, aerodynamics, instrument panel dimensions, and cost of manufacturing, was finally compromised at an angle between the rakish "Silver Bullet" and the more conservative "Response." The contours of the "Reach 2000" body panels were for the most part included, while much of the flashy front fascia styling of Walling's "Pacifica" was adopted. Everyone involved understood that the NS would have to be designed from the *inside out* (as opposed to the traditional General Motors way in which the designers created the exterior dimensions and then let the engineers and others cram their components into the remaining space). Doors, seats, and safety were primary concerns, along with such secondary details as interior storage space, ease of rear seat removal, proper rear and side visibility, and — new to the product list — proper cup holders! Unless those demands were met, the most serenely beautiful body shape in history would be a loser.

In years past many immortal automobile designs have been the inspiration of a single individual, a brilliant stylist whose soaring imagination conjured up a classic collection of curves and angles to create an 812 Cord or a Ferrari GTO or a Buick Riviera. Not so with the NS, which ended up an amalgam of concepts created by the likes of Barrie, McKinnon, Walling, and various members of their staffs. Once the consumer inputs from Bostwick's focus groups had been considered and "hard points" like seating height and the critical windowglass "planes" had been determined, Barrie's Advanced Packaging studio laid down a design that was thematically similar to the final version that would be created by McKinnon's final-design group. While history would credit McKinnon more than any other single individual for the fluid shape of the NS, it was in fact the result of his efforts and those of his associate Steve Holmes, as well as the staffs of Barrie and Walling, all of whom made significant contributions. "They say design by committee doesn't work, but we think the NS belies that," said McKinnon as he perused the rounded contours of an NS long-wheelbase.

Day by day the platform team expanded in size and scope, with small groups of suppliers being brought into the loop, along with other engineering specialists from within the corporation. Now freed from his firefighting duties with the four-speed automatic transmission near-debacle, Chris Theodore took over the team leadership from the retiring John Nemeth, who had done yeoman duty during the initial planning stages. Then Theodore's patron, Francois Castaing, was nearly lost to the company. He was diagnosed with a kidney tumor, and just as he was ascending to a position of real influence, Castaing was sidelined for five weeks after recovering from the ensuing operation. Luckily, the growth was nonmalignant. He would later joke that the entire procedure was done on his desk top in order not to waste time, but the situation was deadly serious, not only to his health, but to the fortunes of the corporation. Castaing was the heart and soul of the shift to cross-functional platform teams and his departure might have caused the creaky alliance between the old and new cultures within Chrysler to crumble. At this pivotal juncture in 1991, the efficiency of the new team concept was still being heatedly debated within the executive and middle-management levels, and the loss of its most ardent advocate could have dealt it a fatal blow.

By late spring 1991, the form and structure of the minivan platform team was firmly defined on the corporate organizational charts. Tom Gale was to head the team, the "Godfather" of the operation who reported to senior management on overall progress. Directly below him was Theodore, whose title was general manager and director of engineering. Seven others would serve as managers of the key areas: Sham Rushwin, a veteran production expert, was the head of manufacturing; Dick Winter, product planning; Frank Sanders, finance; Joe Casola, sales; Peter Rosenfeld, a new addition to the company from the Mitsubishi trading group, was to manage the critical area of purchasing, and old team hands Herlitz (design) and Bostwick (marketing) were to remain in their posts.

Clearly the NS team could not operate independently of other elements of the company. To do so would simply create another chimney. The solution was the creation of five major cross-functional product teams throughout the corporation responsible for Body Interiors, Bodies in White (BIW) and Exteriors, Powertrain, Chassis, and Electrical and Electronics. Each team would be

headed by an executive engineer who would operate in tight cooperation with his counterparts (minivan, small car, large car, and
Jeep/Truck). Rich Schaum's Powertrain team was charged with the
responsibility of developing all NS engines and transmissions,
while Jim Sauter's Body Interiors team designed all climate-control
items, air bags, seat belts, instrument panels, seat mounting, trim
items, etc.

Ernie Laginess's BIW and Exterior Engineering teams would
oversee such items as latches for windows and doors, door handles,
windshield wipers, bumpers, headlights, taillights, and all the exterior trim. Bernie Swanson's Chassis team was to design and develop the suspension — struts, springs, shock absorbers, sway bars,
steering racks, links, and such — while the only senior woman, a
tall, bright-eyed, no-nonsense southerner named Cindy Hess, was
charged with leading her Electrical and Electronics team toward
the creation of advanced instruments, engine fuel management
systems, courtesy light packages, dimmer switches, cooling fan
motors, starters, alternators, and a plethora of other electrically
powered devices.

Spread out beneath the five were eleven more vehicle synthesis
teams led by engineering managers. Examples of these were Bob
Feldmaier's Packaging team (engine compartment design, under-
body, plenum, doors, instrument panels — known simply as the
"IP" — and interior packaging) and veteran Herm Greif's Vehicle
Development team (experimental car build, body structure, and the
critical area of NVH and quality).

In keeping with Castaing's vision of cross-functional teams, numerous other Chrysler engineers, sales and marketing types, finance experts, manufacturing specialists, and representatives from
key outside supplier firms (of which Chrysler had about four hundred) were to act as advisers in their particular areas of expertise.
Slowly, as the program became more complex, the team would expand until ultimately over eleven hundred key personnel would be
on board.

Again the specter of communication — or the lack of it — arose
to threaten the entire team concept. Not only were the various
groups still spread around Detroit, with a complete transfer of all

personnel to the Chrysler Technical Center (already known simply as "CTC") not be completed until early 1992, but the complexity of cross-functional operation demanded a constant interchange of information to be effective. This meant one thing: The key players from the various disciplines had to meet on a regular basis. The solution was to set aside each Wednesday for cross-functional conferences, chaired by Theodore. The meetings came to be known as "Spaghetti Day" after an Italian food purveyor's slogan, "Wednesday is Prince Spaghetti Day." Another spaghetti sauce that claimed "It's all in there," seemed to symbolize the theme of the weekly meetings. The five product team executive engineers reported their progress in six-week cycles (the extra week was reserved for manufacturing and European GS issues). Theodore, joined by Sanders, Rosenfeld, Edson, Herlitz, Rushwin, and Winter, sat at the customary cluster of U-shaped conference tables during the sessions, which lasted all day, dealing in detail with cost, parts sourcing, prototype build status, future development problems and opportunities.

Spaghetti Days would become notorious within the team for their candor and often open warfare. Each week another component of the overall team would have its "turn in the barrel," wherein they would be required to update the rest on their progress and their ability to toe the mark budget-wise. "It got really nasty," recalls Herlitz. "After a while somebody decided that 'cheap shots' ought to be fined. A coffee can was placed on the desk in front of Chris and when somebody said something really off base, the offender had to toss a quarter into the pot. One day the argument got so hot that one of the guys tossed in his Visa card. Others would come into the meeting and throw in five-dollar bills, claiming they were making a deposit in advance." Also included in the meetings were teams from the Windsor and St. Louis factories as well as representatives of key suppliers. Endless problems were hashed out, always with two essential themes: maintaining the schedule and keeping within the stringent budget. Examples: Frank Sanders wanted to know why money couldn't be saved by expanding the so-called air-conditioning cool-down period (the time required for the passenger cabin to reach the required temperature) from three minutes to eight minutes. Chris Theodore announced that by using a cast aluminum front suspension mount, twenty pounds could be saved, but with a $20 cost penalty. "In the old days, weight was no priority," he said. "Now, with ever-more stringent fuel economy standards on the way, it's a major factor, although expensive." Rich Schaum's engine team was required to have a prototype 2.4-liter four-cylinder engine up and running by the end of July. They were a day late — "July 32, 1992," he told the team. Speaking of Theodore's reaction, he recalled, "On that day I remet the angry young man." Ernie Barrie reported that the fake-wood side paneling heretofore so popular on various high-line minivan models would have to go: The new compound-curved flared rear fenders would not accommodate the vinyl decals used on the current, flat-sided ASs. Dick Winter informed the group that by moving the side door handle back a few inches, about $7 could be saved in manufacturing costs. Ernie Laginess warned that the rear lift-gate design would not permit the current factory paint guns to reach a tiny cranny in the bodywork, a flaw that could cost millions to redesign the factory paint booths. And so it went, each Wednesday, with the key team members thrashing through myriads of arcane detail, tires, trim, paint, door sealing, engine mounts, brake lines, manufacturing systems, tooling costs, instrument panel gauges, hookup for left-side door construction, ashtrays or no ashtrays, where to locate the radio antenna, etc., etc. Spaghetti Day after Spaghetti Day, problem piled upon problem, always with the twin swords of Damocles hanging over them: scheduling and cost.

Frank Sanders and his finance types developed a program called "taxes and targets," whereby funding could be constantly moved around within the project, depending on priorities dictated by the team. For example, Cindy Hess's interior-lighting team reported that a new cigar lighter outlet socket with an integrated "halo lamp" and improved wiring connection was on the drawing boards, while a simple 12-volt power outlet socket (for radar detectors, etc.) without the "halo lamp" would save $.70 cents. Decision: the cigar lighter would be offered only as an option and Hess's saved funds would be redistributed within the team. Her group also created an ingenious microprocessor junction block connected to an umbilical cord that ran the length of the NS's centerline, distributing power to everything from the taillights, to the ABS system, to the fuel pump, backlight wiper, and other rear-mounted electrical components as well as the powertrain. By integrating the electronics in a single batch, costs were reduced while reliability was enhanced and serviceability simplified. "In the old days a department's budget was sacrosanct," recalls one engineer. "Once you had the money, you could waste it any way you wanted. Now, with taxes and targets, Sanders and his guys would take away any savings and give it to somebody else who needed it more. The pie kept getting resliced, but it *never* got bigger."

"It was hell, but consider the alternatives," recalls Edson. "Without that level of honest, open communication we would have added years to the project and no one knows how many millions of dollars." It was not for the faint of heart. There was no place to hide. Unlike the old days, when problems could be wallpapered over with circumspect reports and artful temporizing, there was no eluding the harsh spotlight that snapped on each Wednesday. Some members of the team could not handle the pressure and were replaced. Traditionalists still clinging to the chimney system were either retired early or eased into backwater positions in distant corporate outposts. The often lethal barrage of fire coming from behind the desks of Spaghetti Day spared no one, including Theodore. This revolutionary rump court took no prisoners.

Added to the tension of Spaghetti Day was the burden of learning a new and complex computer system. Its intent was to create a total database system linking all the team members as well as the main outside suppliers. Like the other major players in the domestic car business, Chrysler had developed a complex of computers, some of which were CAD-CAM based, but had little or no capability of communicating with each other. Among the most sophisticated systems in the world was the French-designed CATIA (Computer Aided Three Dimensional Interactive Application) developed by Dussault Systems, a division of the well-known French aircraft and aerospace giant Avions Marcel Dussault. The system had been created for aircraft design and had been considered too mathematically based for general application in the automobile business. While Toyota and Honda and Castaing's engineers at

AMC had been using Catia on a limited basis for a decade, it took an alliance with IBM in the late 1980s to enhance the system's capability for Chrysler. IBM's contribution was to expand Catia from a mainframe-based operation while creating user-friendly components that made it accessible to hundreds if not thousands of workstations (or "seats"). In the end over twenty-five hundred such seats inside Chrysler and within its supplier network would use Catia. This meant that beyond the give-and-take madness of Spaghetti Days, the entire platform team could not only interact within itself but could also "speak" to other platform teams.

"We faced two additional challenges in addition to designing the NS," says Edson. "Not only were we going to classes to become fluent with Catia, but the team was still spread out all over Highland Park. While CTC was dedicated in October 1991, only a small part of the team had moved there. The rest of us weren't scheduled to move until the following year."

Catia would be a revelation. Great chunks of time were lopped off the process of creating pre-production prototype vehicles. In the days of yore this critical element in the creation of a new car involved the designers laboriously mocking up full size models — called "clays" — from which dimensions would be transferred to blueprints. These plans would be given to small local specialty shops, which would fabricate limited-production "soft" steel body dies from which stampings would be taken to make the actual vehicles. Depending on the complexity of the design and the bureaucracy involved, as much as a year could be consumed before prototypes were produced. But Catia generated perfect three-dimensional plans from the clays, with infinite variations made with the simple movement of a computer mouse. The capability of the computer often amazed even its most experienced users. It was capable of making extremely accurate measurements of component weights prior to prototype development, based on metal (or plastic) density and thickness information. For example, Ernie Laginess's BIW team was able quickly and accurately to design the rear lift-gate counterbalance system using Catia. All lift-gates are counterbalanced by gas pressure cylinders that are calibrated based on the weight of the door and its center of gravity. Catia measured the weight of the NS lift-gate door to within *half a pound*, thereby avoiding any changes in specification during prototype testing as would have been the case in the past. Catia was also used to estimate weights of springs, brakes, and tires in the initial stages of design.

From the Catia database a series of full-sized die models could be automatically machined from plastic resin or wood. These in turn would be transformed into male and female dies. From there a network of special custom shops, like Astronetics in the Detroit area, created carbon-fiber bodies built to the exact tolerance of production models. By November 1991 the first six carbon-fiber prototypes had been built, more than six months ahead of schedule. Ten metal bodies in white (BIWs — these were simply bare body shells, painted white) would soon follow. They were to be passed out for what were called "QFD" (quality functional development) evaluations by various vehicle synthesis and product teams. A total of 31 so-called F1 Program Vehicles would be hand-assembled by Chrysler technicians while another 147 pre-program vehicles or "mules" would be sent to the proving grounds and other evaluation centers within the corporation for testing. Mules were in fact cobbled-up AS minivans. They appeared to be normal production vehicles, but beneath their bodywork they carried all manner of NS components: suspension systems, drivetrains, electronics, instrumentation, seats, air conditioning, created by the various engineering groups.

Ultimately the Catia network would be complete. Everyone on the team would have access — and input — to the NS database. But even with such sophistication offered by that small, tight information highway, the final arbiter of success would be Spaghetti Day, where human beings, face-to-face, toe-to-toe, hashed out the creation.

A month prior to the first carbon-fiber prototypes being fabricated, NS underwent what was called "Concept Approval." It was then that the major hard-points had been finalized. From then on Herlitz's Interior Design team would work with specific interior headroom and seating measurements. Colors, both interior and external, would be painstakingly selected, not on the basis of the team's subjective moods, but rather by consultations with New York's Color Marketing Group and the Swiss-based International Color Authority. These two organizations were considered preeminent in determining the public's taste in colors as much as two to three years in advance. Designers in the fashion, furniture, textile, paint, wallpaper, interior decorating, and automobile industries took reverential stock in the divinations of both groups and based many of their choices for future color hues and combinations on their pronouncements.

Once themes had been selected, the critical element of interior color coordination had to be addressed. At the base of the NS windshield seven separate trim pieces of the same color were joined. In numerous models that had issued from Detroit (and imports as well) over the years such colors were slightly mismatched. In order to avoid such low-quality pitfalls, a team composed of representatives from the Design Office Color Studio, the supply staff, Manufacturing Interior Trim Engineering, and the primary outside materials suppliers met regularly to insure that all colors matched. Samples were examined under a special "Magnette" color-balanced light and, once accepted, were repeatedly compared to production materials being supplied from Textron and other major vendors.

At the same time, the establishment of the essential vehicle hard-points gave Bernie Swanson's suspension team clearance to begin locating and designing the front and rear springs, shock absorbers, steering box, brakes, etc. that fell under their purview. The vehicle was now moving from a series of abstract drawings and grid forms on various Catia screens to actual rolling stock.

Other support teams were formed to deal with problems ranging from streamlining the quantity of fasteners used in the NS (reduced from 1109 to 612 numbered parts as compared to the AS) to the formation of an Impact Simulator team whose members employed a sophisticated sledlike carriage to test the passenger compartment for crashworthiness and its state-of-the-art dual air bags (with a magnesium alloy housing). A Marketing Launch team, to develop early sales strategies, was composed of personnel from Marketing, Sales, Public Relations, Service and Parts, Chrysler Canada, and advertising agency strategists. A Storage team worked to maximize storage compartments in the NS, based on a survey of four hundred AS owners. An Underhood Appearance team devoted itself to such details as "dressing" the wiring harness and redesigning the transaxle dipstick all in the name of aesthetics.

Among the most critical of the specialty teams was the so-called Weight team, which was assigned the task of saving unneeded poundage in the vehicles. Bulk can affect fuel economy (it was estimated that an extra 0.5 mpg could be attained for every 50 pounds saved) and acceleration (0–60 mph reduced by 0.1 second for every 30 pounds reduction) as well as braking distances, tire sizes, component life, and the number of options offered. The team considered weight-saving options through the use of lighter materials or parts redesign if even as little as 0.1 pound could be saved. If costs less than $1 a pound were possible, the idea was accepted while anything over $2 a pound was rejected.

In order to maintain a constant flow of information among the entire team, a five-man committee called "the Fab Five" (after the University of Michigan's national championship basketball team) was formed by representatives from Planning, Engineering, Manufacturing, Procurement, and Financial Analysis. This group met on a biweekly basis separate from Spaghetti Day to broad-brush future policies and to identify potential problems. The Fab Five would remain in place following the introduction of the NS to deal with further development of the vehicle.

Francois Castaing, as the spiritual father of the platform team concept, was aware that a lack of communication and general isolation among teams could create horizontal chimneys as inert and nonproductive as the old vertical versions. In order to prevent this, he created what he called Technology Clubs, wherein executive engineers, managers, and working-level engineers from the large-car, small-car, minivan, and truck teams met regularly to share information regarding sourcing, personnel, and the exchange of design technology that might be of mutual benefit. It was fully understood that natural human territorial imperatives could ruin the entire team concept if strong lines of communication were not maintained.

The team became convinced that the basic architecture of the NS was correct. Partial confirmation came when Bostwick organized his final focus group in August 1991. It involved 400 hourly workers from the nearby Windsor, Ontario, plant, where some of the NSs would be manufactured. They were selected by lottery and transported, with their families, to the spanking new, still incomplete CTC where they were shown the final version of the styling bucks. They received details of the vehicle they would manufacture four years hence — the first time that level of employee had ever been made privy to such advanced planning. It marked the beginning of a whole new culture of sharing with the unionized workforce.

As the design matured, thousands of tiny, insanely complex problems were discovered. A process called "MITS" (Minivan Issue Tracking System) was developed to catalogue and prioritize the glitches — now simply called "issues" within the team. Example: Herm Greif reported that "the sound quality when closing the sliding door at minus 17 degrees F was objectionable. It sounded as if the door would shatter." Example: A test in November 1991 had revealed that suspension shake in the AS "mules" was inferior to comparable Mazda MPV models. The problem lay in three potential areas: engine mounting, body structure, or the suspension itself. Only further testing would find the source. Example: The engine-cooling fan motor was failing, requiring a redesign of the fan mounting nut and its torque requirements. Example: Early 2.4-liter engines were developing valve guide distortions. Example: A transaxle being tested in a Saudi Arabian taxi fleet developed leaks in its seals at 7,620 miles. And so it went. In all, over three thousand issues — most of them arcane, niggling details — would be revealed and would demand correction, lest they become Achilles' heels that could ruin the program. In this sense, the torque settings of the fan blade nut or the sound of a door slamming in cold weather became just as critical as the proper rake of Tom Gale's windshield, or the fuel efficiency of Rich Schaum's new engine.

The team remained mired in a myriad of detail as 1992 arrived, while tension mounted about the impending announcement of Iacocca's successor. In March the bomb was dropped. Rather than Robert Lutz being elevated to succeed Iacocca, a true dark horse was selected. The financial marketeers, the industry analysts, and the press pundits were all caught off guard as Robert Eaton, the head of General Motors' European operation, was named heir apparent. Word immediately passed through the industry that Lutz, shamed and shunned, would bolt. He was too proud, claimed the conventional wisdom, to stomach such an open rejection. But as is so often the case, the CW was wrong. Lutz took his medicine. He stayed with Chrysler. (Perhaps, in part, speculated some observers, because he had already worked for Ford and GM and was unwelcome there, while no CEO positions among other major automakers appeared open.) Better yet, he formed a solid alliance with his new boss. He would later remark, "I had casual dinners with him and within ten days I knew we could work together." Vastly different in appearance and style, the two men dovetailed across a spectrum of automotive interests. While Lutz was the hands-on "car guy," Eaton was also an engineer with a deep understanding about what made good automobiles.

Shortly after he assumed the leadership at Chrysler, Eaton was asked (obliquely) by a *Wall Street Journal* reporter what he had been doing on the day John F. Kennedy was assassinated. Without hesitation Eaton responded that he was in a dynamometer room at General Motors' Warren, Michigan, Tech Center working on a special 377-cubic-inch V8 for race driver Roger Penske to use in an equally special Corvette Gran Sport race car in the upcoming Daytona twenty-four-hour endurance race. Hardly the kind of reply one might expect from a gray-faced finance type. Still, Eaton was an expert in the big-business numbers game. His years in Europe had produced the kind of worldview that was compatible with that of Lutz. "I knew we'd click as a team," Lutz was to remark shortly after Eaton's shocking selection was announced. At the same time a senior GM executive sniffed, "It's just as well Bob took the job. He wasn't on a fast track here at General Motors." The irony of that statement would generate great amusement in the Chrysler executive suite in coming years.

Eaton's first official act with the NS platform team came a month after his arrival. In April 1992, Eaton, Lutz, Castaing, and Gale presided over what was called a "Theme Approval" meeting, wherein the overall design concept of the new minivan, painstakingly developed over many months already, was officially accepted.

A month later the same group hosted a "Program Approval" meeting wherein the budget was set in stone, along with firm production targets and other long-term strategies. The budget would be $2.0864 billion initially, without additional, expected funding for the European model:

Vendor tools, dies, and material handling	$ 675.8 million
Manufacturing	$ 834.7 million
Powertrain (engines, transmissions)	$ 91.1 million
Acustar (components purchased from Mitsubishi joint venture)	$ 80.9 million
Research and development	$ 247.0 million
Pre-production launch	$ 109.9 million
Update Windsor engine plant	$ 47.0 million
Total	$2.0864 billion

Individual vehicle costs varied, model by model, option by option, but at the opposite ends of the product spectrum Sanders and his number-crunchers developed the following parameters: The short-wheelbase low-line (no options) would require 19.9 hours to assemble — a presentable figure in terms of efficiency, but longer than the best of the Japanese industry. It would cost just over $10,300 to produce. With a price (to the dealer, excluding his markup) of $14,022, the vehicle would yield a modest margin of $3,722 — excluding advertising and promotion, dealer incentives, rebates, etc. The top-of-the-line "premium" van in long-wheelbase form would cost $13,157 to manufacture and would sell to dealers for $21,370, yielding a margin of $8,213 (not considering high-profit option packages). Such a vehicle would require 22.6 hours to assemble. It had been hoped that the NS could be produced in substantially under twenty hours, which was still hardly as quick as the best Japanese benchmark (under fifteen hours). However, the complexity of the machine prevented major reductions in production time. The NS was to be manufactured in no less than thirty-six *different* body styles, on two wheelbases with four different engines (one 4-cylinder, two V6s, and a diesel) and two transmissions. Moreover, the new, more sophisticated design required 30 percent more parts than the T-115. Based on those realities, senior management considered the production time line to be acceptable.

Profit, in the sense that it involves net dollars in a bank account, is difficult to define in the terms employed by the accountants and comptrollers of major corporations. The "profit margin" used by the platform team included only the direct costs related to the creation of the NS. Items like materials, labor, and transportation were in their budget, but not advertising, marketing and promotion, sales incentives, interest on debt, employee benefits, or fixed corporate operating outlays. "Cost" and "expense" are mutually exclusive items in the world of business. The analogy to buying a house obtains: "*Cost*" is the amount expended to construct the building, while "*expense*" involves interest, taxes, heat, light, maintenance. When all expenses and costs are wrapped up, major car-makers like Chrysler consider net profits on their vehicles to be acceptable if they fall in the $750–$1,000 range. While exact corporate profit per vehicle is a serious proprietary secret, dealer profit is easier to compute. In general Chrysler dealers earn a 13 percent gross profit on the vehicle proper and 18 percent gross on all options. The corporation also offers a 3 percent "holdback" safety net, which permits dealers flexibility in unloading slow-selling models "at invoice." Special leasing plans, low-interest programs, and rebates are also used to periodically spike sales.

At the Program Approval meeting, Eaton canceled forever the "old coat, new coat" debate and committed the corporation totally to the NS. Initial production was scheduled to begin in early 1995 at the newly converted St. Louis South assembly plant on short- and long-wheelbase "high-line" vehicles, while Windsor would continue to build T-115s until midsummer, after which short- and long-wheelbase "low-line" vans would begin to be produced. Graz, Austria, would come on line later in the year with 2.4-liter fours and small turbo-diesels for the European market. Following the meeting, the team's key players gathered around Lutz and Eaton as they signed the official document. One of the NS styling bucks loomed impressively in the background. "Here we are, signing off on the single biggest project ever undertaken by Chrysler Corporation and we don't even have a photographer present to record the moment," lamented Lutz. "Sorry sir," came a voice out of the crowd, "no money in the budget for that sort of thing."

6

Enter 692SG

LIKE THOUSANDS of executives on the Motor City fast track, Chris Theodore was up early and on the road before dawn, poking through the thickening traffic on Detroit's rat's nest of freeways, blinking through his rain-spattered windshield and half-listening to J. P. McCarthy, the broadcasting icon who presided over WJR's 50,000-watt morning show. The news on November 24, 1992, was hardly devastating. The city's African-American community was still fitfully trying to eulogize the late Malice Green, a thirty-five-year-old crackhead who'd been bludgeoned to death by four members of Detroit's outgunned and undermanned police force. Sportscasters were bemoaning the tie between hated Ohio State and the beloved Blue of the University of Michigan — while at the same time treating a rare victory by the NFL Lions over a moribund Cincinnati club as if it were a come-from-behind triumph in the Super Bowl.

This meant little to Theodore, who was more focused on such parochial items as General Motors' continued slide from the monarchy of his world. The day before, Moody's had downgraded GM's once-regal bond rating amid swirling rumors of draconian plant closings, model cancellations, and layoffs. In faraway Little Rock, Arkansas, the national press corps remained in a swoon over the recent election, wherein a pair of southern Jaycee archetypes named Clinton and Gore had won the White House following a bizarre battle against a president with a broken political compass and a quirky Texas billionaire haunted by the national debt. Like most of his peers, Theodore was wary of the new administration. They had spoken of bumping fuel-mileage standards to absurd ranges of forty miles per gallon or more. The new vice president had charged, in an environmental frenzy, that the internal combustion engine was more dangerous to civilization than nuclear warfare. That sort of talk, stump-style raving or not, hardly inspired confidence in men like Theodore, whose responsibility lay in planning and creating new automobiles.

According to the radio, the rain would hammer at Detroit for the entire day. Angry nimbus clouds seemed natural to this place. The mood of Detroit was somber, blighted as it was with racial warfare, vast acreages of decaying neighborhoods dominated by lavishly armed street gangs, a profane old hack in the mayor's office, and an automobile industry under assault from a tide of imports. Worse yet, much of the economic boiler system of the city — the light industry, the service businesses, the white-collar middle class, the fancy hotels and condo developments — was moving to the boom towns like Troy, Warren, Sterling Heights, and Farmington Hills on the northern perimeters. What remained was a copse of skyscrapers along the Detroit River surrounded by a gutted urban free-fire zone.

Detroit's image as the powerful, proud Motor City, a muscular, tough-talking town that for most of this century had forged the bestselling automobiles in the world, was badly faded. Now the car business was diffused and fragmented. Aside from a single General Motors plant in the Hamtramck section and Chrysler's $800 million expansion of its old East Jefferson Avenue site, the grand enterprise had fled the city to places like Flat Rock, Michigan, where Ford and Mazda had jointly constructed a giant facility; to Ohio, where Ford and Honda were expanding; to Tennessee, where Saturn and Nissan had planted roots; and to Kentucky, where Toyota was building their hot-selling Camrys. Only four in ten adults in Detroit were gainfully employed, and experts predicted that another 10 percent of those workers would be on the dole by the year 2000. Of all the ambitious public works projects financed by the city since 1985, over half were in bankruptcy or receivership. The credit rating of this cracked and wheezing engine of American industry was the worst of the nation's twenty largest cities.

Detroit's plunge from glory had been chronicled like the slow death of a great empire. In the years following World War II, the city produced nearly 80 percent of the world's automobiles. But this ultimate company town, arrogant and isolated on the Great Lakes coastal plain, refused to acknowledge that its bloated, inefficient, shabbily built products were vulnerable to new technologies from overseas. After all, Detroit was "the Arsenal of Democracy," the home of Yankee ingenuity that spilled out stupefying tonnages of war material from 1941 to 1945 and roared out of the war convinced that its manufacturing know-how would leave it unchallenged.

A Michigan state historical marker in front of Chrysler's Highland Park plant celebrated its role in the Second World War. From that complex had issued forth a majority of the 55,000 tanks produced in Detroit, as well as part of the 2.6 million trucks, 126,000 gun carriages and armored cars employed by the army and marines. The automobile industry's contribution had been prodigious: 4,131,000 engines for aircraft, trucks, tanks, and marine applications; 5.9 million carbines, rifles, and machine guns; 27,000 fixed-wing airplanes, gliders, and helicopters; plus a myriad of items ranging from 12.5 billion rounds of small-arms ammunition to 20 million helmets to 207,000 pairs of binoculars to 100 miles of submarine netting. Now that legendary effort was doomed to sink further into the dim past; Chrysler was closing its Highland Park headquarters, a trend accelerated in a small but symbolic way when someone a few weeks earlier had stolen the marker.

For sixty years Chris Theodore's predecessors at Chrysler had headed toward that lumpy, five-story brick corporate headquarters at Highland Park, a squalid blue-collar suburb six miles north of Detroit's center. There in the hushed, teak-paneled corridors, misnamed "Mahogany Row" within the company, were housed the grandees and ghosts of the great corporation. Illuminated by soft, indirect lights, the place reminded some of an elegant funeral parlor, with mourners rather than high-powered auto execs huddled behind the flush-mounted doors. Like Ford's rusting River Rouge complex, Chrysler's Highland Park headquarters and the engineering, sales, and styling sections that surrounded it would soon become another of Detroit's sprawling vacancies.

Chris Theodore's destination on this November morning was a new, outrageous landmark. The Chrysler Technical Center, in suburban Auburn Hills, loomed above the billiard table Michigan landscape northeast of Detroit like a Mesopotamian city-state, granite-faced and blind to the world. It was a machine-age resurrection of Ur, an arrogant ziggurat, set not against the barbaric tribes in the faraway Zagros, but the predators from Ford who lurked to the west across Interstate 75. Three million square feet, the acreage of seven Silverdomes spread into multitiered, glass-ceilinged arcades and soaring rotundas, the billion-dollar "CTC" as it was called, had been under construction since the mid-1980s. Many derided it as yet another Iacocca excess, a bawdy display when the money would be more prudently spent on new products, debt retirement, modernized factories, pension fund contributions, and other mundanities. By the time the CTC rose out of the moist earth next to Galloway Creek, Chrysler was a shell-shocked war vet, crippled and disoriented, assaulted on one side by a resurgent Ford and a still-powerful GM, on another by the predatory Japanese and their superb machines that Iacocca endlessly carped about being dumped on the American market. Honda had long since fulfilled their goal of displacing Chrysler as a member of the domestic Big Three. And with Toyota, Nissan, and Mazda all consolidating their beachheads with factories on American soil, Chrysler and its feeble satrap, the nearly defunct American Motors, had seemed headed for the scrap heap of the car business, elegant new technical center or not.

But Chris Theodore considered himself to be part of a major renaissance — not just of Chrysler, but of the great city and its bedrock industry. "Detroit Iron" may have become a pejorative cliché to describe badly designed and built automobiles. His company, Lee Iacocca's "new" Chrysler Corporation, may have remained central among the offenders. Lee Iacocca himself, due finally to step down at the end of 1992, may have blundered a dozen ways since his masterful turnaround of the company in the early 1980s. Still, the company's new car, the brilliantly conceived LH sedans, held great promise. The judgment of the marketplace would have to come in before any improvement in the company's reputation would be registered. But Theodore's hopes, and hopes throughout Chrysler, were high.

The LHs were creating a sensation with the automotive press and the buying public even before their formal introduction. Ironically, Chrysler's own market research had warned that the public would be repelled by the LH's "cab forward" concept, which put the driver closer to the front of the car. Too trucklike in context, perhaps smacking of a lack of safety by placing the passengers dangerously close to the nose, warned the pollsters. Yet for once the company leaders had refused to relent, choosing instead to follow the best instincts of design chief Tom Gale and the small, elite team that had created the automobile. They were right, and the nannies who had counseled conventionality were wrong. The LHs (dubbed by cynics as Chrysler's "last hope") were headed for a major success by all measurements.

Now it was up to Theodore and his team of midlevel managers to keep the string — and the company — alive. Since 1984, nearly four million of the Chrysler minis had been sold. But the real war was only beginning. Early rivals had all been wide of the mark, either too stylistically *outré* or wrongly sized or improperly powered to wrestle significant market share from Chrysler. In yet another example of the homogenization of the international automobile business, Ford and Nissan had teamed up to create a new van that was beginning to nibble away at the Chrysler market. Those two rivals were jointly producing a neatly executed package to be sold as the Lincoln-Mercury Villager and the Nissan Quest. The basic design had been rendered by Nissan, while actual production came via a new Ford plant in Avon Lake, Ohio. But the Villager/Quests were being produced on a single 112.2-inch wheelbase, three inches longer than the smallest of the two existing Chrysler models but well over seven inches shorter than the long-wheelbase versions. Ford and Nissan were attacking Chrysler with an expensive, short-wheelbase vehicle similar to one of the weakest-selling models in the Chrysler lineup. A *small, high-priced* minivan. This flaw, the researchers hoped, would doom the Villagers and Quests to niche status within the minivan market.

But another challenge was looming in faraway Dearborn. This one was more serious. Ford was charging toward a 1994 launch of an all-new van, code-named "Win-88." Theodore knew this one would be a player, a heads-up battle against his own secret weapon. The *real* fight would begin in early 1995, when the NS debuted. That would be *the war.*

Theodore was an unlikely general for a major automotive war. Slightly built and fine-boned, with small hands and a mop of wavy swept-back black hair that accented his pale complexion, he had only recently shaved away his thick beard, a rare taboo in Detroit, where crisp, clean Waspish appearance was de rigueur. White shirts, conservative ties, off-the-rack suits, and Marine hairstyles had for decades been the uniform of the day. In the late 1960s, John Z. De-Lorean, the fallen angel of General Motors, had stunned the city by favoring slightly shaggy hairstyles and *blue* shirts. When Henry Ford II appeared at the LeMans auto race in 1966, then-editor of *Car and Driver*, David E. Davis Jr., cracked that he was "wearing sideburns that would have gotten him fired at General Motors."

Unlike some of his associates who now sported tailor-made suits, monogrammed shirts, and flashy cuff links, Theodore's standard outfit was a blue blazer, muted tie, and gray slacks, a contrast to his rebellious, outsider's image. Theodore was hardly the prototypical Detroit engineer who had graduated from a solid Big Ten university and hooked on with one of the Big Three, there to loyally and silently rise through the ranks. The older of two brothers, he was raised in a Jewish neighborhood on the west side of Detroit, the son of a Greek Orthodox immigrant from Crete who ran a tiny whole-sale grocery business. "My father didn't know which end of the wrench to hold, but I was hooked on cars from the start. When I was five my mother found me in the driveway. Somehow I'd jacked up the family Chevrolet and had managed to unbolt a wheel." His dream was to attend the General Motors Institute but he had to settle for the University of Michigan. Studying under David Cole, the highly respected academic — and son of former GM boss Ed Cole — Theodore headed a senior class team that developed a tiny urban car, complete with Wankel rotary engine and an elaborate crashproof passenger compartment. A summer job following grad-uation led to employment with Ford's Heavy Truck Division, where he worked on turbocharging. Following a business slump in 1974 he transferred to GM's Detroit Diesel Division, where he labored through mundanities of advanced design on monster diesel trucks — a role that was light-years away from his stated ambition of designing lithe passenger automobiles.

Restless, he answered an advertisement from Chrysler, which was creating an advance vehicle research team. There he believed his nascent creative talents might be brought to bear. "It was a disaster. I was in my 'BMW' mode, thinking about really quick, nimble, European-type sedans, while Chrysler was still fooling around with big, clumsy, full-frame iron that dated back to the fifties." He dreamed of advanced, unconventional products like a minivan, he claims, but mired as he was in the ossified, aging empire that was Chrysler, his notions were ignored.

But Theodore had been lucky. Had he belonged to an earlier generation, his future in Detroit would have been bleak. Sons of Greek immigrants faced long odds in the strata of midwestern Wasps who had dominated the car business from the time flinty barnyard geniuses like Henry Ford, Ransom E. Olds, David Buick, and the Dodge Brothers created the industry at the turn of the twentieth century. But now, in contrast to that other great American factory town, Hollywood — where the old Jewish hierarchy was giving way to a new class of crisp Eastern MBAs — Detroit's Presbyterian caste was being riddled by ethnics like Theodore. Lee Iacocca was among the first. The master huckster from a middle-class Italian family refused to be denied as he led the gang of young smart-asses at Ford to triumph with the 1964 Mustang. He banged on the gate, demanding total respectability (and power), until Henry Ford II tired of his sledgehammer style and perfunctorily canned him. Others followed Iacocca's brash tactics and while men named Cole and Smith and MacDonald and Peterson and Townsend and Poling still rose to the top, tough guys with more vowels in their names and more pigment in their skin poked and prodded their way into the executive suites. While he seemed the perfect Aryan and therefore acceptable to the clan, Lutz himself was a foreign-born outlander from Europe where it was locally suspected that weird eating habits, libertine sexual mores, and a penchant for small cars with stiff springs would corrupt the entire American love affair with cars. Like chief engineer Francois Castaing, Lutz was

Early design concepts from the initial
planning stages, 1991/92.
(Chrysler Corporation)

Opposite: Bob Lutz (left) and Bob Eaton watch their new minivan "leapfrog" into view at the 1995 Detroit Auto Show introduction. *(Chrysler Corporation)*

Below: Key members of the minivan platform team celebrate winning *Motor Trend* magazine's coveted "Car of the Year" award—the first minivan to be so honored. *(Chrysler Corporation)*

The "Silver Bullet" prototype (minus the left-side door) embodied much of the NS's final contours. *(Chrysler Corporation)*

ARTICULATING SPOILER

MORE SCULPTED BODYSIDE

Renkert 3791

The "Reach" design exercise was judged too extreme for volume production. *(Chrysler Corporation)*

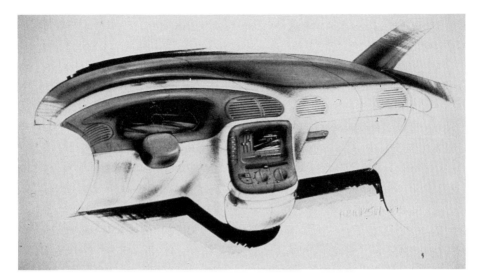

The minivan instrument panel was
redesigned many times to offer maximum
ergonomics for both driver and front-seat
passenger. *(Chrysler Corporation)*

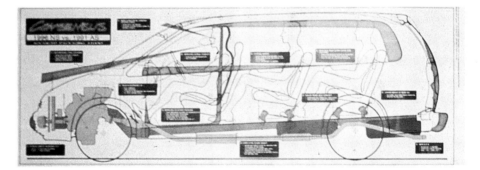

Design office drawing illustrates the
different "packaging" capabilities of the
NS and the older AS minivans. *(Chrysler
Corporation)*

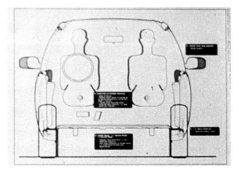

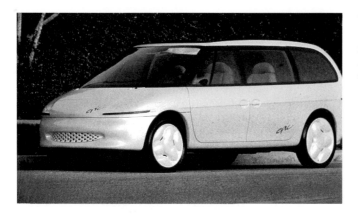

The 1992 "Epic" concept vehicle was rejected as too radical a departure from the then-current AS. *(Chrysler Corporation)*

NS prototype 692SG in its fiberglass shrouding on a test run in Arizona. A lady in South Dakota liked its looks! *(Tom Edson)*

St. Louis workers on the "trim chassis final" assembly line at St. Louis South. The workstations are designed for their ergonomic efficiency. *(Chrysler Corporation)*

"Building the box" at St. Louis South. The heavily automated
welders assemble NS bodies on precision jigs. *(Chrysler Corporation)*

A completed Dodge Caravan rolls off
the St. Louis South assembly line.
(Chrysler Corporation)

known for his fast driving and his contention that Detroit was not necessarily the fountainhead for all automotive wisdom. The exotic birthrights of Lutz and Castaing — not to mention Theodore's — would in decades past have doomed them to junior management roles and exile beyond the royal estates of Bloomfield Hills and Grosse Point.

Nothing much came of Theodore's Chrysler efforts, although he managed to turbocharge a government-funded safety research vehicle, which led him to employment with an ill-fated Long Island company founded on the hazy hopes of building aftermarket turbochargers. After a successful but short-lived contract to turbocharge Fiat Spyder two-seaters and a protracted effort to supply twin-turbo, intercooled units to John DeLorean's monumentally cursed sports car, he returned, nearly broke, to Detroit and a vice president's job at a then-thriving aftermarket custom shop called Cars and Concepts. "We did a Mustang convertible conversion for Ford and more vinyl-top conversions than I like to think about," he recalled, before being offered a job at American Motors. "I rejected it out of hand. 'Me? Work for a shitheel operation like American Motors?' I asked the guy who made the offer. 'Reserve judgment until you meet Francois Castaing,' I was told.

"We hit it off instantly. Francois was my kind of guy. He knew cars top to bottom. He loved 'em. He wanted to build 'em right, despite the mess that AMC was in. I was hired on as chief engineer in packaging the company's new-generation Jeep — called ZJ. That was the gemstone in the operation, and the main reason why Iacocca was so hot to get AMC. When the buyout was completed, Francois and me and a few engineering guys were retained. So there I was, back at Chrysler as a rebel. It was tough. People butted heads. The Chrysler guys, thanks to the minivan and generally good business in the mid-1980s, were figuring they could do no wrong. But we arrived with an ace-in-the-hole: the plans for the ZJ, which looked like a world-beater," he recalled. "That gave us a certain amount of credibility."

Theodore parked his company-provided Dodge Caravan deep in the belly of the CTC and headed into its seemingly endless corridors. Making sure he had a proper, if politically incorrect inventory of cigars stashed in his inner pocket, he made his way to the second floor West Wing, past the capacious marble lobby, teeming with well-polished supplier salesmen and manufacturer's reps, and entered his glass-walled office using a bar-coded identification card. The entire wing, an elegant, glass-arcaded gallery in soft ivory tones, was devoted to his minivan platform team.

The upper three levels of the West Wing were originally intended as scattershot office spaces intended to serve the traditional way of building automobiles — isolated, independent regiments of old pros restlessly interfacing in patchwork dialogues that ultimately resulted in the creation of vehicles packed with compromises from bumper to bumper.

On the fourth floor Bob Marcel was leading the small car team devoted to the creation of the PL, or Neon. It was aimed at the soft underbelly of the economy market. On the third floor, directly above Theodore, was the so-called big car LH team of Glenn Gardner.

Theodore's office was a glass-fronted cubicle, the size of a split-level guest bedroom. It was appointed with a standard-issue middle-management desk, three filing cabinets, a credenza, and four guest chairs around a small coffee table. Chrysler allowed modest personalizing touches, which included the sculptured hunk of a Jeep engine block, a few family snapshots plus some paintings of automobiles — the most prominent of which were a giant Bugatti Royale sedan and the musclebound red shape of the new Viper. (Viper shots were everywhere at the CTC, in offices and workstations, hung like Stalin and Hitler portraits during those despotic regimes as affirmation of one's true faith.) While smoking was not encouraged, there were no rules forbidding it in executive spaces. Several ashtrays were positioned to serve Theodore's lust for an occasional cigar.

Next to him, in an identical cubbyhole, was the burly, thick-necked manufacturing expert Sham Rushwin. The son of a hard-working Lebanese immigrant, Shamel Rushwin knew how to make cars, having callused his hands and bent his back to the tough hourly toil of seven years on the General Motors assembly line before coming to Chrysler. Rushwin was the platform team's builder — formally called "General Manager, Minivan Platform

Assembly" — the man who would coordinate the actual fabrication of the NS vans when they began to spill off the lines in Windsor, Ontario, and St. Louis sometime in mid-1995. It was the job of Rushwin and his staff to make sure that the insane detail inherent in the confluence of thousands of different bits and pieces ultimately resulted in a coherent automobile.*

A few steps away product planner Dick Winter and finance expert Frank Sanders sat in glass-walled offices that opened, like giant fish tanks, on the main arcade. The CTC architects had bragged (without foundation) that no one in the place would work more than eighty feet from direct sunlight, but in the case of Winter and Sanders, their source was at best the glass roof three stories above their heads. Tucked within the recess of Winter's modular wall desk was a gold "Ten Best" medal awarded by *Car and Driver* magazine to Winter for his work on the 1990 Laser/Talon coupes. In the adjacent fish tank was Sanders, the tough, balding number-cruncher with all but the symbolic green eyeshade. He oversaw the $2.1 billion budget for creating the NS like a hungry wolverine.

Theodore's life was dictated by a sheet of paper folded into tiny squares that he carried in the breast pocket of his coat. On it was printed a detailed schedule of the week's meetings. On this day his boss, Chrysler design chief Tom Gale, would chair an early-morning staff meeting, at which Theodore and his staff would brush up on open questions that might come up at a key presentation later in the day.

It was then that the proconsuls of the corporation — Eaton, Lutz, engineering vice president Francois Castaing, manufacturing vice president Dennis Pawley and supply vice president Tom Stallcamp — would hike up from Highland Park for a meeting known

---

*No one is quite sure exactly how many pieces make up a modern automobile. Officially Chrysler lists 1,315 "end items" for the minivan. This number includes the actual number of pieces assembled at the factory. But beyond that Chrysler's inventory of parts built by the corporation — engine, transmission, radio, etc. — totals 3,748. Coupled with pieces built by suppliers, the official total for the minivan is 6,797 individual bits and pieces. But that number does not include literally thousands and thousands of washers, nuts and bolts, gaskets, bearings, fasteners, bushings, and so on that compose the internals of the inventoried parts. Some industry experts estimate that the total is somewhere in the range of fifteen to twenty thousand individual parts for a modern car, but no one, to my knowledge, has ever made an official piece-by-piece count.

as a "Program Review" (official title: NS/GS Program Review, Minivan Platform Engineering Program Management). Theodore and the other heads of the minivan team would take their turns in the spotlight as the General Staff grilled them on the project's progress, with special emphasis on expenditures within the cash-strapped operation.

This was the third such program review since the NS project had gotten under way in early 1990. The first official approval of the new minivan, called "Concept Approval," had come September 23, 1991, after long months of so-called sandbox time in which the details of the new vehicle were laboriously hammered out. "Theme Approval," had come earlier that April, although the official clock on the project did not begin running until May 1992, a few months before Iacocca's farewell extravaganza. It was then that the final budgets for the project were set during what was known as "Program Approval."

The timetable under which the minivan would be brought to market was the subject of intense pressure, for competitive and institutional reasons. Ford's Windstar was known to be scheduled for 1994, so it was crucial that Chrysler bring out its all new minivan as soon as possible thereafter. And it was religious cant in Detroit that too much time was being consumed in the creation of new products. Every automobile company was in a mad race to cut months, if not years, off their sluggish gestation periods. Much public acclaim would accrue to the company able to reduce its design cycles to the three-to-four-year levels of the fabled Japanese. Theodore & Co. were under enormous pressure to lop gobs of time off the NS development schedule.

According to the official company time line, the NS minivan was scheduled to come to market in a mere thirty-one months (126 weeks) after its creation. This would qualify it as one of the most efficient developments in Detroit history and eight months quicker than the critically acclaimed LH cars. But this was an industrywide deception, based on an internal time clock that ignored twenty-four months of early planning. The time line was based on a schedule known as "WBVP" or "Weeks Before Vehicle Production." The official clock only began running with "Program Approval" in May

1992, as final budgets were set and Chrysler officially committed the financial and human resources to create the vehicle. This marked the 126 WBVP *thirty-one month* benchmark. It would lead to the production of prototype vehicles (known as "F-Ones") at CTC at 88 WBVP and finally to the start of the St. Louis pilot production (known as "P-Zero") in July 1994 at 32 WBVP. "Job One," the beginning of volume production, came at 0 WBVP in January 1995.

Thirty-one months to Job One sounded great to the press, but in reality the corporation had been committed to creating the new minivan since the preliminary team was first assembled in the beginning of 1990 — exactly five years or *sixty months* from start to finish. Even though still behind the Japanese, the time line was better by far than anything before accomplished at Chrysler.

Time was but one element of Theodore's challenge. Not only was he the slave to a stringent schedule, but the disciplines imposed by available funds and personnel were enormous. To marshal and organize his available resources, both human and physical, with the constraints of the available budget and time frames created the potential for nightmarish problems. Cost overruns, lengthy delays, or, worst of all, a substandard product could literally wreck Chrysler Corporation. His strategy would be critical in terms of process: He had to organize his team of diverse specialists so that each would complement the other, both in terms of the mission and the countdown to Job One.

To accomplish this, he had to find what industrial management experts called the critical path. It was the theoretical shortest distance between two design points, the connection of the most elemental components of the entire project in a smooth, timely, cost effective time frame. To draw an analogy from building a house: While the lot was being surveyed, other work was proceeding: contracting to dig the foundation, purchasing the plumbing and heating fixtures, finalizing the overall structure's plans and landscaping. But central to the project was the basic construction of the house — the foundation, the walls, the roof — while all the attendant planning and procurement went on around it. A well-run project would not have the carpeting arrive on site before the floors were laid, or the drywall installed before the roof was in place.

It was up to Theodore to orchestrate his team not in the creation of a suburban home, but a $2.1 billion minivan that was to be produced in quantities of over 600,000 units annually for perhaps the next decade. He faced the responsibility to control and coordinate not a small cadre of carpenters and bricklayers, but members of no less than twenty of the old chimneys within Chrysler — designers, financial experts, manufacturing experts, material handling specialists, procurement and supply managers, service and parts people, employee relations representatives, and marketing and product planning professionals, many of whom operated in locations spread around Detroit and across the globe.

To determine the most effective way to link the talents of these diverse experts would be difficult; to succeed would mean that he had found the NS's critical path.

On this gloomy morning, the "Job One" deadline of January 1995 was twenty-seven months (111 WBVP) away. Tom Gale had scheduled the early-morning session in order to summarize the upcoming agenda with the executive staff and to close any loopholes in the presentation that might generate criticism from Lutz and Eaton. He joined Theodore, Rushwin, Winter, Sanders, and the rest of the team leaders in a small glass-walled conference room bare save for a long, vinyl-topped table and a row of upholstered chairs in the well-guarded engineering section of CTC. Gale was a small man with graying hair and a wide grin. He was in many ways the antithesis of the prototypical Detroit "styling" chief. Since GM's legendary Harley J. Earl created the role in the late 1920s after gaining a reputation as a customizer of Cadillacs for Hollywood stars, designers were the flashiest executives in an otherwise gray town. They were singularly exempt from the dress code, appearing decked out in loud Italian-cut suits and explosively patterned ties with Windsor knots (the pinched, single-fold, foldover knot being the industry uniform). Earl's successor, William Mitchell, reached the outer limits by vamping on occasion in skintight white leather on a matching BMW motorcycle. George Walker, the head of Ford styling during the late 1950s, rhapsodized to *Time* magazine that his notion of high fashion was to be seen in a white Thunderbird, with white upholstery, wearing a white linen suit, with a white Russian wolfhound on the passenger seat. Such bizarre profundities were tolerated because "stylists" (now termed "designers") were expected to be eccentrics, at least within the confines of the Big Three executive suites. But Gale, seated at the head of the conference table, was clad in no such peacock finery. Like the rest of those present, he had shed his sport coat and, with striped shirt and conventional tie, blended totally with his associates. Rather than strut his stuff like an automotive Dalí, Gale let his keen esthetic sense and a legitimate passion for automobiles speak for him. His most recent triumphs were the LH sedans, the steroid-bloated Viper, and the popular Talon/Laser/Eclipse sport coupes he had done jointly for Chrysler and Mitsubishi.

Unlike Theodore, Gale was a Chrysler loyalist, an up-through-the-ranks enlistee after leaving Michigan State with a master of arts degree in 1967. He made vice president in 1985 and now held two parallel jobs — the responsibility for overall corporate vehicle design and the specific mission of creating the NS minivan. Gale understood, as did the others in the room, that success of the minivan project was big casino: that unless Chrysler could maintain its position of dominance in that market, other sales blips in the vehicle lineup would be insufficient. Within the little group clustered around the table was centered much of the future of Chrysler.

Gale's approach was relaxed, conversational, and nonthreatening. He reminded everybody of the afternoon schedule, then eased into his concerns about the Clinton administration's possible increase in mileage levels — the so-called CAFE or Corporate Average Fuel Efficiency. Because of classification of the minivans as trucks rather than automobiles, their CAFE standards were much lower, a modest 20 mpg. Talk had been bantered among Clinton campaign aides that the standard might be bumped to 24.5, but Theodore said he was willing to gamble that a compromise might be reached in the neighborhood of 22 or 23 mpg. "If that asshole Gore had his way, it could be higher," grumbled one of the engineers.

Theodore let that pass, but noted that higher mileage ratings might be reached by converting some fleet sales to a CNG (compressed natural gas) system that was currently being tested; a unit that would automatically stop and restart the engine at signal lights, a gasoline/methanol flex-fuel device; the cancellation of the optional 3.8-liter V6 engine and the all-wheel-drive unit, both of which used extra gasoline. Theodore also observed that if electric car technology came on line, it would slightly help CAFE, although it would take six thousand electrics to increase the overall average by 0.2 gallon.

"We're still $42 million over budget," said Gale. "We're getting better. That's been cut from seventy-three, but we don't have any room to maneuver. Eaton and Lutz won't budge on this, so be ready." Two major changes in the plan — the installation of water-based-paint booths and the change from metal to fiberglass gas tanks — would save money in the long run, but the short-term extra cost had bumped up the deficit, and savings would have to be found elsewhere.

It was no fun, being hung out to dry with cost overruns. The week before, Chip Sestok, a member of staff involved with building the European "GS" version of the van, had been pilloried when he noted that a heretofore unbudgeted right-hand-drive model was planned for the British market. The Graz, Austria, plant was budgeted to produce 55,000 left-hand-drive units, which, coupled with the anticipated 560,000 minis coming from American plants, capped production at a hard and fast 616,000 for the first year. Moneyman Sanders and Peter Rosenfeld, who was charged with dealing with the over three hundred major outside suppliers, nearly came out of their chairs at the news. "You are telling me you're going to need $19 million more to get right-hand drive? Where do you expect to get it?" yelled Sanders. "You are telling us something entirely new today," grumbled Rosenfeld. The impact of such a plan — acquisition of special instrument panels from the Netherlands, different wiring systems — was substantial, and Sestok, a lanky man in a Euro-style double-breasted suit and wire-frame glasses, had no choice but to stand in the box and take the fire. Unless money could be saved elsewhere, there would be no right-hand drive. Later at lunch Rosenfeld complained, "Those European guys aren't in the loop yet. They come in here with a laundry list that nobody heard of. That might have worked in the old days, but not now."

Gale worked down through the staff meeting agenda, pausing to note that some serious trouble spots remained in quality, namely proper fit of the front doors, quick, smooth closing mechanisms for the two sliding side doors, excessive wind noise caused by improper window sealing, and a nasty cooling fan imbalance that added to engine sound.

Dave Bostwick, the team's market research expert, noted that while Mercury's Villager was making a modest dent in sales, Chrysler owners remained amazingly loyal. Six out of ten were repeat customers and a steady 50 percent of the minivan market was being maintained. He saw nothing on the horizon that posed a threat until the arrival of the new Ford minivan.

While the Ford van was still supposed to be shrouded in secrecy, the Detroit intelligence network had already transmitted considerable detail about the vehicle. It would be named Windstar and marketed as a companion to the smaller, cheaper, and more truck-like rear-drive Aerostar that was to remain in the Ford lineup. The Windstar was to be built on the Taurus/Sable front-drive platform, an excellent four-door sedan that had been a major success for Ford. It would come in a single, long-wheelbase model and carry a 3.8-liter V6. Like the NS, Ford planned an aggressive sales effort in Europe.

Tom Kowaleski, a slight, sharp-nosed public relations staffer with excellent connections in the automotive press, had interesting spy news. A veteran from AMC with prior service at Ford, Kowaleski was an avid participant in the local sport of intelligence-gathering. Like his associates, one unanswered question nagged at him. Would the Windstar have a left-side sliding door like the NS? This was considered to be an ace-in-the-hole for the NS, and Theodore and his crew continued to puzzle whether or not Ford would attempt the same design trick.

"I'm sure I saw a Win-88 on the Interstate," said Kowaleski. "It was covered almost to the wheels with a tarp on the back of a flatbed, but it was the right size and shape. It was a prototype of some kind, so I cruised beside it, having a close look. There was no left-side sliding door."

The gathering was unimpressed. The vehicle could have been one of several prototypes other than Win-88. Moreover, why would

Ford risk exposure by parading it near Auburn Hills draped in a loose tarp? Perhaps it was a phony, a decoy to delude the Chrysler guys, although Theodore confirmed that his inside sources at Ford indicated that only a single sliding door would appear on the right side of the Windstar. Either way, the Ford van was due a full year before the NS and no one in the room was taking it lightly.

Someone mentioned that the press already knew about the NS left-side door. Iacocca had complained to a West Coast staffer that a *Los Angeles Times* reporter has asked him about the new component, suggesting an insider leak. "Shit," came a voice in the room. "That was Lee. He alluded to a left-side door on the new van in a press conference last spring. He's probably the source of his own leak." (Iacocca was famous for his impromptu and often outrageous cracks to the press. Following one particularly sensational statement, he was chided by the legal department to hold his tongue. "Fuck 'em," he reportedly cracked. "I drove the stock up two points. What have they done for the company lately?")

The meeting broke up and Theodore, Bostwick, Dick Winter, and Kowaleski headed for the CTC basement, an enormous cavern with corridors capable of handling small delivery trucks. There the heart and soul of the project lay — and where their grandstand play for the afternoon session was being readied.

Buried in the bowels of the CTC, in the elaborate fabrication shops, ten NS protoypes were in the process of completion, hand-built machines ready for the harsh testing necessary to ready such a critical vehicle for prime time. Seven of them were in the final stages of assembly. The other three would be merely "bodies in white," skeletal hulks in which various engineering groups — electrical, interior trim, and body development — would carry on static testing of components. Theodore's gem was vehicle 692SG, the first "on wheels" NS minivan, fully equipped and ready to roll, save for paintwork. It had been completed from computer drawings, clay mock-ups, and carbon-fiber prototypes in record time. NS Pre-Production Prototypes would be undergoing testing at 112 WBPV, more than twice as fast as the old standard. This was in the league with the Japanese standard of the industry, but not record-breaking. Still, compared to the elephantine pace of past Chrysler efforts, Theodore knew that the platform team concept had opened the door to beating the Japanese at their own game.

692SG had been built in a corner of a vast, brightly lit area littered with half-completed vehicles. At first glance the area looked like an immense commercial body shop, where repairs were under way on a collection of partially repaired wrecks. Parts were stacked everywhere. A row of bays in a far corner contained the hulk of various prototypes. The future JA midsized sedan stood on jack stands in various states of undress, as did a few LHs and several minivans. 692SG had been fabricated piece-by-piece in one of the bays by a bespectacled craftsman named Harold Burns, a Chrysler technician whose specialty was prototype work of this sort. Burns had put the vehicle together like a giant puzzle, fitting the various bits and pieces as they poured in from outside suppliers and local custom-stamping operations. Each day the minivan had taken shape under the fine eye of Burns and a legion of platform team engineers who had made the long trek from their offices into the CTC basement to marshal their particular components into the proper place, taking note of assembly difficulties, poor fit, impractical positioning, and other flaws that might haunt the production process. Burns had labored over 692SG as if the CTC garage had been in his own backyard and the vehicle his personal kit car.

They found Burns, smiling widely, standing beside his creation outside the CTC's enormous, state-of-the-art paint booth. "I built that thing," he said proudly, although his machine looked awful, a white abomination vaguely resembling an aged Chevrolet Suburban, lumpy and graceless. Chief Engineer Will Knudsen, Burns, and their crew had artfully disguised it with an ugly layer of quick-release fiberglass panels. The reason for the disguise was twofold: to surprise the executives that afternoon by appearing with a running prototype well ahead of schedule and then to test it on the small track along Galloway Creek and later at the corporation's immense proving grounds outside Chelsea and in Arizona. "Wait till Jim Dunne sees this," Theodore mused, referring to the industry's most notorious spy photographer. Dunne is the veteran Detroit editor for *Popular Mechanics* magazine who had specialized in snapping shots of new models months — sometimes years — prior to their introduction. Dunne was believed to have leased a plot of high ground on the perimeter of General Motors' Milford, Michigan, proving grounds, where his 1000mm telephoto lens operated like a ground-based spy satellite. This Ron Galella of the car business was a resourceful reporter, and it had become a good-natured game to try to confound him with weird disguises like that which shrouded the NS. He was not alone. The town was swarming with spies — free-lancers seeking the unguarded shot that might be sold to major magazines, the automotive press, or to the tabloids. Recently a light plane had been spotted circling the Chelsea proving grounds, clearly on a snooping mission. Corporate security forces were baffled by its identity. Its wing registration numbers had been painted over. It was finally scared off when Chrysler put a small plane of its own on patrol.

Under Burns's grotesque fiberglass lay the corporation's great white hope. There was no escaping the reality that Theodore & Co. were now beyond the point of no return. 692SG was a reality in steel. No major revisions were now possible; no veto power in Highland Park was strong enough to alter the course. This hunk of fiberglass and metal was the corporate future.

Eaton, Lutz, Pawley, and Stallcamp arrived on time but without Castaing, whose brother had died suddenly. They had driven north from Highland Park, up I-75 in new LH sedans, and gathered in the CTC styling dome for the "Product Review." It was a yawning, circular room, with a low, Pantheon-like domed ceiling that rose 60 feet above the 120-foot-diameter space. A 42×16-foot movie screen and turntable were concealed in the soft, gray carpeting for audio-visual shows — complemented, if necessary, by a battery of 85 powerful incandescent, fluorescent, and halogen multicolored lights that, in conjunction with a sound system that would do the Rolling Stones proud, was capable of Broadway-style theatrics. A stagelike alcove housed an elaborate, glass-walled projection booth and a long table with microphones set at forty places. Spread around the far perimeter of the room were several bare NS body hulks, some suspension bits, two engines on stands, and a number of display panels for later examination.

Eaton led the way, but it was Lutz, who towered over nearly everyone, who demanded attention. Eaton was a barrel-chested man of medium height, a faintly dour expression pasted on his wide face. If Eaton was reminiscent of a member of the old Soviet Politburo, Lutz was surely a throwback to the Wehrmacht General Staff, a stiff-backed, jut-jawed field marshal radiating confidence and military bearing. These were the players. The platform team fell silent as they entered the room, fading into the carpet as the eminences paraded in, shaking hands and exchanging greetings as they moved toward the dais.

Eaton was still establishing his turf, while slowly encircling his former rival, Lutz. Both men were in a sense outsiders. In an industry where many executives reached the top after moving, church-like, from novitiate to priest to monsignor to archbishop to cardinal within the same company, Eaton and Lutz both came from automotive cultures beyond Chrysler. Of the two, Eaton's career was by far the more mundane. After receiving his B.S. degree in mechanical engineering from the University of Kansas in 1963, he had joined Chevrolet as an engineer-trainee and had stayed with the corporation until his transfer to Chrysler in March 1992. At age fifty-two, Eaton was eight years younger than the flashy and much-traveled Lutz. Born in Zurich, Switzerland, of wealthy parents, Lutz had gained bachelor's and master's degrees at the University of California at Berkeley before becoming a pilot in the Marine Corps from 1954 to 1959. From there he joined General Motors and served in Europe before transferring to BMW as vice president of sales. Having gained a reputation in the international business arena, he moved to Ford in 1974 as the chairman of Ford of Europe and remained with that company for twelve years until lured to Chrysler by Iacocca in 1986. On the surface, a solid détente had apparently been established between them — despite their distinctly contrasting styles. Lutz, the nuts-and-bolts guy, and Eaton, a knowledgeable engineer now more oriented toward organization and finance, had formed an executive partnership to run the corporation while Iacocca was slowly being shoved offstage. The standard hype, the car-biz buzz, the corporate public relations line, portrayed a happy duet of "car guys." It was industry cant that all senior executives in Detroit were "car guys," cursed with such clichés as having "gasoline in their veins," whether or not they could distinguish a gas cap from a camshaft. Iacocca's rap sheet seemed to confirm "car guy" status, with such triumphs as the Ford Mustang in his win column, although insiders knew that he was primarily a marketer and a reluctant supporter of the vivid new line of LH sedans with their radical engineering and styling. He had remained wedded to the squared-up lines and rococo bright-work that formed the dubious trademark of the aging Chrysler New Yorkers and Fifth Avenues that had helped the corporation survive during the 1980s.

Lutz was different. This was a pedigreed "car guy," an un-abashed enthusiast of fast driving and high performance. If anyone was the father of the egregious Dodge Viper, a bare-bones, open-top, monster-motored sports car that had captured headlines for Chrysler a year earlier, it was Lutz. His office was strewn with car models, its walls plastered with paintings of speeding cars and swooping fighter planes, its carpeted floor supporting a Lambor-ghini V12 engine on a special stand — the ultimate affirmation of "car guy" status.

Eaton too possessed solid credentials. He had a predilection for continental design philosophy and driving habits, a solid engineer-ing background, and an enthusiasm for sporting machinery. This smallish, round-faced man appeared more than able to muscle his way next to Lutz as a purified, thirty-second-degree "car guy."

Theodore, looking relaxed, made a few opening remarks, noting quickly the changes that had been made on the NS since Lutz and Eaton had last been updated in July. He reported that nearly fifty of the current model minivans (code-named "AS") were being tested with a multitude of components — suspensions, drive trains, air-conditioning systems, instruments, seats, and so forth designed for the NS. By shielding them inside the present body style minivans (called "mules") they could do early and confidential testing with-out concerns about revealing any proprietary secrets to the likes of Dunne or the competition.

The next great threshold for the project was the "F-One" target — the May 3, 1994, deadline when Sham Rushwin and his manufac-turing team would begin a pilot NS assembly line in the revamped St. Louis plant. This offered nearly a year's lead time to clear the system of any potential glitches prior to the formal introduction of the vehicles to the general public in March 1995. Theodore told the gathering that the March 1995 "roll out" would involve about thirteen thousand minis in both the long- and short-wheelbase permutations being in the hands of Chrysler and Dodge dealers.

Several alterations in the product line had been made since the July program review with senior management. Because of the flared fenders on the NS, the phony wood-grain paneling, much loved by old owners since the woody station wagons of the 1930s, could not be applied in the standard vinyl sheets. This was a significant loss, considering that 50 percent of the so-called high-line minivans — Chrysler Town & Country, Dodge Grand Caravan LE, and Plymouth Grand Voyager LE — were sold with the wood grain siding. Possible alternatives included special paint, chrome wheels, or exotically accented side glass with paint trim. Theodore also reported that cost considerations would cancel a five-speed manual-transmission option until 1998 and that the old white sidewall tires — long a Detroit symbol of opulence — would be dropped entirely from the new NS lineup.

That said, the group left the tables and stepped onto the styling dome floor where, like a gang of tourists meandering through an arcane industrial museum, they moved in a cluster from one exhibit to the next. The first stop was a steel body in white, a bare-boned box bereft of doors, engine, and window glass. Lutz, decked out in a light brown woolen suit, close-cut at the hips, stood out, not only because of the contrasting sea of dark fabrics around him, but because his great wad of white hair towered above every head in the room. Engineer Ernie Laginess announced that the NS body weighed 800 pounds, which was a good number. It had substantially better torsional stiffness and structural rigidity than the current model. This was an achievement, considering that the gaping door cavity in the left side accounted for a 12 percent loss in strength. But thanks to endless simulation on the computer system, plus optimum use of internal bracing, proper gauge steel, and critically located lightening holes, the NS body shell was both lighter, stiffer, and more crashworthy than the current minivan.

Laginess noted that the rear lift-gate hinge system had been changed from a three-leaf to a two-leaf unit, offering a savings of

$2 per vehicle. He did not mention that the manufacturing team was still encountering nagging problems in getting proper paint coverage on the new layout — a subject that had been the source of repeated special meetings. A new front air dam to be added to some Chrysler Town & Country models would improve fuel mileage by 0.3 mile per gallon, but would add a $1 penalty to vehicle cost. In terms of overall CAFE, Laginess said, the extra expense was worthwhile.

The little museum tour straggled around the circle of the dome, stopping at length in front of a carbon-fiber body shell where electrical engineer Cindy Hess gave a crisp rundown of the NS's new features, including an advanced instrument cluster, better wiper-blade control, and more efficient computer programming and wiring harnesses, without once referring to her notes. Lutz and Eaton looked faintly bored as Hess reported that a new solid-state radiator fan relay had been added to offer what she said would provide "pulse width fan speed modulation." Their attention sharpened when she said the unit exacted a $9 cost penalty to her budget, then quickly relaxed when she added that the cooling fan change permitted a counterbalancing savings of $13.50 for the chassis engineering group.

Hess was the only female on the senior design team and was known as tough, capable, and ready to deal, mano-a-mano, with anyone in the place. She seemed totally at ease as she listened to Lutz warn, "LH customers are complaining about weak low-beam headlights. Don't fall into that hole."

Jim Sauter of the interior design team led the group through progress on such trouble spots as the rear air-conditioning system ("The worst in the industry; trying to be best in class"), the new steering post, which would get eleven tilt positions, up from the current five ("We've got some shake in the post, but we think a switch to lighter alloys will cure that"), and a seamless air bag position for the passenger ("There'll be no evidence of the bag on the dashboard other than a small label").

Sauter then moved through a list of cost-saving measurements that typified the minutiae that dogged the people who create mass-production automobiles: A roto-cast (plastic) armrest had been added in place of cloth-covered models to save $10; the right rear movable seat belt anchor had been replaced with a fixed version to save 52 cents; the left and right D-pillar (the rearmost window frames) trim pieces were now integrated into the interior rear quarter panel to save $3.40. It was the kind of mind-numbing detail that, if ignored, could cause a project like the NS to explode beyond its budget barriers like a Benedict Canyon wildfire.

Through all of this Lutz was leading the way, asking the questions, engaging in banter while Eaton looked somber. It was impossible to tell whether he was merely letting the larger, more imposing Lutz posture through the session or if he was being shunted aside by a more extroverted personality. They moved to an NS platform — an elaborately mottled and shaped sheet of steel that formed what in the old days would have been called the chassis. This was the foundation upon which the entire vehicle would ride. It supported the body, engine, transmission, and the suspension. Bernie Swanson, the engineer who headed the team assigned to creating this critical component, explained rather apologetically that there was little choice but to retain the single-leaf spring setup for the rear suspension. This obviously troubled him, as it did Theodore. Here was a state-of-the-art vehicle intended to lead the corporation into the twenty-first century with its rear wheels riding on a springing setup favored by wagon makers at the beginning of the sixteenth! "We had all kinds of neat setups — independents, DeDion, swing axles, you name it," Theodore noted, "but when it came down to cost and simple function, the damn leaf spring was hard to beat. Maybe when we get more money . . ."

Swanson also pointed out one of the villains in the $42 million cost overrun — the new plastic fuel tank. While it would mean an extra $19 per vehicle, Swanson emphasized that it offered significant improvement in emissions, long-term corrosion protection, and, most important, an eleven-pound weight savings. These advantages, he said, more than offset the added expense. Lutz nodded enthusiastically while Eaton seemed to be running numbers through his brain, silently seeking alternatives. He said nothing.

Two engines mounted on stands were next on the tour, one a 3.8-liter V6 that could be a casualty to tougher CAFE standards and Lutz's favorite, Rich Schaum's neatly packaged 2.4-liter four-cylinder. "We won't give up a damn thing to the Japanese with this one," Lutz announced. For decades the Japanese had owned the franchise on small, efficient, silky-smooth four-cylinder power-plants. Detroit had tried on numerous occasions to match them with half-baked, low-budget engines that were not only feeble in power outputs but as lumpy and noisy as tractor motors. Now Chrysler seemed ready. The 2.4 on the stand had all the goodies — four valves per cylinder, twin overhead camshafts, and two balance shafts that would smooth out the power impulses of the intrinsically rougher-firing four-cylinder. "It'll shock a few people in Europe too," smiled Lutz. "They don't think we know how to build small engines either."

Schaum calmly announced that an extra $2 per engine would be spent on the 2.4 liter's air-cleaner resonator to reduce NVH (industry argot for "noise, vibration, and harshness"), but $2.60 would be *saved* by replacing the alloy-cast thermostat housing with a stamped metal unit. Better yet, the engine's exhaust emission output was sufficiently low so that a secondary air pump and air system would not be necessary. The cost savings: an impressive $84. Lutz and Eaton both smiled broadly at the news, not only because of the money, but because both men understood that the elimination of a secondary air pump meant that Schaum and his team had in fact created a clean, high-efficiency engine that could compete on the world stage.

The tour group now numbered nearly fifty as a few stragglers eased into the background. As the group oozed to the end of the exhibits, a pair of doors on the far side of the dome slid open. Without fanfare, 692SG rolled into the room, still encrusted with its fiberglass molding. Eyes began to dart back and forth between the van and Lutz and Eaton. Were they surprised? Did they expect to see a prototype this early in the program? Would they approve of what they were about to see?

Knowing smiles spread across their faces as six coverall-clad team members led by Burns and Knudsen spilled out of the van as it rolled to a halt in the middle of the room. Screwdrivers in hand, they attacked the Dzuz fasteners holding the fiber-glass shrouding in place. Slowly the lovely, smooth contours of the NS began to reveal themselves. "Actually, I kind of like it the way it is," cracked Lutz. Laughter, slightly overwrought, splashed through the crowd. Theodore, who had remained quiet for much of the session, letting his various assistants hold center stage, said to Lutz, "With that long nose on there, we could fit in a trans-verse V10" (the ultra-powerful engine that powered the Viper sports car). "Why not?" answered Lutz, his eyes riveted on the dis-robing.

Eaton and Lutz climbed aboard the NS while the group hovered at a polite distance. Their attention leaned left, to the side of the van that now gaped with the new sliding door. Eaton asked a few questions about structural integrity and the lack of arm space on the seat nearest the door. Would there be an armrest? Assured by John Herlitz, the dapper engineer in charge of interior design, that such a component would be added, the execs poked and prodded their way through the rest of the vehicle, then stepped up to its rak-ish white nose. The ritual signing of the hood began. A fat black marking pen in hand, Eaton scrawled his signature, followed by Lutz, Pawley, Stallcamp, and so on, until the entire group of senior platform team managers had made their marks. It was announced that the hood would be hung in a special display case in the entry of the platform team's first-floor offices.

"We ought to put this vehicle in a museum. That is, if we had a museum," somebody cracked. Like most automobile companies, vehicles like 692SG were treated with considerable indifference. Some significant models were saved, but there had been little con-scious effort at Chrysler to preserve milestone vehicles on an or-derly basis. The future of 692SG was therefore uncertain, heading as it was into a rigorous schedule of field testing in the laboratories and on the corporate test tracks, both in Arizona and in Michigan. It was entirely possible that its end would come against the corpo-rate crash barrier in the CTC safety lab, after which it would be crushed and scrapped. Such was the level of sentimentality in the major-league car business.

Tom Gale, whose sense of history was keener than most of his colleagues', was attempting to rectify the situation. He had formed a small archive committee to catalogue Chrysler's past and, through private donations, to expand and display the corporation's small collection of significant automobiles. An area in CTC had been set aside, but funding was minuscule during the cash shortage.

The NS prototype presentation completed, the players retired to their seats behind a long table on the stage. The give and take of the program review was about to begin. In the fat days of the sixties and seventies this could have involved a "dog-and-pony act" of epic dimensions: elaborately produced motion pictures, lavish soundtracks, computer graphics, and even live entertainment to shield the reality that nothing of consequence was being presented. Those days were gone. A movie screen dropped from the ceiling and a simple mirrored print projector like those used in a thousand high school classrooms was placed before it. In the space-age projection booth, rigged as if to handle a satellite launch, two operators read magazines in open boredom while this most modest of audiovisual displays unfolded. Various speakers, working from Xerox sheets, began to rattle through their presentations.

The session went smoothly, with a minimum of grilling, until Peter Rosenfeld stepped into the line of fire. A former financial analyst for Mitsubishi's trading company, Rosenfeld had come to Chrysler with a harsh dose of reality about how the Japanese do business. "We should deal with them exactly like we treated the Russians in the Cold War," he was fond of saying. Thirtyish, with thinning hair and deep-set eyes, Rosenfeld's job was to streamline the bloated and often inefficient legions of outside suppliers, which, on most Chrysler vehicle programs, numbered over four hundred different firms. Rosenfeld was trying to reduce that to three hundred, but the assignment was nightmarish. The corporation currently used over fifty thousand different types of fasteners — nuts, bolts, washers, wire clamps, tie-wraps, Dzuz fasteners, rivets, etc. — in an insane collection of sizes. Rosenfeld and Theodore were trying to reduce that number to thirty thousand, but the job of tracking that much inventory — in addition to the thousands of other outsourced items — defied an easy solution.

In the end, 70 percent of the approximately fifteen thousand pieces, large and small, that would compose a completed NS mini-van would be manufactured by Rosenfeld's cadre of outside suppliers. This was a larger percentage than either Ford or Chrysler, which, because of their size, had substantially larger in-house parts divisions that manufactured proprietary items on an exclusive basis. This was both a blessing and a curse for Chrysler. A badly run procurement operation ballooned costs while creating uncertain levels of quality and an erratic supply stream. But Rosenfeld and his other platform team counterparts operated with a new advantage; by having a holistic overview of the project's needs, and sustained by the knowledge that their key suppliers were designing components to meet Chrysler's specifications with their own time and money (as opposed to the old system whereby Chrysler simply handed them the blueprints), costs could not only be reduced but quality levels could be constantly monitored.

Rosenfeld's part of the program was stiffly titled "Minivan Platform Volume Management" but the central theme was simple: keeping the cost of component parts from going berserk, as was the industry practice. While the Japanese had perfected their famous "just in time" *kan ban* inventory control, wherein tightly integrated parts suppliers kept their supply exactly keyed to production requirements, the American car business had for years ridden a zany roller coaster. They were either buried in extra parts or were stopping production lines because some tiny, independent supplier of ashtrays in Dubuque had closed his shop after he forgot to pay his electric bill. To avoid such debacles, Chrysler had made a practice of contracting for some components to be produced at the rate of *150 percent* more than the actual vehicles being produced — a costly alternative, but better than the estimated $60 million in lost profits *each week* if an assembly plant was forced to close because of parts shortages and bad forecasting.

Lutz noted that problems existed with the hot-selling Jeep Cherokee. Too many low-line models were being built, while demand for the more luxurious Grand Cherokee Limited could not be met. This entire subject was a hot button throughout the industry, and Lutz quickly swept into action after Rosenfeld noted the penalties for misjudgments in procurement, including higher production costs, excess transportation expense, and supplier overtime. If there was a single area where the Japanese still maintained a significant advantage, it was in this tangle of relationships with suppliers. "We're in danger of wasting enormous amounts of capital to protect ourselves," said Lutz, taking command of the proceedings. He noted the old days, when entire spare assembly lines were kept ready to absorb sudden accelerations in demand, only to fall silent when the market dropped or component shortages arose. "This bothers me greatly," he said grimly.

Tom Stallcamp, the vice president directly in charge of procurement and supply, responded sharply, noting the enormous complexity of the process and adding that the corporate system was rapidly improving. He too had been in the trenches. While men like Rosenfeld dealt with suppliers working directly with their platform teams, Stallcamp was not only responsible for the overall corporate procurement policies, but directly negotiated with major contractors who supplied such universally employed components as tires, sheet steel, and sound systems (which were shared throughout the Chrysler lineup). Now poor Rosenfeld was in the middle, a spectator imprisoned beside this projector and his Xerox sheets while a high-powered debate bounced back and forth between Stallcamp and Lutz — a debate of esoteric manufacturing philosophy. Rosenfeld was like a junior NASA engineer describing a new satellite hydraulic system while Carl Sagan and Stephen Hawking suddenly began debating the Big Bang theory. He stood there, displaying a weak grin, clearly wanting only to gracefully leave the no-man's-land and take his seat.

It was a brief, knife-edged encounter, with Eaton saying little while Lutz loudly pronounced, "We must get the suppliers to shorten their lead time. We need better forecasting. We must force the system to be responsible. We must have lean production!" So ended the lecture. The group fell silent. Even if Lutz had been wrong — and he was not — no one in the place would take him on.

The remainder of the agenda was completed without incident. Frank Sanders summarized the financial picture, noting the budget overrun, but also predicting that savings would be found elsewhere. In years past, a $42 million bulge in a budget of $2.1 billion would have been considered pocket change. But not now. It would be corrected, come hell or high water. The program objective — i.e., the money budgeted — was exactly $2.106 billion. The current status, said Sanders, was $2.158 billion. Vehicle costs, he said, ranged from $9,311 for the Chrysler short-wheelbase low-line model to $11,161 for the long-wheelbase Dodge premium model. Those totals included materials, labor, and warranty coverage. With suggested list prices projected between $14,000 and $23,000, Sanders's figures indicated that the corporate gross profit margin, before incentives, would range between 34 and 36 percent; an acceptable industry figure.

If the minivan sold anywhere near its projected volumes of about 600,000 per year — which discounted a myriad of unanticipated threats such as new rivals in the market, a change of public tastes, a slump in the world economy — it was possible that Chrysler could recoup its NS investment in as little as three years. The vehicle would then generate pure profit for the remainder of its life cycle. But that was a projection fraught with uncertainty, a projection that rattled around only among the corporate financial types, whose billion-dollar computer models were as much based on faith and wishful thinking as that of the men and women who labored to save nickels and dimes on their bare-boned prototypes. Such was the endless blindfolded gambling that cursed the automobile business.

After the lights were snapped off in the styling dome and the 692SG had been driven out, to be taken back to the fabricating shops in the basement, Theodore and a few of the team made a quick stop by Ted's, a favorite bar on the corner of Opdike and Featherstone that had been frequented by the original LH platform team before CTC had been opened. Theodore loosened his tie, nipped at a scotch, and lit a cigar. "We'll keep on truckin'," he said, smiling. "I think we made 'em feel comfortable. Lutz told me on the way out that the program has the potential to be the best in North American history." Somebody mused about the dust-up between Lutz and Stallcamp. "Bob was making a point. It wasn't really a lecture," said Theodore. "But Tom is in a difficult spot. He's been caught short before. Flexibility in this business is always high risk. There's no way to call it dead nuts. I don't care how smart you are. It's not like when I was at Cars and Concepts. There we'd always screw around with a show car until the last hour. Then we'd give it to the painter. We'd expect that poor son-of-a-bitch to make it perfect. To cover up all the flaws. Here we ain't got no painter."

7

Ride and Drive

THE COMPOUND lay amidst the sagebrush and mesquite like a Foreign Legion outpost, low-walled and faintly ominous. Across the flatlands to the west lay the burnt-umber bulk of the Vulture Mountains, one of a series of ragged, mud-colored ranges that dotted the vastness to the west of Phoenix. A trio of flagpoles poked above its faded yellow masonry walls: the Stars and Stripes, the flashy, solar-burst pennant of Arizona, and Chrysler's blue-and-white pentastar. Inside its perimeter sat a cluster of garages and offices and a network of seemingly aimless macadam roads traced across the desert floor. In the world of major-league test sites, the Wittman, Arizona, proving grounds of Chrysler Corporation was considered adequate but hardly state of the art when compared to the immense facilities operated by General Motors, Ford, and Toyota in the Phoenix area.

Thanks to its generally favorable winter weather, southern Arizona was strewn with proving grounds. General Motors had pioneered the area after World War II, homesteading near Mesa on an expanse of desert that now included five thousand acres. Ford was far to the north, along the California border near Kingman. Chrysler's thirty-eight-hundred-acre facility had seemed large until Toyota spent $110 million on a twelve-thousand-acre extravaganza a few miles to the west. Nissan was located near Casa Grande well to the south, while Volvo and Volkswagen maintained smaller operations outside Phoenix. Jaguar worked out of a warehouse in the city, choosing to do its test drives on public highways. Caterpillar and U-Haul trailers also maintained test sites in the area.

Like most major automobile manufacturers, Chrysler possessed a pair of proving grounds. Home base was the sprawling facility at Chelsea, sixty miles to the west of Highland Park and Auburn Hills, off busy Interstate 94. During the winter, its labyrinth of test roads were buried in snow or glazed with ice, which sent the engineering staff trekking westward to the Arizona desert at Wittman. There the generally tepid winter weather permitted unimpeded driving. During the heat-choked summer months evaluations were made of air conditioners, cooling systems, ventilation layouts, brakes, tires, and other components susceptible to extreme heat.

In past decades a trip to Arizona by the engineering staff was considered cushy duty. The anointed were permitted to depart the icy gloom of Detroit for a sunny frolic: days of easy duty on the test track, capped by an early arrival at the motel pool or occasional diversion for a game of tennis or golf. But those days floated away on a tide of red ink that engulfed the corporation in the late 1980s. The subsequent downsizing and budget rigor mortis doomed the trips west to hard work and no play.

This meant little opportunity for Chris Theodore and his squad of seventeen engineers, along with marketing and publications types to languish by Scottsdale's elegant Pointe Resort's multiple pools, bars, golf courses, and tennis courts. They were up early on January 16, 1993, and on the road only to become mired in the swelling morning Phoenix rush hour. After breaking free of the traffic, their little cluster of minivans chugged up State Road 60/89 toward Wickenburg, twenty miles to the west.

The proving grounds lay at the end of a flat, transit-straight road off the main highway. The gate, solid and foreboding, was unmanned, save for a remote voice box and the goggle-eyed lens of a television camera. Theodore leaned out of the lead minivan and, after identifying himself, watched the big gate slide open in the rising morning sunlight.

There was little inside to hide from the prying eyes of the public. To the left a large parking lot was half-filled with ordinary automobiles. To the right, a sprawl of one-story buildings that could have been transplanted from any of a thousand industrial parks from across the nation. In the distance were the outlines of the steel retaining wall that bordered the high-speed 2.5-mile test oval. Behind the buildings, barely visible, were a few test vehicles: strangely disguised Neon compacts loaded with test gear, a prototype Ram T-100 pickup, with its immense bulldog snout that had just been introduced at the Detroit automobile show to mixed reviews. (The corporation had originally considered clothing the new truck in pallid styling derivative of the smooth-edged, carlike pickups from Ford and Chevrolet that dominated the market. But Lutz and Gale, evidencing more of the risk-taking management style that produced the LH, vetoed the layout in favor of the bulky, high-shouldered look that thematically related to the big-rig Kenworth and Peterbilt freight-haulers. "Hell," had said Lutz. "We've only got 6 percent of the market now. Even if 70 percent of the customers hate the damn thing, we still double our share. Then we've got a hit." (Such was the dice-rolling management that now ruled Chrysler.)

Theodore and his team had come to Wittman for what was known in the industry as a "Ride and Drive" — an on-road session wherein the participants would evaluate various vehicles from both the driver's and passenger's seats. The day's mission would be to compare the single running NS prototype — the same 692SG that had been shown to Lutz and Eaton two months earlier — against five other minivans that represented the best in the industry. They included a Mazda MPV, a Toyota Previa, a 1993 production Plymouth Voyager, and one of the new Nissan/Mercury Quest/Villagers (in this instance the Quest version). Also in the test was a 1994 Plymouth Voyager prototype or "synthesis" vehicle that was on the verge of production.

The simple goal was to measure or "benchmark" the 692SG against the competition. Now shrouded in flat black fiberglass camouflage, it looked like a mutant created by deranged schoolchildren when compared to the sleek, refined competition. Lumpy and fat-sided, with a droopy tail, 692SG had been heavily disguised not only because it was to be exposed on public roads around Wittman and Wickenburg, but because it had been driven from Detroit on an arduous, complicated, and protracted four-thousand-mile trip. Organized by senior engineer Will Knudsen, 692SG had been first driven north into raging blizzards, then south into the steamy regions of Arizona. Normal practice was to accompany the test vehicle with a large trailer, generally provided by Reliable Carriers, Inc., a well-known Detroit specialty trucking company that ferried vehicles for Chrysler and other members of the industry. Each evening the prototypes would be tucked away inside the Reliable transporter for safekeeping in a motel parking lot while the crew snatched a few hours rest. But the presence of a Reliable truck inevitably attracted the curious. It was understood within the industry that a Reliable trailer meant that a prototype had to be nearby. In order to nullify snoopers from rival companies or free-lance photographers hoping to snatch a spy photo, Knudsen contracted with the Archer Brothers Racing Team of Duluth, Minnesota, to employ their eighteen-wheel race car transporter as the support truck. The owners, Tommy and Bobby Archer, who were contract race car owners and drivers for Chrysler, stripped their giant red trailer of all identifying decals and ran with the Chrysler crew on the trip. Two teams of engineers were employed, switching places as the little convoy composed of 692GS, the Toyota Previa, the Mazda MPV, and the Nissan Quest straggled westward.

Making the entire trip with Knudsen was Harold Burns, who had fabricated the prototype, and Tom Persons, an evaluation engineer and veteran of such test drives. They had ferried 692SG across the snow-swept Great Plains to log extra miles while checking cold-weather systems like the heater and defroster. Such components could only be thoroughly evaluated in the real world, away from the test labs at CTC. Using NOAA weather forecasts, Knudsen varied the route, seeking the coldest temperatures. They found it — at minus 42°F — near Grand Forks, North Dakota. There, when trying to load the minivan into the Archer Brothers' semi, the hydraulic fluid in the lift-gate froze, requiring the crew to hand crank the vehicle into its overnight hiding place.

Tom Persons was a lean, soft-spoken, prematurely gray Detroit native whose engineering degree came from Lawrence Tech (disdainfully called "Larry Tech" within the industry). "Larry Tech was the poor kid's Detroit engineering school," he mused. His skills in diagnosing and pinpointing design flaws on the test rack rivaled senior engineers like the dour but incisive Herm Greif and easygoing Jack Kerby — veterans of uncounted "ride and drives" such as this. Both men had flown to Phoenix to await the arrival of the test crew.

The trip west, through the icy blasts of January 1993, had been made with 692SG running "like a freight train," said Persons. Save for weak low-beam headlights, which were still a problem on the LH sedans, the vehicle made the trip without a mechanical hitch. However, Persons and Burns were horrified as they rolled into a Holiday Inn in Rapid City, North Dakota, and spotted the motel's roadside marquee plastered with a giant "Welcome Chrysler" message. "I quickly asked them to take it down," said Persons, "although one local spotted our disguised minivan and, after asking if it was a '96 model, noted that she *loved* the styling." Such brushes with the public when driving prototypes were not unusual. Because cold-weather testing is critical to all manufacturers, certain places tended to be favored — remote outposts like Thompson, Manitoba, three hundred miles north of Winnipeg, or the Northwest Territory's Yellowknife, on the shore of Great Slave Lake, favored by Ford, or Fargo, North Dakota, often used by General Motors testers. "Places like Bemidji, Minnesota, get so much use by manufacturers that sometimes you'll see people standing on street corners with their cameras, hoping to get a shot of a prototype," said Persons. "We constantly run into guys from other companies. Here will come this little convoy of vehicles out of a snowstorm and you know it has to be a bunch of engineers from Ford or GM or maybe an import. You know they'll be eyeballing our stuff, trying to figure out who we are, while we're doing the same thing with them. One thing I pledged, no way am I taking an NS prototype to Bemidji."

Basking in the warm morning desert sunshine, Persons's thoughts about the freezing isolation of rural Minnesota were quickly erased by prospects of the pleasant drive that lay ahead. Moreover, heartening news had passed among the assembled group. The corporation had the day before announced a $723 million profit for 1992 ($356 million in the fourth quarter), its best performance since 1988 thanks to the LH sedans and the Grand Cherokee, and a complete turnaround from the disastrous $795 million loss recorded a year earlier.

But the news had generated only modest euphoria in the Highland Park executive suite. Bob Eaton commented with surprising candor, noting that "neither our balance sheet or our credit rating is where we want them to be." He and Lutz then jetted off to New York on what *USA Today* described as a "stock-touting road show" to convince Wall Street of the viability of their plan to sell an additional $1.6 billion of common stock. Chrysler's shares hovered at $40, up from $14 a year earlier, and the corporation was being viewed with new ardor by the financial experts. They had predicted that Chrysler would be the only domestic manufacturer to make a profit in '92, what with Ford's slumping European sales dragging down its bottom line and General Motors' continued collapse despite draconian cuts and bloody internecine boardroom warfare. That same morning the Chrysler team chuckled over the news that Roger B. Smith, the controversial former General Motors CEO, had been forced off the board of directors in a humiliating comedown. Smith, who had retired from the chairmanship in July 1990, had been held responsible for the stupefying collapse of his once-regal corporation, which had hemorrhaged $6.5 billion in 1990/91 and was in danger of seeing its domestic share of market slip to 30 percent — or nearly half what it had been twenty years earlier.

Smith's demise heartened Theodore's little group as they finished their rolls and coffee at the pre-run briefing. After all, Smith, like Iacocca, was one of the old moguls, a man who lived in regal isolation, fat with perks and bonuses. At least Iacocca understood automobiles, even if his taste in styling was suspect. Smith was a finance expert who didn't know a differential from a distributor and didn't care. It was men like Smith who, seeking profit in sacrifice of product, had brought the American automobile industry to its sorry state. It was now up to the new breed of executives rising to power among the Big Three to once again make their automobiles, not their annual reports, preeminent responsibilities.

Among Theodore's Phoenix codrivers were key members of his team — Tom Edson, Bob Feldmaier, Cindy Hess, Ernie Laginess, Bernie Swanson, and Rich Schaum, as well as Herm Greif and Jack Kerby. Also in the group were manufacturing experts Dick Scott and Les Wolfe — part of the team responsible for bolting and welding the NSs into salable products. Two of the corporation's public relations pros, Tom Kowaleski and Mike Aberlich, were also on hand. Both ex–American Motors men, Kowaleski and Aberlich would be key in getting the word out to the automotive press, first through casual conversation and carefully orchestrated leaks, then through organized previews, all with the single intention of blunting the impact of Ford's Windstar, which was to enjoy a one-year head start on the NS.

Jack Kerby would employ a superb stretch of road for the test. It lay south of Wickenburg, a twisting fifteen-mile run to nowhere. The smooth, well-maintained highway probed into the Vulture Mountains, then dead-ended abruptly at a defunct mine. It was a favorite for Chrysler engineers. A hardscrabble trail led onward, but was unpassable by all but a four-wheel-drive truck. With no traffic other than the occasional hunter or hiker, the road offered a thirty-mile round trip for essentially private testing on a public road.

The centerpiece of the test, 692SG — simply referred to by the team as "Type G" — was a long-wheelbase model with the corporation's 3.3 liter, 156 hp V6, also employed in the LH sedans. The Type G was equipped with the new left-side sliding door and, with 300-odd pounds of fiberglass shrouding, was the heaviest of the group of six test cars at 4,375 pounds. This of course would affect handling and performance (and, ironically, *improve* aerodynamics). While the production NS was expected to be quite slippery in terms of wind resistance, the fiberglass-coated, singularly ugly prototype was even better at cutting through the air — in the main because of its longer artificial tail section.

Aerodynamics, long ignored by the industry for the sake of blunderbuss styling, had become a major priority for two reasons. Primary was the search for better fuel economy, which was aided by a vehicle's ability to slip through the airstream with a minimum of what aerodynamicists called "drag." All such measurements were based on a standard called "coefficient of drag" or simply "Cd." The higher the Cd number (anything over 0.40), the worse the aerodynamics. The NS's target Cd of 0.35 was considered to be excellent for such a boxlike shape and a considerable improvement over the current AS (0.41). But beyond fuel economy, aerodynamics played a critical role in reducing NVH. The smoother the external shape, the less wind turbulence and resultant noise. Chrysler had a small wind tunnel at the CTC, capable of testing 3/8 scale models, but any work with full-sized vehicles required a trip to Lockheed's massive tunnel near Atlanta, where test sessions cost $2,000 an hour. Chrysler had plans to build a $35 million full-scale tunnel of their own, but that had to wait for an even stronger ledger sheet. Until then, evaluations of wind noise inside the cabin would be left to the seat-of-the-pants evaluations of drivers and passengers slogging back and forth on public roads and test tracks.

The Vulture Mountain road group was split into six teams of three drivers each. Jack Kerby had worked out a rotation whereby everyone on board would have an opportunity to both ride in and drive six vehicles.

Conversation on the way to the site ranged across a variety of subjects, including a litany of stories about the fast driving exploits of Lutz, Eaton, and Castaing. While Lutz maintained the reputation as the most aggressive of the group, all three men were accomplished drivers and spent hours on the Chrysler test tracks lashing through the bends with various products. It was Lutz, however, who maintained the head-down, wind-in-the-face reputation for speed. "I remember seeing Bob one morning on Telegraph Road. There he was, standing beside a white Stealth, jawing with a cop," said one of the engineers. "Hell," laughed another, "there was the time right along this road that he was hauling ass in a Viper and got nailed by an Arizona highway patrolman for doing some Godawful speed. But he was lucky. Just as the cop was about to write him, he got called off on an emergency. Bob slipped the noose."

They chatted easily as the cluster rolled along the flat, featureless two lanes. The talk centered, as always, on their industry: how GM had pluckily refused to sell V8 engines to Toyota to help save Toyota's floundering, badly underpowered T-100 pickup, or how rumors were flying that no less than Mercedes-Benz, caught short like all European manufacturers by the sport-utility boom, was considering such a vehicle ("The first eighty-thousand-dollar sport-ute," cracked one of the riders). They found it amusing that the Treasury Department had bumped the tariffs on imported mini-vans and SUVs from 2.5 percent to 25 percent in retaliation for Detroit-inspired charges of dumping. This had helped drive the Japanese minivan market share from 13 to 8 percent in less than a year and had further solidified Chrysler's dominance. They were for the most part Republicans, fiscally and socially conservative, as was most of the industry's elite, but this hardly prevented them from celebrating their government's intrusion into trade when it suited their interests.

The conversation turned to the rapidly expanding CTC, where ground had just been broken for a new fifteen-story executive office building that would mark the demise of the Highland Park complex. The structure, to be completed in 1995, would house the executive staff that remained in the same headquarters that had housed the Dodge Brothers and Chrysler executives since 1917. What would happen to the vast sprawl of assembly buildings, offices and parking lots? asked one of the engineers. "Who's to know," replied another. "The place is a toxic waste dump. Tear down the buildings and make a park? That won't work. The facility is obsolete. It's unlikely that anybody would take it over, so the company will probably just put up a fence around it and let it sit." The group fell silent, pondering the prospect of yet another vacant auto plant in Detroit — a city already dotted with similar hulks that served as little more than aviaries and homeless hangouts, the detritus of the new industrial age.

The sun had risen well above the Vultures when the convoy arrived at the test site. The road was clear and open, winding in sweeping curves through the scrub toward the south. Theodore led the pack, which accelerated away, gaining speed across the low hills. He was an accomplished driver and began to push the Type G hard through the corners, causing the passengers to grab their seats for support. "Francois doesn't like the steering," he noted as the van slid around a tight right-hander. "He says it lacks on-center precision. He wants it more like the Mazda MPV." Theodore had chosen to forget the complaint of Bob Lutz after his first drive. "This thing handles like a 1960 Buick!" growled the president. His remarks were tempered after Bernie Swanson discovered a loose lower control arm on the front suspension that was the culprit. But Castaing's criticism involved more serious implications. Steering feel, long ignored by Chrysler, was now considered critical. For years their products had been cursed with vague power boosters that removed any connection between the driver and the road. Now cars like the LH had a tighter, more definite response similar to that found in European sedans. Conventional Detroit wisdom had long maintained that Americans liked low-effort power steering and would not countenance the tighter ratios offered by the continental imports. But when the Japanese followed the likes of Volkswagen and BMW with quicker, more agile steering systems, the domestic industry slowly came around. It had been the same old guard that had ignored the feasibility of manual floor-mounted transmissions, stalk-mounted headlight controls, gas-filled shock absorbers, radial tires, disc brakes, fully adjustable seats, quartz-halogen headlights, firmer suspensions, electrically adjustable rearview mirrors, full instrumentation, more compact exterior dimensions, more aerodynamic body styles, multiple-speed windshield wipers, overhead camshaft, multivalve engines, and fuel injection, *all* of which had been developed and introduced on European cars and *all* of which had been denounced as "too sporty" for American tastes. Now, thanks to the new breed of engineers and executives who were populating the domestic industry, every one of the above items was an integral component on vehicles like the Type G minivan.

Theodore began yanking the wheel hard left, then hard right, pitching the minivan into a series of weird yawing motions. He was trying to evaluate the Type G's steering responsiveness and its ability to recover its composure in radical maneuvers. The rest of the convoy responded in similar fashion, which would have prompted any witnesses — thankfully there were none — to presume all six vehicles had simultaneously gone berserk. As Theodore straightened out, Herm Greif was out of his rear seat, scrambling into the back compartment, seeking the source of a distant squeak. He poked around the headliner, a grim look on his face. "We've got a hole back here causing wind noise," he said. He was tuned for such things, his ears veritable antennae for the groans, whines, whistles, and rumbles that are bound to issue from prototype automobiles. The NS had been carefully designed with a minimum of holes in its unit body, based on the reasoning that any aperture, no matter how small, is a potential source of noise, moisture, and structural weakness. Holes also had to be filled with grommets, gaskets, insulation, sound-deadening material, and paint, all of which cost money. The simplicity of the NS body was in a large part the expression of the necessity to minimize holes. "The sound engineering guys use the analogy of an oak door," noted Tom Edson. "You can have this solid hunk of wood, solid and strong as iron, but one tiny hole will destroy its sound deadening quality. We're looking for an oak door that's absolutely solid."

Theodore stopped in the middle of the vacant highway, then accelerated hard. The 3.3-liter V6 responded with a low growl and the four-speed automatic slipped through the gears without effort. He braked hard and stopped, a frown on his face. Once more he tromped on the throttle and the minivan surged forward, leveling out at 65 mph. "Like they said, it's *slow*," Theodore remarked to Greif. "We've got work to do," he grumbled. The target acceleration was zero to sixty in eleven seconds. Theodore did not heed his stopwatch to confirm that the vehicle was well off the mark, nearer to fourteen seconds. "We've got to get near eleven seconds or the new Ford will whip our ass," he growled. Greif continued to grope behind the dual rear bucket seats. "We've got bad lateral shake back here," said the veteran tester.

"Yeah, and we're still ninety to a hundred pounds overweight," muttered Theodore, implying that the extra bulk affected acceleration. Worse yet, it was possible that trimming that much poundage could affect structural rigidity. Weight was the enemy of fuel economy and performance but the friend of NVH. The trick was to strike a balance between the objectives with proper design.

The convoy stopped at the end of the pavement, just before the road snaked into the scrub toward an abandoned mine. The teams dutifully switched cars, the rearmost trio moving into the lead Type G while Theodore and Greif trudged to the back and climbed aboard what was considered a major rival, the Nissan Quest. It and its clone, the Mercury Villager, were already nibbling at Chrysler sales and getting consistently good reviews in the press.

Again Theodore scrambled behind the wheel and in a deft move adjusted the seat and hooked up the shoulder harness. He wasted no time spinning the Quest around and heading back down the twisting highway. "This thing is good. They did a damn good job, no question about it," he said as he accelerated hard. "Our design guys have torn one down and they figure that Ford has maybe seven hundred bucks more in the package than we'll have in a comparably equipped short-wheelbase NS. That makes it expensive to build, but it's pretty good in all departments. No air bag, and that's going to hurt 'em short term but they'll fix that. Steering has a nice on-center feel and they've done a good job with visibility."

Greif began poking around in the rear, as he had done with the Type G. "Nice and tight back here." Despite Dave Bostwick's contention that the Villager/Quest package was doomed to failure because it duplicated Chrysler's slow-selling, high-line, short-wheelbase ASs, it was already apparent that Ford and Nissan had a success on their hands. It was also apparent to Theodore that Mercury's Villager would dovetail perfectly with the larger, more powerful Win-88 when it arrived a year hence. "I don't care what anybody says, Ford's got two players in our league," he said, rolling the vehicle to a stop at the end of the loop.

They drove on until near dusk, stopping only for a quick lunch in nearby Wickenburg. Rolling out mile after mile, the teams continued their game of musical vehicles, pausing only to change position and briefly to exchange comments about the competition.

Back at the Pointe, they showered and changed and gathered in a small meeting room for an informal debriefing. A tub had been iced down with six-packs of Bud Lite and Cokes, while a simple spread of chips and cheese dip served as hors d'oeuvres. Again, it was no-frills automobile work, shorn of the lavish parties and entertainments of yore. They talked about the 1994 Plymouth Voyager AS minivan first, with complaints centering on the impression of tunnel vision caused by a new, higher instrument panel and its dark blue vinyl treatment. Lightening the color of the panel and removing the tinted sunshade band at the top of the windscreen was recommended. Some disliked the front seats, claiming they were too soft.

A small tide of minor criticisms was unleashed: the rear-window wiper speed was too quick; the lift-gate trim rattled against the glass; the heater/air-conditioning fan noise was objectionable; the cup holder appeared too small for a conventional-sized coffee mug. Suddenly, within the past few years, cup holders had become a major priority in the industry. Road test writers, especially those working on daily newspapers, had become obsessed with the notion of cup holders, often seeming to center their entire judgment of a vehicle on its ability to accommodate a plastic cup of coffee. European manufacturers in particular were slow to react to the trend, failing to see the importance of a cup of regular while on the way to work. They were pilloried in the press for their omission. Conversely, the Detroiters were ahead of the curve, seeking ever more creative ways to accommodate the urges of drinkers and drivers. The new NS would raise the bar even higher by offering holders that would accept even a 7-Eleven "Big Gulp."

The major problem with the AS was Herm Greif's "shake," which centered on the steering column and around the third seat. Compared to the other complaints, which were easily fixable, the shake and "BSR" (engineer talk for "buzz, squeak, and rattle") problems were serious. In an era where consumers were intolerant of the buzzes, squeaks, and body flexing that were omnipresent in American cars of twenty years earlier, Greif's observations demanded attention. After all, it was the AS that would have to hold Chrysler's position against Ford's minivan onslaughts for over a year before the NS reached the marketplace.

"The NVH lab has got some work to do," observed Greif. He was referring to an exotic laboratory, deep in the bowels of the CTC, where a team of specially trained engineers worked in a $22 million, totally sound-deadened network of insulated rooms where all manner of vehicle noise could be isolated and evaluated. The rooms, lined with foam that resembled massive egg crates, were so sensitive that vibrations could be detected from a General Motors truck assembly plant more than five miles away. The lab was considered state of the art in the industry. In fact, prior to the completion of CTC, a team of 150 Ford engineers had toured the lab (at the unauthorized invitation of the contractor) and had essentially duplicated the facility in Dearborn — for a reported $80 million. The CTC sound lab had replaced a crude facility built at Highland Park in 1956 underneath a machine shop. No testing could be undertaken there until the drill presses and lathes upstairs were shut down. No such handicap impeded the engineers at CTC.

The discussion turned to 692SG. Based on the glum expressions and the animated discourse, there was much to be done. Like the AS, 692SG was cursed with Greif's dreaded "shake," traceable to the middle of the cabin, the steering wheel column, and the center passenger seat. Dick Winter, who was responsible for the overall interior planning, was told that the overhead console was too intrusive, that the general shape of the instrument panel — a generous, swooping design intended to permit the driver to reach all the control buttons easily — was less than aesthetically perfect. Bernie Swanson, who was among the tallest of the group, noted that his knee had inadvertently activated the rear-window washer/wiper button. Complaints were registered about the ease of operating the sliding door inside release, especially for women and children.

The list seemed endless. After a day of hard driving by fewer than twenty humans, the machine seemed hopelessly flawed. Some of the complaints seemed niggling. A need for a cup holder for the optional left-side sliding door was expressed, as was a call for more lateral support for the front seats. (The seats were, by universal agreement, not as comfortable as the Previa's, which served as a benchmark for the class.)

Theodore was most concerned about the handling, which he found in general to be acceptable though slightly "ponderous." "The Quest's steering is miles better than ours. Our feel and precision just don't make it. There's too much dead motion on center. We've got more work to do on the whole system," he grumbled. It was well known that Castaing, who was in many ways Theodore's patron, felt the same way. A devotee of European cars with their firmer, tauter suspensions and steering, both he and Theodore were willing to aggressively convert American drivers to the more precise feel of continental machines. Theodore also targeted what he considered to be excessive rear road noise and NVH levels from the powertrain to be inferior to the Quest's. It was clear as the discussion drifted along that the joint Nissan/Ford minivan was the current benchmark; that it more than the Previa or the Mazda MPV represented the best the competition had to offer — at least until the full-sized Ford Windstar arrived a year hence.

"We're way down on power, Rich," said Theodore almost casually to Rich Schaum. The 692SG's 3.3-liter V6 was expected to be the engine of choice for most minivan buyers and, at a rated 156 hp, should have theoretically provided adequate acceleration and passing power. But the sluggishness of the prototype was evident, and heads nodded in agreement at Theodore's observation. "We're working on it, and we think the problem may relate to excessive engine compartment heat. Better venting ought to cure it," said Schaum as Theodore turned to Cindy Hess. "The stalk control confuses the hell out of me," he said.

Again, heads nodded. He was referring to the arm extending from the steering column that controlled the wipers and headlight dimmer. For years American designers had refused to employ simple, ergonomically friendly stalk controls in favor of dashboard-mounted wiper switches and crude large-button headlight dimmers attached to the floorboards. Only in the last decade had the switch been made to the concept long employed on European and Japanese cars. "It looks shitty and I don't like the way it feels. The whole thing is wrong," said somebody. Cindy Hess, the only female in the room and the only senior female engineer on the team dominated by white males,* had no problem holding her own against such criticism. A brilliant electrical engineer with a degree from Auburn, she headed a team whose role was critical to the success of the NS program. While the public might tolerate subtle weaknesses in NVH, power, and interior room, simply because they were not as critical or discerning as the professionals, electronics formed the heart and soul of the vehicle. Electrical problems were the source of most customer service and warranty complaints, especially in contemporary vehicles where everything — from window lifts to seat

*Minorities and women remain rare in the industry, especially among engineering staffs. They are actively recruited, although relatively few seek careers in industry-related disciplines.

controls to power door latches to sound systems to fuel economy to engine performance to even the brakes — is controlled by electronic brains and hundreds of feet of complex circuitry. Worse yet, it was understood inside the corporation that the Huntsville, Alabama, electronics division was one of the weakest in the entire operation and that an unseemly percentage of warranty problems were attributable to that operation.

More complaints from the team were raised about a three-function switch that controlled the instrument panel lighting (confusing) and the size and function of the steering wheel–mounted cruise control switches. These would be corrected, she agreed, but, like the rest in the room, was unable to offer a solution to a problem that had nagged the team from the beginning. It seemed simple enough: the employment of an efficient radio antenna — a component that had been used on millions of automobiles since the 1930s. But the minivan posed a new set of problems. Since its introduction a decade and nearly four million units ago, the AS minivans had employed a single steel wire attached to the right front fender. This simple stick functioned adequately as a radio receiver but was noisy. Its exposure to the airstream caused it to moan and howl at certain speeds, which, based on the new distraction with NVH that permeated the industry, deemed it both archaic and unacceptable. Several alternatives were considered. An antenna impregnated in the windshield glass was rejected as unsightly, inefficient, and costly. A power retractable version was pricey and nearly impossible to mount within the cramped confines of the engine compartment. A third alternative of positioning a small stub antenna on the rear lift-gate was vetoed because of a $10 cost penalty in running a coaxial cable to the radio mounted at the front of the vehicle.

The compromise, as offered on 692SG, was met with little enthusiasm. Hess's team had come up with a fixed unit, mounted in the traditional right-front-fender location, but with a black plastic shrouding that made it appear like a retractable telescopic version. The covering diminished wind noise and turbulence but was bulky and unsightly — a crude, black stick that marred the otherwise clean flanks of the vehicle.

The issue floated among the group without resolution. Shoulders shrugged, heads shook in bafflement. They were running out of steam. Nearly fourteen hours of intense concentration on the vehicle had passed and lethargy permeated the room. Comments lagged. More joking filtered into the discourse. "We've got more work to do on the antenna," said Theodore. "That's for sure. But the big issue here is the shake. Unless we solve that one, we can use a broomstick for a radio antenna and nobody will give a damn."

The conversation moved from the actual to the theoretical, with the issue of traction control discussed briefly. It was a computer-controlled system that in essence functioned in the reverse of antilock brakes. It controlled wheel spin under acceleration (antilock, or ABS, did the opposite, preventing wheel lockup under braking). It was not planned as an option, although it was clear that ABS would be a component of most automobiles by the turn of the century. It was a matter of cost, pure and simple, and when somebody observed that second-gear starts were 90 percent as effective as traction control under most conditions he summarized his remark by comparing the NS to the LH sedans. Theodore snapped, "I don't want to hear about the LH and how we're as good as the LH. We're going to be better than the LH across the board, so forget the comparisons."

It had been a long, hard, and not particularly encouraging day. Tempers were beginning to fray and Theodore adjourned the meeting. They drifted into the gathering dusk and headed for a private barbecue dinner in a distant corner of the hotel. More Chrysler men were already there, part of the small car platform team who had been doing a similar evaluation of the little Neon sedans that were on the verge of reaching the market. Two open bars were well attended as waitresses dressed in western garb passed through the chattering assemblage with hot hors d'oeuvres. The odors of mesquite-fired beef drifted through the still Arizona evening. Francois Castaing arrived quietly and without fanfare. The most senior engineer in the corporation and the man perhaps singly most responsible for the conversion to platform teams was small in stature, with a classic Gallic face: sharp-nosed, with a firm chin and laconic blue eyes. He spoke in low, even tones with a vivid French accent.

Castaing bore none of the persona of the standard-issue Detroit senior executive. He was in fact a near antithesis of the self-confident, fullback-sized midwesterners who had controlled the industry since its inception.

"Francois," as he was universally called within the minivan team, was the purest competitor of the bunch. During his years with Renault, he had been a key player in its massive and highly successful Formula One racing operation. Since coming to Chrysler it had been Castaing who had spearheaded the development of the so-called Patriot racing car with its revolutionary alternate-fuel powerplant and who had been deeply involved in the corporation's short-lived employment of Lamborghini V12 engines in Formula One. One of those exotic powerplants still stood at the entrance of his CTC office. The easy banter swirled around him as he surveyed the scene, a faint half-smile crossing his face. "Meetings like this almost never happened in the old days," he said. "Everyone stuck with their own kind. Engineers with engineers, salespeople with salespeople. No one communicated with anyone. To bring teams together like this would have been unthinkable. Everyone protected his own territory. Everyone walked around with their big black notebooks, afraid that somebody else might see what was inside. The place was full of MBAs," he said disdainfully, "with their endless meetings and their lists and their checkoffs, who in the end knew nothing. We want guys who care about cars, who know about how they work and why they work; guys who will *climb over the wall* to make them the best they can. And no more closed notebooks."

Now the books were open. But to Theodore and Edson and the rest of the minivan platform team the pages were packed with problems; vibrations and shakes, badly executed components, and endless, arcane detail that could doom a vehicle's appeal. Twenty miles away, in the garage of the Wickenburg proving grounds, the well-flogged hulk of 692SG stood silent, the single running example of a machine that was to lead Chrysler into the twenty-first century. Its overall theme was solid, its appearance silky and smooth-edged. But within the artfully shaped sheet metal lay a myriad of flaws — perhaps thousands, both large and small — that would have to be corrected before any semblance of success could be expected. Two years lay ahead before the public would get its first look at the result. Somehow, under the blanket of stars in the clear Arizona night, that seemed an eternity. But to men like Castaing and Theodore, twenty-four months was a wink in time fraught with unthinkable challenges.

8

The Hard Part Begins

CHRIS THEODORE and the rest of the team flew back to chilled, cloud-draped Detroit at the end of January 1993 with one simple reality stuck in their brains. A mere seven prototype minivans were in existence, including the much-flawed 692SG that had been so thoroughly flogged on Vulture Mine road. Seven hand-built machines, each valued at $650,000, that bore little or no resemblance to the production versions that were to begin pouring off the assembly lines two years hence. As with all prototypes, they were more rolling engineering drawings than real automobiles; an artist's first sketch, a writer's first draft, as opposed to a finished painting or an edited manuscript ready for publication.

But the first step had been taken. Ideas had been translated into hard steel, glass, and plastic, and a course, though uncertain, had been charted. The seven vehicles, Type Gs, would be employed by various groups within the team — electrical, suspension, body structure, safety, and so on — to evaluate various components. But the Type Gs could hardly be considered representative of the products to come in quantities of over 600,000 a year if all went according to plan. From *seven* prototypes to 600,000 minivans in little more than two years was a daunting prospect, which would involve a transference from the theoretical graphics of Catia to the hardened steel stampings issuing from three assembly plants spread halfway around the globe. This transference from design to manufacturing was at the core of the automobile business. How successfully engineering concepts could be translated into actual products was elemental in terms of quality, cost control, efficiency, labor relations, and profit.

In the aged structure of the car culture, manufacturing and engineering were two essentially separate worlds. The engineering and design staffs were based in Detroit, home base as it were, within the inner circle of power and influence. Conversely, the manufacturing sector was on the perimeter, isolated in distant cities and operated by men who were beyond the direct lines of management influence. Within Chrysler, all power emanated from the fifth floor at Highland Park. The farther one was from that location — in a very real physical sense — the more detached one was from the fortunes of the company. Worse yet, there existed an open disdain if not hatred between the men who designed cars and those who actually made them. The former were generally better educated and better connected internally than the tough, hard-knuckled, up-through-the-ranks guys who ran "the plants." They were the grunts, the rough-and-tumble men who rubbed elbows with the hourly workers on the line and who battled with the United Auto Worker shop stewards and who took the blame for the shoddy workmanship of the products — although the responsibility had always been shared with the engineers back in Detroit who created components that were poorly executed, cheaply built, and overly complicated to assemble.

It was assumed by industry critics — the financial community, the press, and the public — that if the churlish blue-collar types on the assembly lines would only put in an honest day's work, American automobiles would be the match of any in the world. The people back in Detroit who designed such abominations as the Chevrolet Vega, the Ford Pinto, the Plymouth Duster, the Pontiac LeMans, the Ford Tempo, the Chrysler New Yorker, and literally countless other substandard automobiles from 1950 onward, slipped the noose while the men in the hinterlands — in smoky, backwater towns in obscure factories far from the seats of power — absorbed the blame.

Sham Rushwin understood this schism. He had spent seven years on a General Motors assembly line, watching the dismal process in action. After moving to Chrysler and rising to the managership of the Belvedere, Illinois, assembly plant, where the notably undistinguished Plymouth Horizons and Dodge Omnis were produced, Rushwin was himself victimized by the chimney system wherein designs would be passed over the transom to the manufacturing staff with minimal chance for comment. They were to build cars without complaint, regardless of how inefficient or ill-conceived a design might be. An hourly worker might be given a spot on the line at which he had to employ three different bolt sizes where one might work, or be forced to labor for hours on his back or his knees because no one had bothered to consider assembly-line ergonomics in the design process.

The assembly lines were steaming, deafening, nightmarish places full of sullen men. The chasm between workers and management seemed unbridgeable. The UAW represented its constituents from a purely adversarial position, content to blackmail the corporations through periodic strikes for more pay and benefits. The corporations were sufficiently prosperous so that more money could be muscled out of their coffers without affecting the bottom line. Thus silenced with more money but devoid of feeling or a sense of participation, the workers returned to their forty-hour hells and continued to build awful automobiles.

The dismal cycle began to crumble in the 1980s as the Japanese invasion intensified. Chrysler's pivotal Honda study revealed that there were better ways to make cars: a culture of teamwork that involved every man and woman in the company from the lowliest floor sweeper to the men in the executive suite. It was in theory a cozy idea and it had been paid lip service for decades in Detroit. But as the Big Three faltered, desperate measures had to be taken and, at Ford and Chrysler in particular, massive alterations in the manufacturing culture were made and the hourly worker's influence increased dramatically.

"Traditionally it was the waterfall theory," recalls Rushwin. "The information, the technology, the process, waterfalled down from the top. When it reached us it was more like mist than pure liquid." He described a system wherein the assembly line hummed at a mad pace, like a berserk scene from Chaplin's *Modern Times*. Cars spilled off the end in all forms of ill preparation. The most egregiously flawed were repaired in shops on site, while the less offensive were shipped off to the dealers where, if the customers complained with sufficient stridency, they would be repaired under warranty.

The process had a life of its own, an unstoppable dynamic that was built around the notion that to stop an assembly line was a mortal sin, regardless of the junk belching out the factory door. "We'd have quarterly review meetings where the executive engineers and product guys would come out from Detroit to determine if anything needed fixing. Otherwise it was business as usual," he mused.

That all changed during the crisis years of the late 1980s. "The walls slowly came down," said Rushwin. More power was transferred to hourly workers, producing a reservoir of talent and creativity of amazing depth and breadth. For eighty years the blue-collar workers in the automobile industry had been considered little more than meat on the hoof. They had come, following Ford's revolution just prior to World War I, from the Deep South and Eastern Europe, thousands of uneducated farmboys from the Carolinas and Georgia, gritty illiterates from Poland, Greece, the Balkans, and the Russian steppes, accepting whatever brutal, unrelenting labor the auto moguls handed out. They served silently until the Reuther brothers led the bloody battles that created the United Auto Workers in the late 1930s. Now their sons and grandsons had succeeded them, better educated, better informed, better organized, and infinitely more sophisticated regarding the nuances of the automobile business. Slowly the visionaries within the Big Three realized that this vast asset of intellect was being ignored, and men like Rushwin, who had worked both sides of the street, were the first to try to unlock the door between labor and management. Groups of blue-collar men began meeting regularly with the engineers and management to sort out myriads of issues that added complexity and inefficiency on the plant floor. "Initially, some of the old-line workers and the union guys were uncomfortable with the notion of rubbing elbows with management. The rift was that wide," says Rushwin.

The change was first tried at Windsor, Ontario, where Rushwin and the plant manager, a former Chrysler test engineer named Gino Raffin, developed a series of meetings between hourly workers and line management on the plant floor. Twenty hourly workers, drawn by daily lot, along with Canadian Auto Workers shop stewards, supervisors, and representatives from outside suppliers, sat down around a big square table and hashed out issues of mutual concern. Each day dealt with a different subject: Mondays, car bodies; Tuesday, paint; Wednesdays, trim; Thursdays, chassis; and Fridays, assembly. "It took time," says Rushwin. "A lot of hourly guys had never even talked to a guy in a white shirt and tie, much less told him what he thought. It just wasn't done. The class structure was too strong. It sounds easy, even logical, to break down that culture, but nearly a century of habit was hard to break. In the end we saw union grievances in the Windsor plant reduced from two thousand a year to no more than ten or fifteen."

Rushwin remembered an incident typical of the final hours of transition from the old culture to the new. "When we built the new AS — the reskinned T-115 minivan that was introduced in 1991 — the company was so strapped for cash that we couldn't afford pilot vehicles" (vehicles built prior to production on the assembly line to test the system and to evaluate parts and components). "They just sent the hourly guys home for a few weeks and changed the plant over for what's called a 'hard launch.' When they came back, the line was cranked up and they began bolting together cars they'd never seen before. That was common practice in the old culture: guys working by rote on machinery they didn't know or care about.

"As usual there were quality problems. Suddenly the yard was filled with four thousand minivans with a major rattle in the rear shoulder-belt mounting. Major noise. The vehicles couldn't be shipped. One of the hourly guys suggested a simple fix using a little rubber washer. Rather than wait around, we sent him and a crew out into the lots and made the fix. In the old culture that would have been unthinkable. The problem would have been sent back to engineering staff in Highland Park where'd they have had a series of meetings and then issued a directive to the plant. They would have recommended a rubber washer to be installed by the *same* hourly worker who had the idea in the first place!"

It was Bob Lutz who first referred to this "new industrial democracy." The words were not hollow. Chrysler, thanks to cruel empirical lessons, understood that a participatory workforce meant added productivity and quality. The fact that four hundred Windsor hourly workers and their families had been invited to see mock-ups of the NS as early as November 1991 attested to the fact that the men and women in the factories were being included in the new culture. Now, as the monster plants in St. Louis and Windsor were preparing to shift from production of the aging ASs to the new NSs, hourly workers were beginning to work side by side with the assembly-line designers to insure that workstations were as ergonomically efficient as possible.

Two years lay between the humming assembly line and the platform team's trip back from Phoenix. This time there would be no hard launch, but rather a series of carefully staged production cycles, each intended to steadily "ramp up" (favored industry jargon) toward full capacity of 560,000 units from St. Louis and Windsor, plus another 55,000 from the Graz, Austria, plant. (That total number would be increased in early 1994, based on optimism within the corporation.)

This was hardly revolutionary, although it did involve a level of caution and a deliberate process sometimes not practiced in the industry. Eaton, Lutz, and Castaing, in company with Theodore, recognized that there was too much at stake to rush the job. Chrysler's reputation for quality (or lack of it) was too fragile to gamble, even though every day of delay meant more inroads into their market territory by Ford's Windstar.

The plan was both complex and protracted. It would involve a pilot assembly line for prototype production in the basement of the CTC, as well as the trio of assembly plants. From a handful of Type Gs would evolve a steady escalation of NSs, each slightly more numerous and each closer to the production versions that would ultimately reach the public. The system would work this way:

Vehicle Type	Description/ Mission	Time Frame WBVP	Location	Vehicle Quantity
Type G Pre-programmed Skinned Prototype	Hand-built prototypes using hand-built parts for initial vehicle and component testing	115 wks	CTC	7

Vehicle Type	Description/ Mission	Time Frame WBVP	Location	Vehicle Quantity
F-One Program Car	Hand-built with prototype "soft tools." Test vehicles, auto shows, publicity and advertising photography. Also *120 "partial properties"* (nonrunning, incomplete bodies built for various design teams)	91 to 79 wks	CTC	31
P-Zero Pilot	Built with production tools and dies. All-white paint. Used for crash testing, EPA, and internal evaluation. Long wheelbase only	24 to 15 wks	CTC	47
P-Zero Pilot	Same. Short wheelbase only	17 to 13 wks	St. Louis	40
C-One Pilot	Built with full assembly line fixtures and tooling. Approved paint and interiors. No serial numbers. Used for internal evaluations	11 to 8 wks	St. Louis	265
PVP (Production Verification Pilot)	Essentially production level vehicles, used for limited rental car fleets, training, public relations, etc. Serial-numbered vehicles	0 hour 1-30-95	St. Louis	325
V-One (Volume Production)	Full production vehicles	0 hour 1-30-95	St. Louis	600,000*

*Includes annual production from Windsor, Ontario, and Graz, Austria, later in the year.

With several hundred "mules" and Harold Burns's handful of Type G synthesis vehicles running around, the real work was about to begin. Test vehicles serve two basic purposes: to evaluate function and viability of the whole vehicle and its thousands of separate components, and to create a manufacturing process from which a viable mass-production system can be created.* It is one thing to design and hand-build a few perfect machines and quite another to duplicate that machine by the millions, without major flaws.

The mass production would take place in the three assembly plants, but that was over twenty-four months in the future. In the meantime a small pilot assembly plant had been created in the lower level of the CTC, a miniature of that which would be built on a grand scale at St. Louis and at Windsor.

Building an automobile involves three elemental steps. First, about three hundred pieces of sheet metal have to be welded together to form the frame and body shell — "like building a box" says production engineer John Nigro, a broad-shouldered, good-natured team member with an easy smile. Then comes the application of paint. Much of the welding and painting can be done by robotics, after which begins an intensive process called "trim chassis final," during which about a thousand subassemblies like the engine, transmission, suspension, brakes, wiring, and wheels are fitted along with glass, seats, upholstery, trim items, and electronics to make a complete minivan.

Chrysler's mission was fiendishly more complicated than Ford's Windstar. Their chief rival was building the Windstar at a single plant — Oakville, Ontario — with one engine — a V6 — and in one body style on a single wheelbase. Conversely, Chrysler was setting out to build two body styles, with four and five doors in long (119.3 inch) and short (113.3 inch) wheelbases with five engines, three transmissions, and a plethora of option levels. (A sixth engine, the 2.0-liter 4-cylinder from the JA/PL series, would come in 1997 with right-hand-drive models from Graz.) To make such a system work in three factories on two continents required intricate planning with little room for error. Hence the critical nature of the CTC pilot plant. While it was impossible to duplicate a complete St. Louis or Windsor style assembly line with their thousand workstations spread over 2-million-plus square feet of factory, the CTC

*The late John R. Bond, the editor of *Road & Track* magazine during the 1950s and 1960s, once observed, "Any engineer can design a water pump for a Rolls-Royce, because it can be hand-built in small quantities with cost no object. But it takes a genius to design a water pump for a Chevrolet, which has to be produced, cheaply and efficiently, by the millions."

facility was built to contain a series of robotic welders and sufficient workstations (about twenty) so that the entire assembly process could be compacted into a space about one-twentieth the size of the real thing.

"Building a box" was the most critical element in the entire process. A series of sheet metal components created by Chrysler's three stamping plants at Sterling Heights and Warren in Michigan and at Twinsburg, Ohio, were to be welded up on eighty-six exotic robot welding rigs specially designed by suppliers Pico and Detroit Center Tool — both longtime vendors to the Big Three. The initial stampings would be produced with so-called soft tools, i.e., stamping dies made from a less expensive kirsite nickel alloy capable of producing about 250 panels each before losing their precision. Kirsite permits a company (the process is employed universally throughout the industry) to use less expensive, less durable dies until the exact fit of each panel had been verified. After that the team would spend $143 million for 608 chrome-steel "hard dies," each capable of stamping out as many as *three million* pieces before needing replacement.

The F-One vehicles built at CTC would employ soft tooling manufactured by eleven different tool and die vendors around the city. The stamping would be trucked to CTC and mounted on "framing jigs," where they would be welded into place by the robotic and hand-held guns — spot welded and fusion-arc welded into a "box" that would form the minivan's unit body. The average vehicle involves two to three thousand individual welds, each with variations based on the welding gun's tip pressure, the metal thickness, and the coating on the metal. "It takes time to make a good weld," said manufacturing engineer Ted Kleppert, noting that each robotic welder performs from 17 to 22 welds at each station, its high-voltage nose snooping around the expanse of metal like a giant, orange-colored reptile. The framing jig, which moved along the assembly line, was to stay at each robotic welding station exactly 55 seconds.

The positioning of the sheet metal panels on the framing jigs is determined by a "PLP," or primary locating point. These PLPs must be accurate to within 1 millimeter to insure proper fit of the doors, glass, suspension, and so forth. They would be checked in the CMM room — a space kept at exactly 70°F where a laser machine run remotely by computers checked tolerance to within .01 millimeter on 288 points in and out of the body structure. (Some initial bodies were found to be 11 millimeters *too low* at the rear — a fitful and unpredictable problem that was to nag Nigro and his crew for nearly another eighteen months.)

Once the prototype bodies had been welded up, they moved along the small assembly line, where hourly workers and engineers and supplier representatives worked together to complete the vehicles. This joint effort was something of a revolution for Chrysler. "In the old days our pilot plant was located on Outer Drive, while the engineering staff was at Highland Park, fifteen miles away. There wasn't much exchange of information," says Nigro. "Now everybody is in the same building and we build the pilots together." So too for the major outside suppliers who design and manufacture almost 70 percent of Chrysler's vehicles. "In the old days we'd give a supplier a design and tell him to go make it as cheaply as he could," recalls Tom Edson. "Now we tell them what we need and how much we're prepared to spend. They design the pieces and work with us to make sure they're at the proper quality levels."

The assembly of thousands of parts, each serial-numbered and set for an intricately sequential fitting on the vehicle as it moved along the assembly line, required planning so that it met five basic parameters: (1) proper fit, (2) simple and efficient to assemble, (3) easy to maintain, (4) cheap to manufacture, and (5) reliable. Much of this related to the methodology employed on the assembly line. In the old chimney system, where various engineering departments and suppliers seldom communicated, a workstation on an assembly line might require workers to use, for example, both 6mm and 8mm bolts, where with proper planning a single common size could be employed. A seemingly elemental problem, easy to solve, but one that haunted the industry for decades.

In order to pre-plan the detailed assembly of the NS, Theodore's team created what was to become known as "The Wall." It was in essence a detailed set of photographs, drawings, schematics, and text sequentially outlining the entire assembly process from the first welding jig to the final roll-out of a finished vehicle. The Wall would be located in a hallway in the bowels of the CTC. It described each of the 408 workstations that would be created at St. Louis and Windsor. Each workstation was described in categories, including the basic process, safety rules, special requirements, names of the operators, the tooling needed, part numbers to be assembled, material-handling requirements, conveyor heights, and error-proofing regulations. A detailed schematic drawing of each operation was also included. The CTC Wall would be over two hundred feet long and would be copied and displayed at both assembly plants when completed. In order to find a proper location, engineer Alan Willey hiked for weeks through the 3-million-square-foot complex searching for a several-hundred-foot expanse of bare wall. "I was up in the executive penthouse and down in the service bays before I found the spot, outside the central computer room," he recalled.

The Wall was to serve a number of functions. From it, teams of engineers, material-handling experts, human-factor professionals, finance types, and manufacturing professionals could graphically see each workstation, and thereby evaluate the way every facet of the assembly process evolved. Worker ergonomics, for example, could be dealt with, thereby reducing the bending and squatting that cursed old assembly lines, contributing to worker fatigue, inefficiency, and $5 million per year, per plant, in worker compensation claims for assembly-line injuries and lost time.

As fastener engineers, tool engineers, industrial engineers, conveyer specialists, material-handling and packaging people worked with the platform team engineers, a massive database was developed whereby graphic displays for The Wall would be transferred to each workstation at the factories. There assembly-line workers could consult the same pictures and diagrams on 8×8-foot panels that dropped from the ceiling. Moreover, workers were given the same capability as their Japanese counterparts — the critical ability to stop the line when they spotted a problem. In the old days this was no more possible than a Union Pacific yard worker stopping the Super Chief. As Rushwin said often, "*How* you build it is at least as important as *what* you build." Long ignored by Chrysler, which had paid long and dearly for a reputation for shabby workmanship, The Wall was intended as a radical cure to a process that was *ad hoc* at best.

"In the old days you'd fire up an assembly line and make it up as you went along," says Rushwin. "We'd move guys around on the line until you got some semblance of efficiency. Other than some loose-leaf binders, nobody had any notion of the total process. It would take at least six weeks of production to refine the system, and then it wasn't right. But you let it go, hoping somehow it'd be okay or somebody would fix it down the line or in the dealerships."

Each Thursday members of the platform team would trundle down the CTC escalators (there were no elevators, other than for executives in the building, making for a more open, social environment: "People don't talk on elevators; they do on escalators," noted one Chrysler executive) to The Wall, where a review of progress would be made. They would check manpower assignments, conveyer design, streamlining of tools and fasteners, and the critical area of material handling. (Chrysler was moving toward the Japanese "just in time" supply system, meaning that each workstation had to maintain exactly the right level of components.)

By visually tracking the entire manufacturing process via The Wall, the platform team was able to coordinate their design functions with the manufacturing experts from the plants and the outside suppliers. "In the dark ages the lack of communication prevented engineering changes on the line," says Tom Edson. "So some worker would be required to install a 7/16th-inch bolt, then lay down his impact wrench and pick up another one to install a 5/8th-inch hex head. Some guys on the line had to work with as many as eleven different bolt sizes. When you consider that the cost of acquiring and storing a part is estimated at $21 each, the priority of commonizing parts and simplifying the manufacturing process with systems like The Wall becomes clear. It was habit. Different engineering departments favored different-sized fasteners. They had a comfort level with certain components and there was never any need to change. We started out with 1,100 different fasteners on NS. By working with the various team members and the manufacturing guys, we cut that number to 600. Chris Theodore would like to cut it to *six*."

Cutting, slicing, paring, trimming. The team knew there was still great waste within the system, but part of the fat had long since been trimmed, along with sections of old bone. More could be done in the way of streamlining the process, but that involved experimentation, fits and starts, and retracing ground when shortcuts failed. There was no textbook to consult, no fail-safe methodology to be followed.

Within the realm of assembling automobiles, there were few secrets. Assembly lines tend to follow a set pattern, regardless of where they are in the world. They resemble in a broad theme the same system Henry Ford and his team of visionaries had perfected in 1914.*

Every manufacturer, from Japan to the United States to Germany, employs essentially the same process — body assembly, paint, and trim chassis final — to make their automobiles. There is, within the capabilities of late-twentieth-century robotics and manpower, no other viable alternative. Therefore when Rushwin and his team, which included manufacturing experts Les Wolfe and Bruce Donaldson, began to work with St. Louis plant manager Joe Mollahan and his staff to lay out the snakelike assembly line in the gargantuan, 2.8-million-square-foot vacant hall, they understood that certain rigid parameters — regarding maximum line speed, available manpower, the number of workstations as specified by The Wall, etc. — could not be tampered with. It would take their entire manufacturing budget of nearly $835 million to get it right, including the creation of a near-duplicate setup at Windsor and a smaller facility at Graz, Austria. By the end of 1995 they would, if all went according to plan, have created an industrial machine capable of punching out over two thousand minivans a day.

The money on the table was serious. "This is high-stakes poker," mused a team member when somebody mentioned that a currently

---

*Contrary to popular myth, Ford himself did not invent the moving assembly line. It was employed first by Ransom E. Olds (Oldsmobile) and then by Henry Leland (who created *both* the Cadillac and Lincoln marques) using a process common in the meat-packing industry. A group of Ford executives, C. H. Wills, James S. Couzens, P. E. Martin, Charles Sorensen, William Knudsen, and perhaps most important, Clarence Avery and Walter E. Flanders, perfected the process for the Model T. But it was Ford himself, a legitimate barnyard genius, who recognized the advantages of mass production and gambled the future of his company on its success.

popular Clint Eastwood motion picture was heading toward $100 million in gross sales. "Chump change," he mused. "The Hollywood moguls think a hundred mil is high bucks. Hell, we spend that much on racking." *Racking?* What could that possibly be? And how could it be that expensive? "Racking" is an industry term for the fixtures, mountings, crates, and "racks" employed to transport sheet metal components, engines, transmissions, axle assemblies, windshields, and so on from the supplier sites to the assembly plants. Each one of those components must be packaged for truck and rail shipment so that they will arrive undamaged and ready for installation. Each rack had to be specifically designed and manufactured for NS components, much like the tooling dies, the welding robots, and the assembly-line carriers that transported the unfinished bodies through the assembly process. The budget for NS racks was *$91.5 million.* "That would be like the Hollywood moguls spending that much on film cans," mused another member of the team.

It was the small stuff, like properly designing nearly $100 million worth of disposable racks that would determine the success or failure of the NS program. There were a thousand similar details to be attended to, from training manuals for dealership mechanics (now called "technicians"), to public relations strategies, to door-latch design minutiae, to shock absorber valving, to EPA-approved air quality in the paint booths, to wind noise around the radio antenna. Each demanded attention, with a thousand more unseen problems lurking around the next corner.

The final trials of 1993's late winter saw most of the general themes of manufacture already set; the broad outlines of how to make the NS were in place, save for one central problem. In order to maintain a constancy of supply in the face of such unforeseen problems as strikes, supplier shortages, and weather emergencies, Bob Eaton wanted both St. Louis and Windsor to have the capability to produce long- and short-wheelbase models. The original plan set down at the time of Program Approval a year earlier called for long-wheelbase minivans to be built at St. Louis while Windsor made only short-wheelbase versions. But this lack of flexibility concerned Eaton, and he had later specified that each plant be capable of producing both sizes.

Frank Sanders, who was responsible for keeping the entire program's budget under control, saw trouble. The requirement that each factory, separated by over six hundred miles, have sufficient inventory sourcing to manufacture a full line of minivans threatened to knock the budget "out of bed," in Sanders's words. Sanders was an ex-Marine, the dreaded "beanie" on the team who broached no nonsense when it came to holding the line on expenses. "Cowboys," his term for the parenthesis on a balance sheet that indicated negative cash flow, were verboten. "The executive engineers; they're the enemy," he had joked in reference to the Swansons, the Hesses, Schaums, and Feldmaiers who had to make the Eaton edict work while toeing Sanders's budget mark.

"In the old culture we'd have simply done what Eaton wanted and spent the money. We wouldn't have met the objective financially and nobody would have known where the money went. It would have simply disappeared and suddenly the program would have been 50 percent over budget. That wasn't going to happen to the NS." Ironically it was Sanders himself — the self-described "dumb beanie" — who solved the problem of how to produce a sufficient supply of long- and short-wheelbase minivans. He proposed a so-called price class flex plan, whereby both factories would build long- and short-wheelbase vans only in the "highline" or "midpriced" trim level. According to his plan, all premium (expensive) vans, in all wheelbases, would be made at St. Louis, while Windsor would build the "low-line" or cheapest models. Each plant would make the high-volume, midprice "high-line" models, thereby reducing the investment of having each plant equipped to build every model in the lineup. Thanks to Sanders, the most popular models could be manufactured at both plants, while the lower-volume, cheapest, and most expensive NSs could be built separately.

Sanders's input was a classic example of the advantages inherent in the cross-functional team concept. Here was a financial expert making what was traditionally a manufacturing decision. In the old culture, an individual like Sanders would have been totally isolated from problems relating to product mix and the complex world of assembly plants. In terms of offering a solution within that realm, he might as well have been working for an entirely separate company. How and where and what models of the NS would be built would have been dealt with within the jealously guarded domain of Sham Rushwin and his manufacturing staff. It would have been the height of presumption, if not downright impossible, for Sanders to have intruded into such a decision-making process. But now, within the team, his notion of "price class flex" was received like a revelation. Rather than being rejected or reviled, Sanders was celebrated, not only in high humor for being a "dumb beanie" but for generating a supremely practical solution for what could have been a ruinously expensive shift in policy.

While skeptics remained within the corporation and even within the outer perimeters of the NS platform team itself, inputs like Sanders's were steadily hammering away at the ancient Chrysler chimneys. If the NS could succeed, both financially and industrially, it could mean the old structures might crumble forever.

9

Nowhere to Hide

By THE SPRING of 1993, what had begun as John Nemeth's platoon of dreamers doodling ideas in a vacant room in Highland Park had exploded in size and scope. Now Chris Theodore was heading battalions of men and women spread across the United States, each operating as an extension of the tiny team formed up by his now-retired predecessor. Not only were nearly one thousand engineers, manufacturing experts, financial types, marketers, and sales professionals laboring inside the CTC, but the project had now spread to St. Louis, where a new assembly line was beginning to be chalked on the floor of the vacant factory, and to several hundred suppliers inside and outside the corporation who would fabricate everything from body panels to floor mats to door handles for the NS.

During the 1980s, when it had become stylish to doom the United States to Third World status as Japan seized control of global car markets, American work ethics had been mercilessly denigrated. Our workforce was, according to the conventional wisdom of the day, a collection of lazy, ignorant, churlish louts organized into bureaucratic and unionized Gordian knots. The white-collar staff came late and left early, while languishing through long lunches between brief interludes of useless paper-shuffling. This was utter nonsense. Within the precincts of the automobile business, workers had exerted Trojan-like amounts of energy while on the job. Sadly, it was the process that was wasteful and redundant, and much of their labor was consumed in pursuit of the trivial and the counterproductive.

This had all changed, at least at the leaner (and in some cases, meaner) Chrysler Corporation. Members of the minivan platform team worked hard enough to make the average Japanese appear like a laggard. They were at their desks or engaged in meetings no later than 7:30 A.M. and generally remained until after 6:00 in the evening. Lunches, in the elaborate, glass-walled cafeteria with its eclectic selection of dishes, lasted no more than half an hour, unless a lunch meeting was scheduled for one of the meeting rooms that lined the upper mezzanine of the great gallery.

Their agendas — meeting schedules, trips, conferences, etc. — were set by a central computer, which could be updated and accessed at any time. The dress code varied by the day, with coats, ties, and classic business garb expected during the midweek while Mondays and Fridays were reserved for casual wear. Open shirts, sweaters, and slacks were permitted, and while they were not recommended, some engineering staff pushed the envelope by favoring well-pressed jeans. Their work area, vast, soft-hued, and low-ceilinged, was a labyrinth of neat workstations, separated by low partitions. The room was filled with the murmur of human activity, but classic office noise — the rattle of telephones, the clack of typewriters, the clank of copy machines — had long since been replaced by the mute, microprocessed technology of the Third Wave. Voices were never raised and the traditional conclaves around the coffee machine were as archaic as green eyeshades and slide rules.

During the brief hours that the team operated independently, the members attempted to normalize their lives in midlevel homes scattered throughout suburban Detroit. Program manager Tom Edson's wife was pregnant with his third daughter. Chris Theodore and his recently divorced ex-wife were struggling with his teenage son by his first marriage. The boy was operating with typical teenage rebelliousness, flirting with trouble and generally frustrating his father's efforts to persuade him to toe the mark. Friends assured him this was a temporary insanity associated with late male adolescence, but it proved a depressing distraction, only counterbalanced by the purchase of a second home on the shore of Lake Huron, which he dreamed of as a refuge from the daily struggle with the NS.

While the organization, the working environment, and the process had changed, the elemental challenge had not. The NS minivans, now numbering thirty-one Type G synthesis vehicles being tested throughout the team, were riddled with problems. The MITS tracking system listed 944 "issues" that had to be solved prior to production. Worse yet, the project was still over budget, $11.7 million within Ernie Laginess's body and exterior group alone. Laginess's cost overrun related mainly to the price of vendor tooling. This had been budgeted at $283 million and was now edging toward $298 million — an intolerable excess that would demand that the suppliers who created the stamping dies, presses, and so forth slash their prices. Acustar, the Chrysler division that was also to supply tooling, was $3.8 million over budget, as were other suppliers, bringing the total deficit to $16.3 million beyond the overall body program cost of $1.78 billion (the largest single component of the NS project). Cost savings in other areas reduced the total shortfall to $11.4 million, including the added expense for a new Mexican production facility for the 2.4-liter engine. In the old culture, this would have been a tolerable "ballpark" figure. On this day in early 1993, it was not acceptable. The price would have to come down, unless savings could be found elsewhere within Sanders's taxes and targets system.

Ernie Laginess's body program was not only the most expensive single element in the NS project but potentially the most rife with problems. His team had identified 350 "issues," almost double those found in the chassis group and two-thirds more than those that remained in the manufacturing sector. Cindy Hess's electrical team, John Herlitz's interior group, and Rich Schaum's powertrain operation were all in relatively good shape, with less than 100 issues each, although some issues were potentially both expensive and difficult to solve.

The MITS tracking system and Sanders's budget expanded and contracted on an almost daily basis. As one issue would be solved, another two might turn up. So too for the budget. As one cost item might go down, another might rise, often in concert with the price of solving an outstanding issue. Each Wednesday's Spaghetti Day session would deal with this ever-shifting platform of issues and cost. Some days the situation would seem to be approaching stability, where costs and production issues would be in balance; on others the entire process seemed to be spinning out of control.

Some of the issues centered on maddening detail that often consumed days of haggling for solutions. Example: How to paint the left-side fuel door (the little flap covering the gas filler) and its housing and spring assembly during the assembly process. This involved multiple knotty issues: shrinkage and deformation of the housing, door sag, unpainted sheet metal under the housing, and potential paint chipping. Such minute elements of fabrication that seemingly should have been solved decades earlier posed special challenges with *each* new car design. This one took multiple team meetings over a monthlong span before it would be solved.

On a broader, more complex front, the Type G synthesis vehicle testers were reporting excessive wind noise and water leaks around the doors and windows. Some of this was to be expected on early prototypes, but unacceptable operation of the sliding doors, bad lift-gate design, inefficient windshield wiper design, and sloppy interior fabrication had to be solved.

Worse yet, there were major problems with an integral component of the NS's chassis structure. Included in the design was a giant aluminum casting that served both as an engine-mounting structure and as a locating point for the front suspension. It was a daring engineering concept, intended to save weight and increase production efficiency, but Swanson's suspension team reported cracks in the castings of three different test vehicles. Herein lurked a major potential disaster. This 26-pound hunk of complex cast aluminum was the largest single mass-produced piece of the metal ever employed in a chassis. The primary NS steel suppliers, Bethlehem, Thyssen, US Steel, and Stelco, increasingly nervous that their traditional turf as prime material vendor to the automobile industry was steadily being invaded by the aluminum and plastics interests, had fought hard to compete with a comparable design. But the 20-pound weight savings, in an area where handling, fuel economy, and ride are all degraded by extra poundage, pointed the way to the new radical concept. Better yet, the improved precision of the complex casting, when compared to a welded-up patchwork of steel, made aligning the front suspension easier (and cheaper) during the assembly process. New casting techniques would be necessary, including the design of all-new machinery to cut, shape, trim, mill, and drill the outsized hunk of aluminum, 39.4 inches long, 20.7 inches wide, and 12.2 inches high. Development problems like the cracking seemed inevitable. In all, it was a risky and audacious change in design techniques. Staying with the old-fashioned steel component was the safer course, but Theodore was a strong advocate for the aluminum casting and he enjoyed the endorsement of both Lutz and Castaing. Had it not been for them, the larger, heavier steel component might have been employed, but now Chrysler was preparing to join Honda, BMW, and other industry leaders in using large aluminum components, despite the $20 cost penalty in this instance.

Now there were cracks. What was causing them — fatigue, stress, corrosion, poor heat treating — remained a mystery, but one that demanded a solution. The program was too far along, too integrated — too committed to aluminum — to revert to steel. No one in the industry had ever attempted to employ an aluminum casting of such size in such volume production. One of the engineers who had seen the outsized female sand-casting molds said they reminded him of "coffins." To insure strength, the units were being heat-treated for as much as ten hours each, which slowed the entire process. Treatment time had been cut to six hours, which might have caused the failures, but the time penalties, already significant, made lengthening the process a poor option. Skeptics remained on the team. The great hunk of aluminum, while light and state of the art and a thing of beauty, seemed to pose too many risks. "If those things can't be heat-treated within a reasonable amount of time, we'll have to tie up all the Domino's Pizza ovens in the entire state of Michigan," mused an engineer.

The team was hardly alone in its challenge to make aluminum an integral part of automobile fabrication. The metal's light weight and corrosion resistance made it particularly attractive to designers, despite the reality that it tended to be less strong, less rigid, and more difficult to shape and weld than steel. It had been employed for years, perhaps most notoriously with the Chevrolet Corvair, the pancake, air-cooled, Porsche-inspired engine of which was prone to block warpage and leaks. Undaunted, GM tried a small-displacement V8 for its early 1960s compacts and a four-cylinder for its Vega subcompact a decade later, both of which exhibited similar failings. (The British Rover Co. bought the tooling for the V8 and uses an improved variation of the engine to this day in its Land Rover SUVs. Australian Jack Brabham also employed a highly modified version to win the World Formula One racing championship in 1966/67.) Despite GM's spotty successes, the worldwide industry was committed to making aluminum work in automobiles, and its usage was increasing by the day. Numerous imported cars employed aluminum extensively, and Chrysler was using the metal for its giant V10 Viper sports car engine. Ford and GM were working hard to manufacture new generations of aluminum-block powerplants to mate with their transmission housings and other drive-train components that had employed the metal for years. Even as the NS project rolled forward, Tom Gale's advanced design group was creating prototype roadsters to be marketed as Plymouth Prowlers with a body made of aluminum. The plan was to employ the vehicle as a test bed to develop advanced welding and bonding methods for mass production. But none of that would solve the cross-member cracking.

Bernie Swanson's suspension group, which would participate in solutions regarding the cross-member, felt the pressure. Swanson, tall and lean, with swept-back white hair and sporting a crooked smile, was operating with a small engineering group that numbered seventy-two men. Traditionally a project like the NS would have involved over four hundred suspension engineers assigned similar duties. "In the old days we were all concerned about the lack of hard engineering knowledge among the leadership," said Swanson. "It's different now. Castaing, Lutz, and Eaton talk our language. Our solutions would be their solutions. There used to be so much bureaucracy that nobody had to make a value judgment. Everybody had protection. We worked in isolation. There was no accountability. None. I remember when I was a young engineer working on designing the Volare suspension. There was an advanced suspension design group and a production suspension design group. They hardly ever talked to each other. When we advanced guys showed the production guys what we wanted to build, the production guys laughed their asses off. What we wanted to do couldn't be done. Those days are gone forever. Now there's nowhere to hide." In this open environment, Swanson and other team members would solve the problem. There was no alternative.

As the team grappled with the cross-member and a myriad of other issues surrounding the NS, word continued to filter in from Dearborn regarding the Win-88 project, now known as the Windstar, from a widening circle of the automotive press and from those within the industry. The NS design office had blown up a series of spy photos published by Jim Dunne and others in order to determine external features and, more important, to attempt to evaluate the internal dimensions of the new threat. The photos, plus intelligence being received through Theodore's sources and others, confirmed that the Windstar would be built on a single wheelbase, from a revised Taurus platform using the same 3.8-liter V6 engine. It appeared to be over an inch longer than the upcoming NS long wheelbase, based on their analysis. (It was in fact 1.6 inches longer.) The styling, camouflaged as it was, suggested conservatism and a vague resemblance to the curvaceous lines of the NS, at least in profile. The team wondered if the classic measurement — the 4×8 sheet of plywood — would fit inside with the rear seats simply pulled forward, as had been rumored. This could be trouble, because the NS would not accommodate the wood without removing the rear seats entirely. Two more components puzzled them. Would the Windstar feature a left-side sliding door and would the sliding door track(s) be concealed in the window frame as Toyota had done with the Previa and Chrysler planned to duplicate? Either way, the Windstar was unquestionably the most serious challenger to Chrysler's minivan dominance yet, although they were comforted by the knowledge that Ford planned only one wheelbase and a single powertrain as opposed to the multiplicity for the NS. The new threat would be manufactured exclusively at Ford's relatively new facility at Oakville, Ontario, on the southern fringes of Toronto's vast urban sprawl. This was mildly ironic in that, for the short term at least, a majority of that quintessential American automotive creation, the minivan, would be produced in Canada.

The Windstar would be a player, regardless of its size or styling. Ford was too strong, too savvy, and, like Chrysler, too battle-scarred to be wide of the mark again. They were on a hot streak. Like Chrysler, Ford had completed a massive downsizing during the late 1980s. Like Chrysler, their hierarchy of classic auto moguls had been replaced by more internationally oriented executives with engineering backgrounds. Like Chrysler, their old patriarch, the late Henry Ford II, had expressed the same tepid enthusiasm for the radical, aerodynamic Taurus as had his old nemesis, Lee Iacocca, for the LH sedans. Their new leader, Alex Trotman, a Scots-man by birth, was widely respected within the industry as a savvy "car guy" with a contemporary worldview. Yet, because of its immense size compared to Chrysler, Ford was still wrestling with excessive cost overruns and a chimney culture that refused to disappear. The minivan team mused over reports that Ford was spending nearly $6 billion to create its so-called Mondeo world car, a smallish four-door sedan that could, with minor modifications, be sold in every market from San Francisco to Stuttgart to Singapore. Six billion for a single model, as opposed to an expected less than $2.2 billion from Chrysler to create a multitude of minivan variations and a new powerplant. The *Wall Street Journal,* in an openly critical story on the Mondeo, quoted the renowned automotive financial analyst Maryann Keller as observing, "I don't know how Ford managed to spend this much. The Mondeo seems to be a product of the old-fashioned way of throwing money at something to get it done." Such news heartened Theodore because it implied that dollar for dollar, Ford was still incapable of matching Chrysler in terms of product creation, although he fully understood that Ford enjoyed a significant lead in manufacturing quality. In terms of fit and finish, Ford was openly acknowledged to lead the domestic industry by a wide margin and to be rivaling the best from Europe and Japan. Regardless of the technological brilliance of the NS, Theodore and his team understood full well that unless it was properly bolted and welded together, it would be a loser among the increasingly quality-conscious public.

Regardless of Ford's burgeoning reputation for solid fabrication, the Toyota Previa remained best-in-class, quality-wise, among current minivans. Despite its shortcomings — an intrusive, noisy, low-power four-cylinder engine, *outré* styling, etc. — the Previa was built like a large, ambulatory Rolex. Among the mass producers of automobiles, Toyota was the envy of the world in terms of quality. While some of its products were styled so conservatively as to border on the prosaic, each example appeared to have been carved from a single ingot of metal. Toyotas represented the best in stolid, totally reliable day-to-day transportation modules (while its Lexus luxury car was easily the equal, in terms of fit and finish, of the best from Mercedes-Benz). The entire product line, including the Previa, consistently finished at or near the top in every industry-wide survey of production excellence. Therefore it was the Previa that Theodore & Co. chose to "benchmark" reliability and function of the primary NS systems and specifically areas of high risk like the sliding side doors, the front doors and lift-gate, the wiper systems front and rear, the instrument panel (simply called "IP" within the industry), layout and trim, seat comfort and construction, and the seat belt design and mounting.

The NSs intended for use in the initial long-term test cycles, which were to last a year and would involve repeated evaluations of the major vehicle systems, would be F-One vehicles that were about to be assembled in CTC's pilot plant. These machines, using so-called soft tooling, would in theory replicate the actual production models due roughly eighteen months hence. This time there would be no self-serving rationalizations, no "not invented here" delusions that had so often cursed such evaluations in the past. All too often such tests had been conducted not to make hard-eyed comparisons, but to justify what had already been created and to conceal from top management known deficiencies. This would not happen with the Previa vs. NS. In the internal memo outlining the mission, the final statement was icy and to the point: "This is a benchmark and a *reality check*, not a statistical study."

As the summer of 1993 blossomed over southern Michigan, the team began to see progress. Working with outside supplier foundries and aluminum vendors, the team redesigned and strengthened the cross-member internally to eliminate the cracking, although other issues rose up among the fleet of F-One vehicles as the testing schedules intensified. Leaks, poor door fits, wind noise, and

Herm Greif's dreaded "shake" remained major issues. Bare bodies, "bodies in white" as they were called, were shipped across the border to Ortech, a small firm in the Toronto suburbs, where they were mounted on a platform and subjected to insane levels of vibration. There the issue of "VSR" — vibration, shake, and rattle — would be searched to its source. Unless the body structure, now lighter and potentially weaker than the old AS because of the yawning cavity for the left side door, could be made rigid, there would be no possibility of eliminating VSR on the production vehicles. This had to be solved within the soft-tooling cycle or uncounted millions would have to be spent later. This was an unacceptable risk.

As the engineering team grappled with the multiple leaks, cracks, and rattles, the marketing and research experts continued to monitor the current market and to devise strategies for the launch. Dave Bostwick maintained his Chrysler monitor study, an ongoing program wherein current minivan owners were surveyed, via evening phone calls, to determine their general mood. This, plus several other tracking studies, gave Bostwick's small team constant updates on the general minivan market and on minivan owner attitudes. Tom Kowaleski was also devising plans to keep the Chrysler minivan in the public consciousness during the interim year when the Windstar would be the new kid on the block and Chrysler would have to soldier on with the aging AS. He scheduled a tenth-anniversary celebration of the old machine, which had been brought to market as a 1984 model. Moreover, he was devising a strategy whereby some of the impact of Ford's planned introduction of the Windstar at the January 1994 Detroit International Motor Show would be tempered. He was planning a series of press "backgrounders" on the NS in early December 1993 wherein several of the fiberglass styling mock-ups would be shown to reporters from major daily newspapers, news magazines, the monthly automotive magazines, key columnists, and financial analysts from Wall Street who specialized in the automobile business.

His goal was simple: to blunt potential enthusiasm for Ford by showing the press and others Chrysler's plans to trump Ford — although the card would not be played for another year. Backgrounders of this sort were hardly uncommon in the industry, and in fact he and his public relations counterparts throughout the business made a practice of leaking snippets of information about new models sometimes two to three years in advance. For the most part the automotive press used these leaks with discretion and honored the news embargoes imposed by the companies. But this plan to preempt the Windstar introduction was more than a clever gambit; it was a critical element in keeping Chrysler's image alive. "I want every member of the press who writes about the Windstar to remember seeing the NS and to have in the back of their minds, 'Yeah, the Windstar is neat, but let's not forget what Chrysler has up its sleeve,'" said Kowaleski.

This would not be easy. Ford was generating a powerful public relations campaign of its own, touting the fact that the Windstar would be the first direct hit in history on the Chrysler minivan. In making the claim they chose to ignore their own Aerostar and Mercury Villager as well as GM's wide-of-the-mark APVs from Chevrolet, Pontiac, and Oldsmobile. Moreover, word was filtering into the trade press that Honda would enter the minivan market in late 1994 with a smallish vehicle based on the Accord platform. Honda, packing a powerful reputation for quality and technical innovation, could not be discounted, although it was believed that the steadily increasing value of the yen against the devalued dollar, plus grousing from Washington about Japanese minivan dumping tactics, would force Honda to take a low profile. Honda would surely offer a solid product, but in terms of a volume assault, the Windstar was the only serious threat on the horizon.

As Kowaleski and the marketing staff struggled with the more abstract problems of sales strategies, Tom Persons and his team of test engineers were on the road, making evaluations of the F-One in real-world conditions. Testing was to be undertaken not only on Chrysler's two proving grounds, but on public highways with vehicles equipped with fiberglass cladding to defy the curious. Persons gained the dubious honor of being the first driver to receive a speeding ticket when he was nabbed in south Texas during a hot-weather evaluation. "The cop never even asked about the vehicle," he mused. Cold-weather tests were scheduled for early October 1993, but unusually mild weather in Northern Canada forced Persons to take a vehicle to Alaska — which was a logistical nightmare. Shipping by rail or sea would consume too much time, as would the 4,000-mile drive up the Alaska Highway. The only choice was air freight. One of the F-One NS prototypes was driven to Nashville, Tennessee, where it was loaded into a United Parcel Service Boeing 747 freighter and flown to Fairbanks. This elaborate travel scheme came perilously close to being an expensive waste when a warm spell also spread over Alaska. General Motors and Ford had been forced north as well, and Persons spotted one of GM's prototype Cavalier compacts and a well-disguised Windstar lurking in the airport freight terminal awaiting colder temperatures and snow. Impatient, Persons tried the automotive equivalent of the aged gag about selling refrigerators to Eskimos. He rented a refrigeration truck in Fairbanks and loaded up the NS. As he edged the prototype up a pair of spindly ramps, it came to him that one false move would wreck the machine valued at nearly a million dollars and delay the test program by weeks. The absurdity of loading a vehicle into a refrigerator truck in Alaska came to him. "This is nuts," he chuckled to himself. "What kind of business am I in?"

Cold weather finally arrived and the truck was discarded, but the snow pack remained light and Persons returned to the lower forty-eight seeking more foul winter weather. He found it in the Dakotas, where a blizzard had swept out of Alberta to close roads and send temperatures plunging. "We did most of our testing after dark. We used various Chrysler dealerships as bases of operation. I remember one night when it was thirty-six below zero and the heater wouldn't work. We drove until we about froze and took the NS back to a dealership in Fargo, North Dakota. The shop was empty. We used the mechanics' tools to make the repair and put 'em all back so they'd never know. When that trip was over, the only people outside Chrysler who'd ever seen the new minivan up close were three janitors in North Dakota."

While Persons and his little crew battled snowbanks and broken heaters, John Herlitz and his interior design team were wrestling with colors and fabrics for the multitude of NS models. Their workroom on the top floor of the CTC appeared to be an upscale paint, carpet, and wallpaper store, with movable panels hung with color swatches and fabric samples. The selection was stupefying: hundreds of subtle variations on a single hue, multitudes of cloth and vinyl samples, all labeled with the garble of flashy names that had become so much a part of the automobile industry — Burgundy, Rosewood, Cirrus Spruce, Silver Fern, Equestrian Camel . . . Debates centered on such issues as whether to offer two or three different headliners, each varying in color, composition, and, most important, cost. How many leather interiors? How many paint schemes? How many different variations in carpeting? The interior environment, the hospitality factor as it were, was critical to any vehicle design. Traditionally the American industry was more attentive to this component than the Europeans and the Japanese, who tended to coat their vehicles' instrument panels and doors with oppressive expanses of black vinyl while upholstering their seats with monochromatic brown or gray cloth, vinyl, or leather. Even Mercedes-Benz and Lexus, considered the *ne plus ultra* of luxury cars, offered little in the way of trim save for a patch or two of polished Zebrano hardwood scattered through the interiors. The Chrysler team understood full well that brothelized trappings of velvet, velour, and weirdly tinted vinyl had gone the way of whitewalls and spinner hubcaps. But the interior of a minivan could become cavelike with the wrong color combination and create an atmosphere bordering on the claustrophobic. Grown men and women arguing over issues like preferences for Cirrus Spruce or Silver Fern might sound frivolous, but their final judgments would be as critical as any hard choices being made in the test labs four stories below or on the proving grounds.

External paints were being made in concert with PPG, the primary supplier of a new water-based process that would not only be more environmentally friendly but would permit the paint shop workers at St. Louis and Windsor to work at room temperature, as opposed to the 100°-plus ovens required by the old method. The elimination of the much-loved fake wood paneling on the upscale Chrysler Town & Country minivan (a holdover from the traditional 1930s vintage station wagon) still posed problems, but was headed for a solution by substituting special paint schemes and different cast aluminum wheels in place of bogus wood trim. Theodore had also approved a method for adding an accent stripe to the flank of the Town & Country that would save millions. The traditional way of applying striping was with a vinyl appliqué. But this was expensive — $23 per vehicle. The team devised a simple jig whereby a worker would *paint* the stripe for 35 cents. But there were problems. The construction of a jig that would conform to the curved surfaces of the minivan was difficult. Moreover, Dave McKinnon and his designers had tapered the striping in various widths for aesthetic reasons, making application more complicated. It was determined to begin production with conventional tape, while pursuing development of the paint process. "We wanted paint," said McKinnon. "Not only would it be cheaper, but the customer perceives value in paint versus tape, so it would win on two counts." But the tape would remain for the foreseeable future.

By the end of October 1993, vehicle development had proceeded to a point where Theodore scheduled another "ride and drive," a two-day 500-mile round trip from the CTC to the pretty Lake Michigan coastal town of Traverse City. The fall foliage was still in bloom, the weather crisp, and the road relatively clear of tourist traffic as the nine-vehicle convoy with its twenty-four passengers got under way. As in the past, Jack Kerby had devised the route and set up the rotation schedule for drivers. Two fully disguised NSs — F-One vehicles 6059 and 6062 — would lead the pack, while a brace of production version model ASs would also be in the fleet. A third current minivan, a European "ES" model, carrying a 2.5-liter Italian-made VM turbo-diesel and a five-speed manual transmission, was also in the group, as were four of the principal competitors — a Mazda MPV, a Toyota Previa, a Nissan Quest, and the updated Chevrolet Lumina APV with an electric right-side sliding door (a component rejected by Chrysler as too expensive and potentially dangerous for small children). Jokes were made on the hand-held VHF walkie-talkies about Jim Dunne lurking in the bushes as the caravan headed north. Kerby was a veteran of such jaunts, although he had seen the purpose of such trips change, like so many other components of the NS process. "Years ago the separation between engineering and manufacturing was so great that sometimes they seemed to be working for two different factories," he mused as the flatness of southern Michigan gave way to the rolling rural desolation of midstate. "Design and assembly were worlds apart. We didn't worry about BSR [buzz, squeak, and rattle] like we do today. We just designed the things and sent 'em to the plants to be made. The basic policy was, you show us BSR and we'll fix it."

The group trundled northward, stopping only to change drivers every half hour and to chatter constantly about the strengths and weaknesses of the vehicles. The competition was by now familiar to the team. The Lumina's new power door was the source of interest, but no one considered it a serious threat, nor did it elicit second thoughts about not including it on the NS. For many of the group, the European diesel was a surprise. It was more powerful and quieter than expected. "The Europeans are much more aware of fuel economy than we are, but they also expect decent performance. The little VM ought to work pretty good in that market," said Theodore as he butted a cigarette during a stop. "It's like the rest of the program. We just can't fuck it up."

The trip was delayed half an hour when a power-steering hose on NS6062 ruptured, requiring a quick, unscheduled pit stop in a roadside radiator shop. Under way again, the group made easy, relaxed progress northward. Talk on the radios loosened, ranging from familiar personalities to roadside curiosities. At one point an aged American Motors Gremlin chugged past, southbound. It was a strange, bloated, boxy machine that had turned out to be too large to attract compact buyers, yet too cramped to sell in the conventional sedan market. Like many AMC products, the Gremlin had been created for a niche that didn't exist. "Hey Chris," cracked a voice over the radio, "is that one of your designs?" Laughter spread through the convoy as another voice interceded, "Fifteen yards for piling on."

The overnight turnaround was at the elegant Grand Traverse Resort, perched high on a windy bluff overlooking the vast, cottage-lined bay that was its namesake. Before dinner the team gathered in a large oak-lined conference room to hash over the day's drive. The talk immediately centered on the wind and road noise that cursed both NSs. Part of the problem, on 6062 at least, was a loose front suspension strut, which would be fixed overnight, but the trouble went deeper. These were prototypes, employing hand-built pieces from various suppliers. Jack Kerby noted there was trouble with some CTC welding fixtures, which produced tolerances on some fittings well beyond the hoped-for minimum of one millimeter. That contributed to the poor sealing around the doors. There were more complaints about the radio antenna and once again ideas of relocation were discussed. Could it be stuck in the windshield posts — known in the industry as "A-pillars"? Someone noted it would not fit in European car washes in that position. How about in the back, on the lift-gate? Too expensive. Concealed in the front fender? No room. Integrated in the windshield? Unacceptable signal reception. And so it went. They seemed cursed with a steel rod poking from the right front fender like an ugly nose hair. The challenge was to silence it as much as possible.

An argument swept through the room about the position of the cruise control on-off light. Cindy Hess's team had placed it on the steering wheel, where some claimed it was difficult to see. Several of the team wanted it moved to the instrument panel, others recommended leaving it on the steering wheel hub, but redesigning the light. The subject was left unresolved, save for Hess's understanding that the light needed improvement. Such was the power of the team — and her group in this case — to place the light anywhere they wanted provided it fulfilled its mission and stayed within its budget borders.

It was generally agreed that the handling on both NSs was better than the competition and improving by the hour. Francois Castaing's demand for European-style steering responses was being answered by Swanson's Suspension team. The roominess and visibility from all seating positions was confirmed as a strength, as were the sound system and acoustics. Overall, the package seemed on target, but a myriad of details demanded solution, the worst of which was wind noise.

Theodore let the conversation swirl around the square of tables until he finally stepped into the ring. Scanning a scrap of paper on which he had scrawled notes during the trip, the leader began to unload his frustration as the room fell silent. He agreed that the sealing around the door openings needed major work, then irised down to specifics. The radiator fan was too noisy, as was the radio antenna. The tachometer needle was "notchy." (All NS models would employ electronically controlled analog instruments, save for top-of-the-line Chryslers, which would offer digital readouts.) The power door-lock buttons feel "clicky," he said, leaving Hess to presume that they should be actuated with a more subtle movement. The power-steering pump was noisy, as was what he referred to as "off idle noise" — the engine sound produced at initial rpm's just after moving away from a dead stop. The list went on. Theodore didn't like the tire noise being produced by the low-line 15-inch Goodyear tires. (The new minivans would offer both Goodyear and Michelins in 15- and 16-inch sizes, with corporate costs ranging from $120 to $130 for sets of five. A glitch in these plans would arise when Michelin briefly considered dropping their "OE" or "original equipment" supply for the NS to concentrate on aftermarket replacement sales, but relented under Chrysler pressure. They would remain as OE suppliers on the high-line and luxury models, where the somewhat quieter ride of their radials was viewed as a premium.)

Theodore also wanted the headliner fasteners hidden to give a smooth expanse of surface and complained that the passenger door panel was "busy" and "uncomfortable for an armrest." The column-mounted shifter action was unsmooth and needed improvement. He noted that the vehicles now had no less than seven heater/air-conditioning vents, yet air flow was poor. He reminded the team that the current AS models were particularly weak in this area and noted, in his low-key, almost subdued manner, that improvement was a priority with the NS. It was not Theodore's style to raise his voice, yet he radiated an attitude of confidence and authority that transcended his slight frame and relaxed demeanor. Heretofore the observations being exchanged in the room were accepted and discarded as opinion. Some would be acted upon, others forgotten. But when Theodore spoke, pencils and pens scrubbed paper everywhere in the room. His remarks would not be forgotten. "And I don't know about the rest of you, but I got some shake on the driver's side mirrors and the brakes tended to squeak at low speeds on one of the vehicles." (Theodore was identifying a problem that would haunt the team until weeks before volume production.)

The meeting ended casually when Theodore completed his remarks and the team drifted down the broad, carpeted hallways of the hotel toward dinner. Peter Rosenfeld, the supply expert who, with Frank Sanders, was one of the so-called bean counters on the team, was a relative newcomer to Chrysler and openly admitted that many of the engineering nuances escaped him. He looked concerned as he left the room, his deep-set eyes dulled with fatigue. "I guess I'm worried about where we're going to fit in the market," he said. "The team will probably fix all that stuff we just talked about, but long term I worry about a series of attacks within the minivan segment. Ford is coming at us with the Villager and has 10 percent of the minivan market. The Windstar is sure to take more. We've got 50 percent now, but with each new vehicle, that percentage is sure to drop. That's bound to dull our 'all things to all people' approach. The only alternative is to continually expand the minivan segment, so that maybe 35 percent for Chrysler gives us the same volume. Sometimes I can't see that happening, but then, I'm the eternal pessimist on the team."

Rosenfeld was certainly at odds with marketing analysts at Chrysler, who projected that by 1998 the domestic minivan market would be at 1.8 million vehicles annually. It was acknowledged that intrusions by competitors like Ford, GM, Honda, Nissan, and Toyota would cut Chrysler's market share to below 40 percent — but that volumes in the 650,000–700,000 range could be maintained with that percentage. The projection for vehicle preference — 25 percent low-line, entry-level models, 60 percent well-equipped, midlevel "family" models, and 15 percent upscale luxury versions would still pertain. It was difficult to dispute such evidence. The corporation maintained the largest database in the world on minivan customer preferences. Like the rest of the car companies, they understood population trends, age groups, demographic splits, gender preferences, and so on as well as anybody, and it was graven in stone that Americans would continue to embrace minivans in increasing numbers. It was the corporate savior, the crown jewel, the centerpiece of the pentastar emblem, as it were, and there was no choice but to defend that segment of turf like grim death. At least $2.1 billion of the company's still-thin assets were being placed on the line, with the possibility of more to come if, as was rumored, Eaton and Lutz decided to increase capacity worldwide. Windstar or no Windstar, Rosenfeld's worries over being nibbled to death, tiny segment by tiny segment, notwithstanding, the corporation would stand or fall on the expectation that the NS would hold its own well past the turn of the century.

As the team returned to Detroit and the grinding, day-to-day search for detailed solutions, Tom Kowaleski and his public relations group were completing their plan to defuse the Windstar introduction at Detroit. Once a backwater event with none of the panache associated with the extravaganzas at Frankfurt, Geneva, Tokyo, or even Chicago, the Detroit International Automobile show at the downtown Cobo Hall convention center had exploded on the world scene within the past decade. It was now considered on a par with the best in the world and auto-makers — imported and domestic — saved their best wares for display at Cobo. As plans were being laid for the upcoming January 1994 show, it was understood that Ford would make a giant splash with the Windstar. Chrysler would counter with its zoomy midsized JAs — the Chrysler Cirrus and Dodge Stratus — but it was Kowaleski's mission to steal at least part of the spotlight from the Windstar. His only alternative was his long-planned sneak preview. "Backgrounder" invitations were sent out in November, setting the date for the four-day session in early December, exactly a month earlier than the Ford hoopla. The press would come in small groups, no more than fifteen to twenty at a time, and be hosted in the styling dome at CTC. There, four full-sized fiberglass mock-ups, produced by the local craft shop AutoNorth, would be on display — a long-wheelbase Chrysler Town & Country, an LWB Dodge Caravan, a short-wheelbase Voyager, and a sporty version of the Dodge, also on the SWB. Two interior styling bucks would be present as well, to afford the press a look at what the passenger compartment of the new vans would be like.

This was risky business. While in recent years the traditional press embargoes had become looser and looser, Chrysler had pioneered the option of showing journalists future products far in advance of introduction. The advantage was clear: to create an early "buzz" about the corporation's future product mix. But there was a downside. If the press — which could be capricious, petty, and sometimes notoriously ignorant about the nuances of car design — deemed that the vehicle being revealed was in fact wide of the mark and unworthy of enthusiasm, any chance for generating excitement at the time of the regular introduction was dead.

The press arrived at the CTC in small, cheery clumps and were escorted up the maze of escalators to the fourth floor, there to be led through a series of locked doors and stark off-white corridors to the styling dome. Chris Theodore, Tom Edson, Bob Feldmaier, and Kowaleski led the briefings, explaining the major features. For the so-called buff books — *Car and Driver, Automobile, Road & Track, Motor Trend* — they highlighted the multiplicity of engines, the better handling, improved suspension, and so forth. For the general press — *Time, Newsweek,* women's magazines — emphasis was placed on the dual air bags, the fourth door, advanced child seats, 5 mph bumpers, multiple safety features, enhanced interior room, and so on. It seemed to work. The silky lines of the full-sized models elicited compliments, as did the neatly executed interiors. But the final judgment would be reserved for over a year, when the so-called Long Lead Preview would be held, and the critics would for the first time drive actual production machines.

Theodore spoke confidently about the vehicles, but in the back of his mind he was still grappling with the bugaboos of noise and shake. Beautiful as the mock-ups were, glistening under the soft lights of the dome, he knew only too well that the new Ford he was trying to overshadow would embody at the least two things: it would be well fabricated, with excellent fit and finish, and it would be quiet. Ford had made major advances in producing cars with low levels of wind and road noise in recent years, and there was no doubting they had transferred that technology to the Windstar.

The first impression of the NS seemed to have been positive. The press had departed apparently impressed. But their printed verdicts were a year away. And it was within that twelve months that Theodore and the team had to make the reality of the NS conform to its steadily rising expectations.

While Kowaleski and his staff were artfully attempting to divert attention from the Windstar, Tom Stallcamp, the corporate vice president of procurement and supply, was moving forward with a plan called SCORE, an acronym for Supplier Cost Reduction Effort. By maintaining a strong link with a compact group of external suppliers ranging from the dozen so-called tier one (tires, steel, glass, paint, carpeting) majors down to the tier three (fasteners, gaskets, moldings, etc.) and giving them maximum flexibility in terms of design and costing, Chrysler was realizing massive savings. "We're operating at the opposite end of GM's 'tin cup' approach," said Peter Rosenfeld. "They give the supplier exact specifications and then beat 'em into the ground on price. We bring the supplier into the design process, give them the opportunity to make it at a reasonable price, and negotiate from there," he said. In December Stallcamp told the industry journal *Ward's Auto World* that SCORE would produce $504 million in cost reductions in 1994, with savings totaling $900 million since the program was introduced three years earlier. By reducing the total number of outside suppliers from 3,200 a decade earlier to about 1,200 (with 90 percent of the sourcing coming from only 150 first-tier companies) Stallcamp predicted that another $750 million would be saved in 1995.

Much of this bonus would come as more and more Chrysler executives and the corporate suppliers adopted "lean production" — a Zen-like process called *"Kaizen,"* developed by the Japanese, in which minimal labor was devoted to achieve maximized goals. The smallish (3,600 employees) Chrysler supplier Fruedenberg-NOK, the Plymouth, Michigan–based manufacturer of seals, gaskets, and molded products, had been cited by Bob Eaton as "the best exponent of lean production in the United States and a benchmark for the corporation." In search of ways to integrate *"Kaizen"* into the corporation, a series of human resources sessions were organized for over one hundred top management members (rank "92" and up in the management hierarchy) at the Edison Inn in Port Huron. The sessions, wherein senior vice presidents set the egalitarian tone by greeting their underlings at the door and carrying their bags to their rooms, were designed to generate an atmosphere of problem-solving through small teams.

The attendees were split into groups of a half-dozen each and assigned unique tasks involving role-playing ("If you were Walter P. Chrysler") and the assembly of complex, Lego-like structures, including a quasi-heart defibrillator. The intent was simple: to expand Chrysler's cultural revolution from the old top-down management policies to the new broad-based teamwork, while creating a sense of vision for the corporate future. "Some of the guys took umbrage at what they considered childish games," recalled Tom Edson. "But overall the results were positive. We came back to Detroit with a feeling that creativity comes from all kinds of sources and that tightly structured authority could be a major roadblock for creativity. The Port Huron sessions were one more step in breaking down the old culture." They were so successful, in fact, that the program was expanded to include nearly two thousand of the top management people within the company and the program was maintained for almost two years.

But feel-good psychology and executive problem-solving could carry Chrysler only so far. As men like Edson left Port Huron and began the ninety-mile drive across the snow-dappled flatness of the Great Lakes plain toward Auburn Hills, the cozy warmth of camaraderie gave way to reality. Chrysler was facing its greatest challenge in the modern marketplace and no amount of executive baggage-handling would keep Ford away from the door.

10

Showtime in St. Louis

THE DETROIT International Auto Show opened in January 1994 with a public relations firefight between Ford and Chrysler. The Chrysler public relations team fought valiantly by introducing the JA-body Chrysler Cirrus midsized with a massive, six-figure show-biz launch featuring white-maned Peter Graves and a "Mission Impossible" theme. But it was the Windstar, the much-anticipated, much-rumored challenge to Chrysler's minivan dominance, that held center stage. At stake was the multibillion-dollar minivan market that had long been the exclusive terrain of the struggling Highland Park company. The Cirrus promised to join the LH sedans, the Grand Cherokee, and the audacious Ram pickups as a solid seller, but a grim reality lingered behind the flash and glamour of the auto show: the aging AS Voyagers and Caravans would have to hold the field against the Windstar and its neatly styled Mercury Villager for a full year before the NS came to market.

Early reviews of the Ford challenger were positive. While slightly sway-backed around its A-pillars and tail heavy, the Windstar was a solid package. Theodore and Edson were comforted by the knowledge that it would come in only one wheelbase and that but one engine, the Taurus 3.8-liter V6, would be offered initially. Further solace came with the news that no left-side sliding door would be offered, although Theodore was receiving intelligence that Ford was having second thoughts about the omission and was considering investing an additional $750 million to add the door as an option. Even then, it would not be available until 1997 at the earliest. Better yet, they were delighted and not a little shocked to learn that the Windstar's rear compartment was one-quarter of an inch too short to accommodate a 4×8 sheet of plywood, a failing that could surely be exploited in the NS promotion campaign. Still, the press lauded the Windstar's carlike handling, its relative silence, and its excellent fit and finish, although some journalists grumped about the impression of bulk created by the package, both inside and out. But that was niggling detail contrasted with the massive threat posed by the Windstar, and no one at Chrysler deluded themselves otherwise. The first head-on threat to their dominance was in the game.

The Highland Park management planned an aggressive response. In early January the Product Planning Committee chaired by Eaton listened to Theodore and Edson explain that despite the entry of the Windstar into the market they believed that Chrysler's program was "product constrained," i.e., lacking sufficient production capacity to meet what they believed to be an expanding market. Funding was frozen at $2.3 billion (an additional $200 million had been added to the Graz GS program to include the 2.0-liter Neon engine — the sixth in the lineup — in the 1997 product mix, although production would remain at 55,000 units per year). Domestic production was set at the originally approved 560,000 vehicles from St. Louis and Windsor, which, said the team, would not be sufficient to meet long range market demand. The committee agreed, adding $300 million to the project to fund additional tooling capacity, assembly-plant modifications, and expanded vendor tooling capability to bump annual production at both plants by 110,000 units to 670,000. It was a decision laden with *chutzpah*, considering that only days earlier their archrival had introduced the most serious threat to their sales position since the first T-115 rolled off the line a decade earlier. Moreover, Honda, always a player in any league, was on the way to market at midyear with its smaller, high-quality Odyssey minivan.

More money hardly eased the pressure on the team. It meant finding ways to produce 110,000 additional vehicles for proportionately the same price of doing business. Lutz had been adamant about holding the retail prices at essentially the same level as the current AS. Windstars were costing over $25,000 with decent trim options, and Lutz demanded that only a few high-line NSs exceed that limit. "Don't play numbers games with me," he warned the team. "Don't let the costs get out of hand and then try to justify them on the basis of profit margins. The customer doesn't care about how much we make; he wants a reasonably priced vehicle, so hold the line." With that edict, the team understood that production costs had to be held down, and that any upward slippage could not be justified by adding to the sticker price at the dealer level.

Meanwhile, management changes were in the works. Tom Gale, the spiritual, if not hands-on inspiration of the minivan's styling, was being promoted to handle international operations — an area of major expansion in Eaton's long-term strategy — while retaining his design-chief status. His role of "Godfather" of the minivan team would be assumed by sales and marketing vice president Ted Cunningham, a tall, gregarious, well-respected corporate executive with little or no manufacturing experience. While popular within the company, there were those on the team who openly questioned whether he had sufficiently broad knowledge of the business to take Gale's place. In order to allay concerns and to better acquaint himself with the nuts and bolts of manufacturing, Cunningham spent a week working on the assembly line at the St. Louis minivan plant. "It was amazing," he recalled. "The heat was tremendous. For years the guys on the line had been working through the Missouri summers with no air conditioning. The working conditions were terrible. No wonder we had quality problems." Based on his experience Cunningham pushed hard to improve working conditions at both St. Louis and Windsor and to have areas of the factories air-conditioned to improve worker efficiency.

As Cunningham slowly moved into Gale's role, while still maintaining his primary job as sales and marketing boss of the corporation, other men were on the move as well. John Herlitz, who had led the design team on the minivan, was elevated to vice president within the design department and with considerably expanded responsibilities. And by the end of the year one of Chrysler's legitimate heroes would step into retirement. Glenn Gardner, the man who had generated billions in profits for the company with such triumphs as the original T-115 and the LH sedans, was heading south to a life of golf and general tranquillity in Windermere, Florida. Gardner's departure would enjoy none of the fanfare of Lee Iacocca's Las Vegas party. Despite his illustrious career, he would leave Chrysler with only a perfunctory celebration. His final campaign, the LH sedans were smartly styled and selling well, but the dreaded Chrysler curse of poor quality was beginning to blight their reputation. Gardner's large car team seemed unable to make the kind of quick corrections necessary to get the vehicles up to par, and both Eaton and Castaing were reportedly irritated about Gardner's rather cavalier disclaimers of responsibility. He would leave, still a hero, but in some ways a representative of the old culture, which maintained that quality was always someone else's burden.

"There is something about this goddamn industry that makes me crazy," Chris Theodore was to lament. "We seem to get it to 99 percent of our goal and slack off. Francois said the French noticed it when they ran American Motors, and it sure as hell is evident in this company. I don't know what the hell that is, but we can't let it happen to the minivan." Adding to his own personal pressure was his impending marriage. His young fiancée, Tracy Antos, was organizing a large wedding, to be followed by a two-week honeymoon in Greece — including a stay on Theodore's father's native Crete. He worried about that absence's being costly in terms of maintaining the team's intensity as St. Louis geared up for production and the final six-month countdown began. Wedding or no wedding, the grand, crazed machine that would begin to burp out NSs at the rate of seventy per hour was beginning to sputter into life.

As winter broke in Detroit and spirits began to rise, reality intervened on a daily basis. The dreaded MITS issues list had exploded to over three thousand, a function of the growing number of parts pouring in from outside suppliers and the more exacting standards being imposed on production-level components. Some were tiny issues that could be solved by a phone call, while others posed dilemmas, like the racking problem at the Sterling Stamping Plant. Some of the shipping racks were out of specification. This meant that the panels could be bent or damaged on the bumpy rail or truck ride between the plants. Correcting that would drive the racking budget to $135 million. And there was the side panel glue. A flawed bonding agent was permitting some trim on certain models to fall off during proving ground tests. Unlike previous models, where body side molding and trim were attached by mechanical fasteners, the NS employed special adhesives, which not only simplified assembly but reduced weight by as much as 13.5 pounds. It demanded correction, as did alignment problems on the lift-gates and failures of the gas-filled hinge props. The list went on in what seemed absurd detail: a list so long and complex that it appeared insoluble. Only intense, hour-by-hour pecking and probing could begin to chew away at the myriad of problems.

Defying the semichaos surrounding the project, Theodore scheduled a May 1994 ride-and-drive for senior management at the Arizona proving grounds. It would be a night run, with the NS prototypes appearing on the public highways bereft of fiberglass disguises for the first time. The vehicles, while far from perfect, would undergo more scrutiny from Eaton and Lutz. This had been done in eight-week cycles since the program began. While other platform teams chose to review their progress with senior management on a much longer interval basis, Theodore chose a strategy of keeping the top executives totally appraised of progress (or lack of it). It was a gamble, because stumbles and setbacks would only add pressure to the team, but Theodore knew that Eaton and Lutz hated surprises and both were sufficiently sophisticated in a technical sense to abstain from panic or rash decisions. They had to know, problems and all, about what was going on with the corporation's biggest gamble in history.

They arrived, as usual, in separate Gulfstreams. Eaton landed first at Phoenix's Deer Valley private airport in his tan-and-white ex-Iacocca G4 (it had long since been shorn of its blue-and-white corporate livery in the name of anonymity), while Lutz roared in moments later aboard the older, slightly smaller G2. Out spilled a retinue of VPs, who, after a briefing by Jack Kerby in an upstairs meeting room, crowded into a fleet of ASs and a new Windstar and headed for the lush Wickenburg Inn deep in the desert near the proving grounds. Following a relaxed dinner, the group headed across the darkened parking lot to the cars. Two NSs, looking sleek and cleanly contoured without their shrouding, were to lead the pack. The rest, a Windstar, a Previa, a Mazda MPV, a Chevrolet APV, and a few current ASs, were to serve as the usual benchmarks. Eaton and Lutz, as expected, started off in the NSs both powered by standard 3.3-liter V6s. Tom Pappert, the burly VP of sales, trailed behind as the little convoy bounced over the three-mile-long dirt road leading from the inn to the main highway. Once on the macadam, the two NSs squirted into the darkness. Pappert tromped on the throttle to keep up. "Goddammit, do Eaton and Lutz *always* have to drive a hundred miles an hour wherever they go?" he growled in semibemusement.

The group hammered through the Arizona night for three hours, stopping every thirty minutes to change vehicles. They would stand on the darkened roadside, a small cluster of men unknown and unnoticed by the passing traffic, an aging gang of car nuts behaving more like hot-rodders organizing an illegal drag race than a collection of multimillion-dollar, Fortune 500 executives. "Can you imagine Roger Smith or Henry Ford or Iacocca doing something like this?" somebody said to Bud Liebler during one stop. "Hell, in the old days if we didn't have 'em back in their hotel suites in time for cocktails, we were in deep trouble," he chuckled.

It ended, near midnight, back at the inn, where a debriefing was held in a small conference room, furnished only with a U-shaped formation of bare tables and a small bar in one corner. Eaton and Lutz both poured themselves hefty glasses of scotch and lit up large, expensive cigars before beginning their remarks. "Watch out for Windstar, you guys, it's a helluva vehicle," said the chairman. This remark, candid and alarmingly trenchant, was a radical departure from the cant that generally issued from auto executives of such rank. Acknowledging the competition, much less praising it, was *verboten*. Men like Eaton simply were not supposed to make positive remarks about the enemy, regardless of how valuable such observations might be. In the past, careers had been ruined by such candor, but now, in the new age at Chrysler, such open honesty was not only accepted but expected. The comment came as no surprise. Everyone in the room understood that Ford had a contender and that the intervening year before the NS reached the public would be tough. Even tougher was the short-term challenge of making the NS as well-fabricated as the Windstar, which, while large and faintly numb to drive, was solidly built and beautifully finished. Lutz remarked about the NS's weak low-beam headlights, a problem that also plagued the LH sedans. Theodore explained that Sylvania, which was responsible for the design, was having trouble with the complex computer-designed interior mirror system that permitted the oddly contoured lights to produce proper levels of illumination. "They had it once and lost it," he said. "They swear they'll get it back."

Both Eaton and Lutz liked the NS's handling and its steering feel. They commented on mechanical components like veteran engineers, chatting about spring rates, sway bars, camber angles, shock valving, with a comfort level generally unknown in the executive suites. Overall, their impressions were positive, and Theodore and his team groped across the darkened landscape to their rooms feeling satisfied that the powers-that-be were comfortable with their progress. But clearly, much remained to be done.

Not only would the NS have to be manufactured by the tens of thousands, but it would have to be sold to a public already inundated with a broad selection of fine products. Americans were getting spoiled. Gone were the days when the marketplace was loaded with shabby products. Almost thirty manufacturers — American, Japanese, German, South Korean, English, Swedish, and Italian — were flooding the country with generally good vehicles. Only a handful from South Korea, Italy, and Great Britain could be described as below par in terms of quality, dealer service, and reliability.

The power of Chrysler's persuasion in this clutter would be left in the hands of two major advertising agencies. Both enjoyed a long and generally comfortable relationship with the corporation. Both were located in a large office complex in suburban Southfield on the edge of the John Lodge Expressway. Chrysler/Plymouth's agency, Bozell Worldwide, was an outgrowth of the venerable firm of Kenyon & Eckhardt and had handled the $50-million-plus minivan account since 1981. Bozell's offices overlooked its rival, BBD&O (Batten, Barton, Durstine & Osborne), which generated all

Dodge advertising. BBD&O, located in a flat-roofed four-story building to the south of the Bozell skyscraper, operated with a similar budget and, like the rest of the sales and marketing arm of Dodge, viewed their counterparts at Bozell as friendly enemies.

So it was in the trenches — the dealerships — where dollars actually changed hands between the company and the public. While the designers and manufacturing types viewed the three brands — Chrysler, Dodge, and Plymouth — without loyalty or rancor, rivalries were on plain view among the sales and marketing groups at the two advertising agencies and within the four-thousand-member dealer body.

Chrysler/Plymouth had been joined at the hip since the 1920s, while Dodge and Dodge Truck enjoyed a similar relationship dating to the pre–World War I infancy of the industry. Within the minivan structure, Dodge, Chrysler, and Plymouth vehicles had been sold in the context of what was called "nameplate engineering," i.e., identical mechanical innards with only minor trim and label changes to separate them. Now change was afoot. After considerable wrangling inside the corporation about ridding itself of the sagging, rather incoherent Plymouth name, the decision was made to return to the original structure of the three brands: Plymouth as a cheaper, entry-level vehicle, Dodge in the midrange, and Chrysler as the luxury brand (although surveys indicated that the latter's image had been so badly corrupted by various mediocre products that the public had ceased to equate it with such prestige marques as Cadillac, Lincoln, or the upscale imports). Pricing, trim levels, and marketing strategies would differentiate the Plymouth Voyager, Dodge Caravan, and the Chrysler Town & Country to a much greater degree than in the past. The current Voyagers and Caravans were being sold with nearly parallel strategies to essentially the same consumer groups. But under the new plan the three brands would seek distinctly different — and hopefully broader — segments of the minivan market.

Of the two agencies, BBD&O seemed to have a slightly less challenging assignment. It was responsible for a single brand, Dodge, while its counterpart at Bozell was burdened with the job of building two distinct campaigns for Plymouth and Chrysler, as well as broader strategy for Chrysler corporate affairs. BBD&O's creative boss, Dick Johnson, was a veteran of the Detroit advertising wars. Beefy, with a bemused expression, he sported a pair of reading glasses balancing on the tip of his nose. Like many in the advertising business, Johnson preferred jeans and open sports shirts and smoked with politically incorrect regularity. His small team of men and women, working with Dodge's director of advertising, Jay Kuhne, had begun to form up their campaign with particular care because of one simple reality: For as much as six months after the NS was to be introduced, the age and obsolescence of the ASs would only be amplified, potentially killing sales. "We were trying to reinvent an icon," recalls Johnson. "We had to be very careful with words like 'revolutionary' and 'all new' because this buyer group is not as trendy as some others. They value their boxy vehicles as both unique and especially functional. By implying that we had 'changed everything' as we had done with our Intrepid LH sedan campaign, we were playing with fire. We knew what happened to 'new Coke.'"

Relying on data from Dave Bostwick's group and twelve consumer clinics conducted on their own, advertising recognized clearly that Caravan minivan owners were by nature conservative family types aged thirty-five to forty-four. Safety and function far transcended styling and performance as buying priorities. "These things are extensions of their homes," said Johnson. "The boomers who will buy the NS are looking for a vehicle that is a kind of '90s lifestyle enabler. The growth of minivans and sport-utility vehicles is an expression of a need for utility in personal transportation; kind of Swiss Army knives of the road. So our challenge was to create a campaign around what we called 'the new original' — a concept that implied evolution, not revolution, a sort of 'gold-standard refined,' that would say to the minivan buyer this is the logical next step."

Because the creative types at the agency were privy to the progress of the NS's design, it was apparent that the mass of new features would have to form the basis of the campaign. Unlike Leo Burnett's Oldsmobile Aurora campaign, which was just reaching the national television audience with million-dollar, computer-generated graphics of cars and people floating through space and across abstract paintings, both BBD&O and their counterparts would zero in on feature-oriented advertising, eschewing graphic pyrotechnics and overwrought cuteness in favor of explaining the new left-side door, the increased interior space, the 50 percent greater glass area, the reduced turning radius, and the plethora of options.

By the end of May a retired Chrysler technical writer named Lee Sorenson had completed a 90-page "Smart Book" packed with detail about the NS's features. It was to be employed throughout the company as a reference document for advertising copywriters, the public relations staff, sales and dealer training, and for cross-referencing among the engineering and design staffs. Sorenson's orderly exposition of the NS, from its shock absorbers to its optional roof rack, was to be invaluable as the agency decided that a campaign based on a matter-of-fact explanation of the vehicles' vast list of features and the attention to detail was obvious strategy.

"In the old days we'd sit here wondering what was going on at the factory until we'd get a call and be shown the new vehicle. They'd say, 'Here it is, now make some pretty ads to sell the damn thing,'" chuckled Johnson. "Now that's all different. My staff was privy to the NS's progress right from the start." He was referring to a hidebound corporate culture that had for years tied advertising in knots, forcing agency creative types to work with a tiny body of preapproved and predigested "facts" that had been vetted by the marketing and legal departments to a point where virtually nothing of substance could be said about a given product. Recalled one veteran, "Because we had so little flexibility in what we could create, you'd get entire advertising campaigns in which nothing serious could be said about the automobile. Worse yet, you'd be forced to rehash that same material over and over. We were told, 'Don't reach beyond the data that's been provided by the factory. Don't rock the boat.'"

Johnson agreed. "Five, ten years ago, if a copywriter wanted details on a certain component from a Chrysler engineer he'd have to go through our chain of command, which would in turn go through the corporation's chain of command until the two could finally talk to each other. That might take weeks. Now my guys have the engineers' phone numbers. All they have to do is pick up the receiver and dial. It sounds simple, but it took years to get to this point."

Johnson and his staff of forty copywriters, art directors, and researchers were operating in a new culture and it made their job easier. "The minivan platform team is full of motorheads who really want to make good cars," he said, reclining in his lushly furnished office, his sneakers resting easily on his desktop. "We've got thirty-eight major dealer associations to answer to. Most of those guys have gotten religion. Once it was strictly 'trash for cash.' Now they understand it's a case of product, product, product, which is why our campaign will be totally straightforward, with emphasis on features. We'll use the tagline 'We've thought of everything.' "

As Johnson's production team geared up dummy print ads and storyboards for television commercials, the art directors had chosen candy-apple red as the theme color for their minivan campaign. Like Bozell, the actual advertising would be bought and placed by Chrysler's Pentacom media-buying division, but it would be up to the agencies to recommend introduction strategies. This posed a problem. Because there were no major sporting events — World Series, NCAA playoffs, Super Bowl, Olympics, etc. — scheduled for the spring of 1995 when the campaign was set to break, Johnson's team decided a new strategy of "road-blocking" major time segments of prime time, a saturation bombing of audiences of top-ranked shows, coupled with 4–8 page color inserts in major news magazines, parenting and family publications, and enthusiast journals. "We're going to tell America that the NS is 'just as original as the original' and thank God we've got the stuff to back it up with," said Johnson.

Across the expanse of concrete and macadam that composed the Southfield office park, the creative staff at Bozell faced a more complex problem. Not only were they assigned the task of creating distinct, parallel campaigns for the Chrysler and Plymouth minivans, but the history of the agency burdened them with more political baggage than BBD&O. Bozell was the outgrowth of an alliance with Kenyon & Eckert, a venerable New York–based agency that had handled the Lincoln-Mercury account ("The sign of the Cat") when Lee Iacocca was still at Ford. A respected K&E executive named Leo-Arthur Kelmenson was a close friend and political ally of Iacocca's. He had played a central role in the agency's shift to the larger and more lucrative Chrysler account when the Chairman moved from Dearborn to Highland Park. But this friendship seemed to hamper any agency efforts to streamline the advertising process or make their campaigns more compelling. Quite the opposite, because the creative side of the Chrysler account remained in New York while the so-called account side (sales, marketing, client liaison, etc.) was based in Detroit. "It was a nightmare," recalls a former staffer who became frustrated with the system in the late 1980s and moved on to a more flexible agency. "We could only work with product information provided in official corporate briefs. If we wanted more data, we'd have to go through an insane chain of command, up through the agency, then to Detroit, then down through Chrysler bureaucracy with side trips through both their legal department and ours. To find out a simple fact about say, rear seat foot room, might take a month. Worse yet, Bozell was considered to be 'Lee's agency.' We were dragged in for all his pet projects like Ellis Island and the Statue of Liberty. And we kept using him for all those up-close-and-personal ads that we knew had long since lost their impact. We had guys assigned exclusively to Iacocca to prepare his copy and polish his image. Keeping him finessed was a full-time job. He was a major distraction for the agency and no doubt affected the advertising."

As Iacocca moved offstage, clearer heads took over and slowly Bozell moved toward a more focused mission. The creative people transferred to Detroit, where they were able to operate in closer proximity to the company. The antiquated lines of communication were streamlined and small teams of copywriters, marketers, and product experts were created to enhance the impact and credibility of the advertising. Shorn of the strictures embodied in the imperial Iacocca regime, the agency began to zero in on a similar product-oriented approach to BBD&O's. Their "minivan store" campaign, developed in 1992, had effectively linked the Plymouth and Chrysler minivan brands when the two vehicles were essentially the same and an upscale Voyager could come almost as lavishly equipped as a Chrysler Town & Country. But now the mission was changing. The new marketing strategy called for sharply dividing the identity of the two brands, aiming Plymouth at the entry-level mini-van buyer while positioning the Town & Country as an upscale luxury product. This had begun when Chrysler/Plymouth general manager Steve Torok had, in 1992, managed to elevate the leather-trimmed Town & Country from a paltry 300 units per month to ten times that level. By marketing the vehicle at nearly $30,000 a copy, a whole new minivan segment had been created with projected high-profit sales of 80,000 annually. At the same time, the Plymouth image had lost its identity as an entry-level automobile, much as GM's Chevrolet brand had become blurred over the past few decades. Bozell's challenge, led by minivan creative director Gene Turner, was to sharply delineate the identities of Plymouth and Chrysler. Working with corporate brand manager Ken Laurence, Turner's group again employed clinics — four in all at Boston, Cincinnati, Dallas, and San Mateo, to confirm what they already knew: that function and utility were the key elements, encompassing useful seating arrangements, interior roominess, and accessibility through the new left-side sliding door. The same age and demographic groups being sought by Dodge and BBD&O were the Chrysler/Plymouth targets as well — over four million owners in all. Using the theme line "the ultimate minivan," Bozell planned to introduce the Town & Country during the running of the Preakness horse race on May 20, 1995. This would follow a mass mailing to owners of competitive minivans a month earlier, as well as a 250,000 distribution of an elaborate hardcover promotion book produced by Ross Roy, an established Detroit production house specializing in sales material for Chrysler and Ford.

Bozell planned to employ golfer Tom Kite as a spokesman for Town & Country and to use a series of platform team engineers in television spots, much as Ford, GM, and others had done over the years to give authenticity to their claims. A redesigned Plymouth logo, better focus on its entry-level identity, and the outlay of about $200 million in advertising, marketing, public relations, and sales

training would be spent on the NS launch. That would boost the total NS minivan outlay to $2.8 billion.

Would it work? "This is the biggest crap game in the world,"
said Steve Torok inside his cluttered office on the top floor of the
Walter P. Chrysler building in Highland Park. There the
management of Chrysler/Plymouth and Dodge divisions were
jammed together in a welter of crowded offices and secretarial stations positioned in the corridors. Soon the entire entourage would
be transferred to the fifteen-story office building being built at
CTC, but until then Torok and his Dodge counterpart, Marty
Levine, were doomed to operate in the jam-up of humanity in the
outdated building where the NS had first been laid down four years
earlier. A round-faced man in his forties with an easy smile, Torok
has risen through the ranks, mainly as a marketing and sales expert. "We are trying to make long-term capital investments in what
is essentially a fashion business," he said. "This business is highly
sensitive to external factors beyond our control. You make your
best guess and take the consequences. You are looking at a man
who, ten years ago, as a top market planner in this corporation recommended *against* building a second plant to manufacture T-115
minivans based on our detailed analysis of the market. At the same
time I *advocated* building a second assembly plant for the long-
forgotten, unlamented St. Regis. Fortunately for the company —
and my career — my input was ignored."

Torok scanned the parking lot outside his office, now almost
deserted as the company's transfer to Auburn Hills accelerated.
"The changes around here are unbelievable. This was a classic,
top-down company, profit-oriented, with no passion, like the postal
service. There used to be a joke around here that we'd go bank-
rupt and close the entire place down and there'd still be five
hundred guys who didn't get the word working on engineering changes for the K-car. Now that old culture is gone. We've
changed, but all the dealers, for example, are still with us. Their
goals are entirely different. They're much more conservative; more
inclined to sell what already works than to try new approaches
and new products. They've got much-shorter-term needs. We look
down the road two or three years for a return on our invest-

ment. They're looking at the future in terms of weeks and months. Getting all this in sync — the design, the manufacturing, the supply, the marketing, and the dealers — is a challenge nobody has met totally."

It would be up to men like Torok and his counterpart at Dodge to actually sell the NS while keeping the aging AS alive in the hearts and minds of consumers and the dealers for much of 1995. They would have an extra $100 million with which to fend off the challenge of Ford's Windstar while launching the NS in grand style. But more than a year lay between the time the first NSs rolled into the showrooms. A mass of hurdles lay ahead. Two major factories had to be fired up, supplies had to be purchased and inventoried, and a mass of nagging design problems had to be solved.

The real action, the hard-knuckled labor involved with actually making automobiles, was under way four hundred miles to the southwest, in the St. Louis suburb of Fenton, Missouri. There Sham Rushwin's associates, Les Wolfe and Bruce Donaldson, had set up shop in a deserted factory cafeteria. With about 150 engineers and UAW hourly workers, they were building piece by piece the first assembly plant for NS production. Sprawling across hundreds of acres on the north side of Interstate 70, the stark white bulk of Chrysler's Missouri assembly operation was actually two complete factories known inside the company as St. Louis One and St. Louis Two. Separated by a giant water tower in the middle of the complex, St. Louis Two (or South, as many call it) was to become the locus of NS manufacturing operations. A hulking building without windows, its flat roof studded with smokestacks and ventilator pipes, the plant had been vacant for five years following the last K-car, LeBaron convertibles and Daytona coupes, that rolled off the line. Its northern counterpart had been producing AS minivans at the rate of about 1,100 a day for nearly a decade and would be shut down and converted to the assembly of the increasingly popular T-100 Ram full-sized pickup. The cavernous 2.8-million-square-foot St. Louis South facility was now being fitted with an enormous, mile-long assembly line that would within a year be capable of spitting a completed NS minivan out the door at a rate of about 72 per hour. The workforce of roughly fourteen hundred men and women per shift would weld, screw, bolt, and clip 1,315 different pieces — so-called end items — into the vehicles as they waddled along at exactly 1,560 feet per hour or .295 mph. The line was theoretically capable of a "gross" production of 78 vehicles per hour, presuming no glitches or delays. But the production team estimated a "net" rate of 72 per hour, which meant that each vehicle would spend exactly 42 seconds at each one of the 408 workstations — each exactly 20 feet in length.

The factory's low roof was now being rigged with a network of white-painted steel girders that would form a mile-long conveyor that snaked above the gray concrete floor. This would act like an industrial ski lift, transporting the semicompleted vehicles from one workstation to the next. Hanging from the conveyor were 350 steel carriages, painted bright orange and resembling immense ski-area chairlifts without seats. Among the white I-beams were vine-like forests of air hoses that hung from the ceiling, each connected to masses of blue-hued air guns and impact wrenches used in the high-speed attachment of nuts and metal screws.

"Truth be known, there aren't any secrets here," said Bruce Donaldson as he strode along an inert line of carriages. "Major automakers build cars essentially the same way. You'd see the same thing at Toyota or Ford or GM." The St. Louis assembly line snaked its way, west to east, across the plant, beginning at a rail spur where steel body panels from Chrysler's three stamping plants at Warren and Sterling Heights, Michigan, and Twinsburg, Ohio, rolled in. From there the panels were jigged up in what were called "subassemblies" and sent through a series of 375 robotic welders to "build the box" of sheet metal. The use of computer-controlled robotic welders was nearly doubled in the NS assembly, as compared to the old AS, which streamlined the process and reduced emissions. The new units were powered by compressed air or electricity, as opposed to the older high-maintenance hydraulically powered units that employed toxic hydraulic fluid and were considerably noisier. The body shops at both St. Louis and Windsor were capable of increased, computer-controlled flexibility. An additional 54 panels (31 percent more than the AS) were required for the four body configurations of the NS (long- and short-wheelbases, with and without the left-side door), yet all could be produced at each plant. Better yet, the addition of the fourth or left-side door required only two new workstations and eight additional workers. Once the "box" had been welded up and the roof attached with spot welds and special structural adhesive (which eliminated the need for additional hand-brazing and metal finishing), the units tracked their way upstairs and into the immense, tunnel-like paint shops.

For decades the American automobile industry and Chrysler in particular had been cursed by a reputation for poor paint quality. Chrysler automobiles often left the assembly line coated in enamels exhibiting what was known in the trade as "orange peel" — a mottled, rindlike surface that degraded the entire appearance of the vehicle. Drips, smears, and cloudiness were not uncommon, while even the cheapest Japanese imports boasted paint that glistened after years of usage. Slowly the American industry had upgraded its paint by investing in new technologies and employing what was known as "clear coat," a finishing layer that added depth and luster to the color.

In order to elevate the NS to world-class levels of quality, it was understood from the beginning that the paint had to be radically improved. In order to attain the goal, $200 million was invested in revamping the St. Louis paint shop, while an additional $50 million was spent at Windsor. The modifications involved a conversion to waterborne color coats as opposed to the traditional solvent-based paints. Not only did the new process enhance the brilliance of the paintwork, but it reduced volatile emissions by substantial degrees and eliminated all lead and chrome content. Moreover, a major effort was made to reduce the solvents employed in the paint booths by 50 percent and to cut all toxic ingredients associated with sound-deadening, sealing, and paint priming. De-ionized water replaced solvents in the paint purging systems.

The NSs were to be primed using an electro-coat process that immersed the entire body structure in a tank containing a water-based epoxy primer solution. By charging the bodies electrically, the primer could be deposited evenly over the entire surface, with no sags or runs. This "E-coat" reduced emissions levels to 66 percent below federal standards. The next step in the process, an epoxy-polyester antichip powder, again eliminated the need for environmentally dangerous solvents, while the final waterborne "appearance" coats were not only cleaner but were applied in humidity-controlled chambers at 73°F, offering a vast improvement in working conditions from the old days when paint booth temperatures rivaled those found in foundries and steel mills.

Once the bodies had departed the paint booth, the doors and lift-gate were removed in what is called "doors off" assembly. This permits workers to install interior systems like the heater/air-conditioning units, steering, instrument panels, wiring, headliners, and trim without having to work around the cumbersome bulk of doors. The system eliminated a critical two feet of wasted walking distance while permitting workers to install door trim and window mechanisms at waist height, rather than having to stoop when the doors remained fixed to the body. Computer programming had the assembled doors rejoin the vehicle near the end of the assembly line.

As the doorless body shells chugged, trainlike, out the paint booths and back downstairs toward the area called Trim Chassis Final, another separate part of the plant was devoted to assembling the lower unit of the vehicle that contained the engine and transmission, exhaust and brake systems, and the front and rear suspensions. These components were mounted on wide, flat fixtures called pallets. With such units, which had been developed in concert with hourly workers acting as consultants to the engineering staff, the drivetrain components could be bolted together by raising the entire unit electrically and automatically bolting it in 28 PLP (primary locating points) to the body. The pallets could be adjusted to accommodate both long- and short-wheelbase minivans and, by the exact location of PLPs, created a more accurately assembled vehicle than in the past.

The pallets held the components in an inverted position, permitting workers to hook up wiring, install brake lines and controls, fit suspension pieces, and so on without having to work above their heads while stuck in below-the-floor pits as in the past. By increasing the ergonomic ease of installation, worker fatigue was reduced, with a commensurate rise in efficiency. The chassis pallets, once completed, rejoined the main assembly line to begin the lengthy, labor-intensive Trim Chassis Final. There the drivetrains were fitted, along with instrument panels, seats, interior and exterior trim, radios, all wiring looms, windows, tires, and wheels, as well as the earlier removed doors. The vehicles passed along the assembly process in a "hot car" mode, meaning that after the electrical distribution systems and the instrument panel were in place, an external 12-volt power source was connected, giving workers an immediate indication if all systems were working properly. Any defects would be instantly detectable and corrected on site. Once the on-line checks were completed, the battery cables were attached and the vehicle readied for normal operation.

After the front and rear fascias were bolted in place, the vehicles would be filled with fluids, have their headlights aimed, wheel alignment checked, engines started, and be driven off the line to the marshaling yard for shipment to the dealers. The complexity of the entire process dogged Rushwin and his staff. Once St. Louis was set up, a duplicate assembly line would have to be created at Windsor, Ontario, and a third, much smaller facility at Graz, Austria. Windsor, an aged, 2.5-million-square-foot facility located just across the river from Detroit, would come on line in midsummer 1995. Work was progressing on a new paint facility and other modifications to the old factory that had been a key element in Chrysler's manufacturing process since it had opened in 1928. Located on Tecumseh Road, in a working-class neighborhood, Windsor sprawled over 120 acres, and extra space was at a premium. Plant manager Gino Raffin, a tough former test engineer at the Chelsea proving grounds, was in constant contact with his St. Louis counterpart, Joe Mollihan, as they tried to dovetail their two operations. Windsor had produced over three million minivans since 1983 and its workers prided themselves on being the best in the business. Raffin had led the way in empowering his Canadian Auto Workers (CAW) to become more involved in the manufacturing process. Even now, almost eighteen months before full NS production was to begin, shifts of as many as 140 Windsor hourly workers were in St. Louis working side by side with company engineers and their Missouri counterparts in setting up the assembly line. Their inputs would then be utilized when they returned home. In the meantime, Windsor would continue to pump the AS models out to keep Chrysler in the minivan game while St. Louis came on line. Once the two major North American facilities were up to speed, St. Louis would build so-called high-line and high-volume models while Windsor produced high-volume and "low-line" NSs. This was hardly as simple as it sounded. Each plant had to produce four major body styles in nightmarish combinations of trim levels, paint, engine and transmission setups; three and four doors, short and long wheelbase, and with and without air conditioning. St. Louis was set to build 125,000 different variations on the theme; Windsor about 25,000. (This was in fact an improvement on complexity: The current AS could be built in over 250,000 combinations.)

Continually stung by low ratings for quality by J. D. Power and other polling services, Rushwin's team was making a major thrust to produce world-class vehicles. A series of "BIC" teams (Best in Class) had been established and were shuttling back and forth between Detroit and St. Louis aboard commercial flights and corporate jets in such magnitude that a nearby Holiday Inn had a block of 150 rooms reserved for the foreseeable future — with two more hotels on standby for spillover. In the old days, no more than six engineers would be assigned permanent status at the assembly plant to monitor quality. Now St. Louis would get thirty engineers to watchdog day-to-day operations. Along the line itself, large graphic displays of The Wall were hung at every eighth workstation to give workers an instant reference to the approved process. Donaldson and his designers had set up the assembly line so that all work could be done at heights ranging between 30 and 40 inches off the floor. At those levels, ergonomic efficiency could be optimized. A yellow rope resembling an emergency subway alarm ran the entire length of the line and served a similar purpose. This "quality alert system" permitted any worker at any time to stop the line if he or she spotted a problem.

Such systems had been in use by Japanese workers for decades, but had only recently been utilized in some American plants. When a worker determined that a problem was serious enough to stop the line and yanked the cord (or pressed a button in the more auto-mated body shop), a large lighted display board in the immediate area was illuminated, informing supervisors of the exact location of the stoppage, while a computer calculated the delay and displayed the amount of overtime needed to compensate for the QAS (quality alert system) stoppage. The computer also pinpointed potential chronic trouble sites along the line, which aided production ana-lysts to fine-tune certain assembly procedures at workstations that experienced above-average "pulls."

At the same time a group of outside suppliers were working with Peter Rosenfeld and Tom Stallcamp's staff to develop what was be-ing called a "supply delivery schedule" based on the Japanese "just in time" system that had revolutionized the industry in the 1970s. Within a one-hundred-mile radius, forty-six vendors had created either manufacturing facilities or supply depots so that parts could be delivered in four-hour cycles, meaning reduced storage on site for Chrysler and higher efficiency in terms of excess inventory, transportation costs, and down time due to shortages.

Also referred to as a "pull" system, "just in time" (or simply JIT) embodied a complex program to keep in-plant inventory at a minimum. As vehicle orders were received at the assembly plant, a computer operated by production control engineers would send part and subassembly orders to the supply network. Presuming there were no unexpected bottlenecks in the network — which only existed in a perfect technological world — parts would arrive at each workstation on an as-needed basis. This JIT plan was in-tended to reduce costs of maintaining large inventory supplies at the factory, but it also embodied serious risks. If but one of the suppliers failed, the entire system would stop. There would be no on-site backup parts inventory — a risk amplified by Chrysler's heavier-than-average dependence on outside suppliers. Such a problem would slow the introduction of the NS and threaten to bring the entire program to a halt.

The JIT policy was but one part of a Japanese-created manufac-turing philosophy called "lean production." Chrysler internal memos defined the phrase in simple terms: "If it's not required, don't do it." This Zen-like drive for simplicity manifested itself after months of intense planning in everything from the design of workstations to minimize worker movement while maximizing comfort, to using threaded fasteners exactly the proper length to reduce the time needed to tighten them, to employing studs and clips in place of nuts and bolts and threaded fasteners where possible — all to reduce worker time and effort. The aforementioned plan to halve the number of nuts, bolts, and fasteners employed in the NS was yet another example of the drive toward simplicity and bare-bones assembly techniques. Stallcamp's protracted and complicated campaign to reduce the number of tier one suppliers from 450 to about 300 was also part of the lean production campaign and one that was expected to pay long-term dividends once the chaff had been separated.

Like an immense erector set, the horizon-to-horizon vacancy of St. Louis South was being filled with a spiderweb of steel that would transform bits of metal and plastic into real automobiles. If all went according to schedule, the first P-Zero prototype would be framed up on the third day of November 1994, triggering a series of increases in volume called "ramping up," culminating with full production of short-wheelbase NSs on March 27, 1995. Windsor would come on line in July of the same year, almost four months to the day later.

Meanwhile, back in Detroit, in the basement of the CTC, engineers were evaluating noise levels as well as the critical areas of electromagnetic compatibility, wind resistance, and crashworthiness in a network of high-tech laboratories. Barrier crashes to evaluate body structure, fire safety, door-latch strength, air bag and seat belt mountings, glass integrity, and so on were being carried out on a regular basis. One of the first to be impacted against the concrete was the Harold Burns 692SG, the first hand-built minivan that had served with such honor from the moment it was revealed to Lutz and Eaton two years earlier. It was an ignominious end for a milestone car, the first vehicle of what promised to be hundreds of thousands of clones. The ugly, noisy death crash completed, the crushed carcass of 692SG was hauled away to a little graveyard on the edge of the CTC test track, there to lay in a rusting heap until it was trucked to a scrapyard for meltdown. All that was left was its original hood, hanging in the lobby of the minivan platform team's offices one floor above the impact laboratory. Its white surface smeared with the signatures of the team, the hood would serve as a memorial to a prototype machine that would in many ways symbolize the destiny of the entire corporation.

11

Boulders, Rocks, and Sand

THE WEDDING was large and raucously Greek. Chris Theodore and his bride, the former Tracy Antos, were married in Detroit on a warm day, July 24, 1994, and spent two weeks as planned honeymooning in the Greek islands. Distant family members smothered them with hospitality as they traveled to his father's native Crete before returning to the car wars in Auburn Hills. Already Tracy was expressing concern over the intense pressure being exerted on her new husband by his work at Chrysler.

She spoke openly to friends about her hope that he would retire soon, before the toll on his health became too great. But retirement to his beach house on Lake Huron was far from Chris Theodore's mind. He was on a fast track at Chrysler, and if the NS program could be concluded successfully, there was no telling how far he could go in the company. After all, he was closely allied with Francois Castaing, the vice president of engineering. Becoming his successor was hardly out of the question. At age forty-four, he was a relatively young man with a bright future in the car business — provided the NS reached the market as a properly designed vehicle, manufactured within budget. Those elemental parameters meant success. Without them, puttering among the sand and stones on Huron's rugged shoreline was probably a reasonable alternative.

The bags had barely been unpacked, the snapshots processed, and the passports stowed away when reality rose up and smacked him in the face. John Nigro and the team of engineers assigned to the exacting job of setting up the St. Louis body shop reported that a strange anomaly had been discovered. As the P-Zero bodies were being fabricated at the CTC, the CMM tolerance-measuring machine was identifying what was described as a "sag" in the rear segment of the short-wheelbase vehicles' main body shell. Some of the bodies in white were 6mm out of specification, meaning that the back of those minivans, should they ever reach production, would droop nearly 1/4 inch. With body tolerances targeted at a maximum error of 1/2 millimeter, the so-called sag was intolerable. With a body that distorted, external trim would be misaligned, doors and windows would not fit, suspension pieces, brakes lines, and so on would be wrongly positioned and prone to failure. In a word, the body, the main component, the very skeleton of the SWB NS, was not acceptable with less than six months left before volume production was to begin.

"I went nuts," Theodore later confessed. "It was the only time I really lost my temper during the whole program. I pounded the table. I swore. I stalked out of the room. It seemed unreal. We had come this far, worked this hard, and made this kind of progress only to find that the goddamn bodies were out of tolerance." Finding the problem, much less fixing it, was to be a nightmare. Time would be lost. Credibility would suffer. The *Detroit News* got wind of the problem and announced that the launch of the NS would be delayed from January 9, 1995, to February 13. The trouble was not identified, although the story was essentially correct. But Theodore knew the delay was likely to be longer than the *News* predicted. Tom Kowaleski fielded the ensuing flurry of press inquiries by refusing to confirm the story, but offered, as a "Chrysler spokesman," a terse statement saying, "We are not going to go until we are ready to go." Adding to the story, the *Wall Street Journal* speculated that the delay would cost Chrysler the production of about three thousand units and noted that the fat profits being generated by the corporation with its LH, Grand Cherokee, and Dodge Ram pickup would more than offset any minivan losses over such a short term. This was little solace as Nigro and his team began to root through the data and to microexamine the flawed bodies in search of clues. Could it be a production problem at the stamping plants? This seemed unlikely, because the error was not appearing on all the bodies. If a stamping die was out of tolerance, it was logical to assume that all the panels would be cursed with the same error. These were production "hard dies" that were in question, not the kirsite "soft tools" employed in the earlier F-One prototypes. A flaw in the production tooling would cost hundreds of millions to repair. Yet the problem encompassed more than one set of hard dies, each of which was punching out the panel in question. Each would have to be reexamined. All passed. The problem was elsewhere. Could there be damage in the shipping process, perhaps bending in the racks as they were transported from the stamping plant to the assembly line? More time was consumed in a search for trouble within the racking system. That seemed to be working properly. There was only one other possibility. It lay within the complex of welding fixtures and framing jigs that gripped the sheet metal panels as the robotic welders tacked them into position. A network of pins on the framing jigs called "primary locating points" (PLPs) had to be precisely placed in order to produce a perfect weld and a square and true body structure.

Finally, after a panic-laden search, the trouble was found. It was a PLP jig that after repeated cycles in which the body panel was inserted for welding, was distorted no more than a few millimeters — a dimension undetectable to the unpracticed eye. This error, once it was welded in place, would be amplified as the flawed panel moved through the assembly process. Now that it was isolated, the guilty PLP could not be simply replaced, but had to be redesigned to ensure that failure would not be repeated. More time lost. More added expense.

Now the new Chrysler management was prepared to absorb losses in time and money that would have been unacceptable in the old days. The tradition at Highland Park and throughout the domestic industry was that once a launch date for a new vehicle had been set, not hell or high water would alter it. Dealer introductions, advertising campaigns, shipping schedules, and marketing strategies were all centered around a specific date — generally in the traditional September–October time frame when new products were revealed to an eager public. Those dates were carved in stone. In the past, if a flaw like the one that faced the team was discovered, the process would still thunder ahead regardless of the risk of poor quality. "We would just force the issue," said Edson. "We'd try to tune the trim dies to compensate for the error, doing it on the fly. You'd never know quite where you were, because you'd get what we call 'drift' with the fixtures." In other words, the dies and the stampings would float slightly in the imprecise die fixtures, causing inconsistent, ill-fitting bodies and trim, an ailment endemic to American automobiles. A common visual symptom of this was distorted bumpers and body cladding and varying gaps in door frames, hoods, and trunk lids.

With the NS, Chrysler was halting the production schedule to make a proper fix, regardless of dealer protests or sniping from the press. Too much was at stake to risk complaints about more below-par fit and finish from a company that had abused those standards of quality for decades.

More trouble. Bernie Swanson reported that the front disc brakes were producing a squeak at low speeds. They were fine during normal operation, but in passive situations, like easing into a garage and gently applying pressure to stop, there was this tiny squeak. "It was crazy," Theodore recalled. "Here we had a brake of a type we'd been producing for damn near forty years throughout the worldwide industry. There were no secrets to disc brakes. One brake was basically like another brake, but ours had this irritating squeak. When I heard about it I called the president of Kelsey-Hayes, who was supplying the brakes. I found him in China. I raised hell. It turned out one of their engineers had made a small change in our specifications. That was the source. Then some of the master cylinders started to leak. Do you know how long this industry has been making master cylinders? We've been using hydraulic brakes since the 1920s — *seventy years!* And we got a leak. Not on all of 'em, maybe 8 percent of the units. But if you're seeking zero defects, 8 percent might as well be 100 percent. We got it fixed — it was a flawed o-ring — but it was more aggravation with a situation you just don't think can be the source of a problem."

As the end of the program came into sight, all the broad-brush strokes that had created the NS with all its features and its splendid utilization of space were on the canvas. Now came the detailing, the shading and shadowing that would create a true work of art. As they irised down to a final, perfect vehicle ready for volume production, all manner of insane, unexpected, unreasonable problems were rising up.

The team was still saddled with a mass of MITS issues. Ernie Laginess's body in white team was facing problems ranging from rearview mirror shake to weakness in the sliding door upper hinge track. "I want that track strong enough so Godzilla can't break it," demanded Theodore. Jim Sauter's interior group was grappling with a whistle emitted by the air-conditioning evaporator, poor fit on some interior front door panels, and a buzzing sound in the heater core. Worse yet, one of the engineers had cut his finger on a sharp edge of an air-conditioning outlet on the instrument panel. In addition to the brake howl, Swanson's chassis team discovered troubles with a new track bar that was producing unseemly noises. Five different gusseting systems were tried, resulting in "five quiet vehicles and five noisy ones." A plea was made for more test vehicles at the proving grounds, but there was a shortage of Type Gs and P-Zeroes, all of which were being utilized for testing by various teams.

Rick Rueter's powertrain team reported that the rear engine mount was producing problems. The newly designed cross-member was ill-fitted and rubbing against the engine and a chassis member. "This is a classic example of bad communication, of groups within the team not talking," grouched Theodore.

He sensed faint malaise overcoming his team. They had come far. They had laid down the elements of the best minivan in the world, better than the Windstar, better than the Honda Odyssey that was now reaching market. The Odyssey embodied Honda's traditional jewel-like fit and finish and featured a left-side rear door — albeit one that swung on conventional hinges rather than slid. But the vehicle was smaller both in terms of interior and exterior dimensions than the short-wheelbase NS and was available only with a smallish, 2.2-liter, 140 hp four-cylinder engine that lacked torque and hauling power. Surely the Odyssey would appeal to Honda loyalists, but no one on the NS platform team believed it to be a contender in the high-volume minivan market. The fact that the Windstar and Odyssey both failed to surpass the NS in terms of model selection, options, or interior capacity seemed to create in some members of the team a sense of slackness that seemed to drift through operation, as if the job was about completed and little else except small tidying up was left. But Theodore understood the old adage: The devil is in the details. Literally thousands of tiny items that could curse the entire project remained to be solved. At one meeting Cindy Hess made the mistake of comparing a component to one used on the LH, citing that it had worked well on that vehicle. "If I ever hear about something on the LH being good enough for us, there'll be hell to pay," Theodore snapped.

Lighting a cigarette in the solitude of his office, he looked momentarily defeated, seemingly crushed by the weight of handling the largest project in the corporation's history through two years of development. "We Americans seem to quit too soon, to say 'We won, it's over, let's celebrate' before the job is finished. It frustrates the hell out of me."

Tom Edson, always able to put Theodore's passion into perspective, put it this way: "A project like this is like draining a pond. First you get to the boulders and you clear them away. Then the water lowers until you get to the rocks. When all the water's gone, all that's left is the sand. What we've got now is sand."

Each week's Spaghetti Day, held in classroom 4E in the west wing of the CTC, produced more problems and, thankfully, more solutions. In the name of cost-cutting, cancellation of the load-leveling suspension was discussed (but not implemented), as were a number of expensive paints, including candy apple red and a luminescent gold. The all-wheel-drive option, a limited production item at best, would be delayed until the 1997 model year. Some of the rocks and boulders were being cleared away, and the program seemed to be getting back on track as the crisp days of October 1994 wrapped around Detroit. The framing jig PLP problem had been corrected and the body shop at St. Louis was finally certified for full production with hard tooling. Swanson's brake howl problem was solved by a decision to employ the heretofore optional heavy-duty brake package throughout the line, at a cost penalty of $13 per vehicle. Slowly, the MITS issues were giving way to intense work and a new schedule for assembly-line start-up of P-Zero vehicles was reset for November 3. If no further disasters were encountered, the time lost would not involve major penalties. And if all continued according to plan, the first long-wheelbase PVP (Pre Volume Production) NS minivan would begin to be framed up at the St. Louis body shop on January 10, 1995.

While plans remained in place that NS production would reach the 670,000 mark at full capacity, market analysts predicted that domestic minivan sales were destined to level out at about 1.2 million units annually from all manufacturers. If this was the case, a dangerous glut of vehicles loomed on the horizon, especially when General Motors came to market with its updated and improved products in 1996. Chrysler's market share had dropped from 45.3 percent at the beginning of 1994 to under 43 percent, with further erosion predicted. If that projection of 1.2 million units was correct, Chrysler's nearly 700,000 units would mean they had to be capturing well over 50 percent of the market — a long shot considering the increased competition from Ford, GM, and the imports. Clearly something would have to give. The opening shots in a price war had already begun, with rebates being offered on the AS short-wheelbase Voyagers and Caravans, with more predicted in the new year. Word was passing through the industry that Ford was planning a short-term closure of its Oakville, Ontario, plant to cut Windstar inventory, especially on its slow-selling low-line models.

As Theodore and the team appeared to be getting the production cycle on track, the corporation eased into a state of relative euphoria. The third-quarter financial report was excellent. Profits rose 54 percent over the prior year, totaling $651 million. This gave Chrysler a net cash balance of $4.2 billion after another $1.2 billion had been added back to the badly scavenged pension fund. The stock was floating in the mid-$40s, well below what some market analysts had predicted, but still solidly positioned for growth.

Kirk Kerkorian, an old ally of Iacocca who held 32 million shares or 9.2 percent of Chrysler's common stock, was openly pressuring the board of directors to reinvest some of the surplus cash and to increase dividends beyond the 25 cents per quarter. He also demanded a two-for-one stock split. Eaton resisted, desiring instead to build a $7.5 billion war chest in anticipation of the next inevitable slump in car sales. The seventy-seven-year-old billionaire had been cleared by the SEC to increase his holdings to 15 percent and thereby position himself for all manner of mischief, including a hostile takeover battle that could wreck the company's finances. Eaton countered by investing one billion in a stock buyback and declaring a dividend increase.

Eaton was publicly wary about what Kerkorian's goal was. In November he told *Ward's Auto World* reporter David C. Smith, "I would not want to hazard any speculation about what Mr. Kerkorian might or might not do. We're just going to have to wait and see how the situation develops." Not far back in the shadows lurked Lee Iacocca, who held about 2.9 million Chrysler shares, roughly 1 percent of outstanding common stock. He sat on the board of Kerkorian's MGM Grand Hotel and would surely be a player in any game of control or stock manipulation that might ensue.

As 1994 neared a close, Ford's assault on the minivan market seemed blunted, at least in the short term. The Windstar, priced in the mid-$20Ks and out of reach of many low-line Plymouth Voyager and Dodge Caravan customers, had slumped in the showroom after a fast start. *Automotive News* reported that inventories of the vehicle had leapt from 54 days to 89 days (60 days being considered optimum), while dealers were being provided with aggressive leasing deals to stimulate sales. By the end of 1994 Ford was projected to produce about 212,000 Windstars while Chrysler would build over 600,000 Voyagers, Caravans, and Town & Country models of the AS. But that was only part of the story. The aging Aerostar would bring another 219,000 vehicles to market that combined with 140,000 Mercury Villagers and Nissan Quests (jointly produced) would give Ford a total minivan production of over 570,000 units and put it in the minivan business with a vengeance. Moreover, it was known to be preparing a major springtime assault on Chrysler when the changeover from the older AS models to the new NSs would cause the greatest vulnerability.

It was axiomatic in the industry that minivans had a specific "season" for sales, beginning in March and extending to July. After that, when family vacation plans were complete, sales, according to Ted Cunningham, "shut off like a switch." Within this window of vulnerability Ford was preparing its next major offensive. Angst began to permeate the sales force. Some wondered whether the NS was too evolutionary, too derivative, too similar, appearance-wise, to the Windstar to generate much public excitement. Others were concerned about the rising public fascination with sport-utility vehicles, some of which offered nearly as much interior space and functionalism as minivans, with more performance and external panache. Sales of Chrysler's Jeep Grand Cherokee and Ford's Explorer were booming, with new, improved entries pouring into the market from every major manufacturer.

The corporation's curse of poor quality would not go away. *Consumer Reports*, which seemed to harbor a perpetual grudge against Chrysler, announced that the entire product line was below par and that the LH sedans, which they had once recommended, were being excised from their list due to poor fabrication. Chrysler responded by assigning Bozell Worldwide to create a quick-hitting, three-week, $10 million television and newspaper campaign touting Chrysler owner loyalty. After all, the corporate marketers had data that their customers had a higher loyalty rate than Honda, Toyota, or Nissan owners and that 74 percent of their minivan owners claimed they would buy another. The corporation line regarding the J. D. Power rankings was something of a reach: It claimed that over 300,000 import owners had been "captured" in 1993 and, because they tended to be younger and more discriminating than traditional domestic buyers, they often "graded harder" on consumer surveys like Power's. This of course failed to explain why these same tough-minded customers had given consistently higher scores to the import brands they had deserted.

The campaign was a timing disaster. The centerpiece was a full-page ad in *USA Today* headlining letters from Chrysler customers celebrating their vehicles. In the same issue, October 10, appeared a feature story citing J. D. Power surveys of quality and customer satisfaction, plus other consumer group findings. All ranked

Chrysler well below average. The story noted that complaints about Chrysler products outnumbered those generated by all other manufacturers. The juxtaposition of the ad and the story was a major embarrassment. Bud Liebler, always the point man in such situations, protested the judgment of the *USA Today* editors, claiming that it was customary for big media to warn advertisers if a critical story would conflict with an ad. He told the press that he was "frustrated and angry," which did little to blunt the impact of a situation that only amplified the reality that Chrysler had a long way to go before its reputation for quality would rival that of the market leaders.

Another salvo arrived in an *Automotive News* story bylined by veteran reporter Joe Bohn, citing an unnamed platform team engineer, who claimed that an October crash test of the NS conducted at the CTC safety laboratory had resulted in major failure. According to the rules set down by the government, major corporations are allowed to administer their own crash tests and to submit the data to officials at NHTSA. A follow-up in the December 13 edition of the *Detroit Free Press* showed a Jim Dunne spy photo of the vehicle (actually one of the disguised vehicles that had been offered to certain members of the press for preliminary test drives the same week) and speculated that the failure — which involved a 30 mph crash with unbelted dummies — might again delay production of the NS. Once analyzed, the news was no more important than Dunne's picture of a vehicle that had been on the public roads for several months. Theodore quickly responded by noting that "vehicles often fail crash tests. If passage was assured, why would they be conducted in the first place?" he asked rhetorically — a question the press should have posed to itself. He noted that of the seventeen P-Zero vehicles crash tested, only two had failed and the corrective measures had already been taken. In the case of the flaw treated in *Automotive News*, a small "dart" was sliced in the front frame members to improve what safety experts call "crush" — the ability of a body structure to absorb energy by sequentially folding up under impact. This permitted the steering column to tilt upward at the proper angle, thereby reducing injury to the test dummy.

Internally, the event was considered part of the routine development process and had been quickly forgotten. But what upset Theodore was the fact that such proprietary information had been given to the press. Clearly, there was a leak within the team. Moreover, it was an individual with access to data from Ernie Laginess's body structure group and Sauter's interior systems group. Was it a mole or simply a disgruntled employee? Either way, he or she had openly violated company policy and was subject to immediate dismissal.

The source of the story was soon revealed. An engineer named Paul Sheridan stepped forward to claim responsibility and was immediately fired. The corporation publicly described him as a dissatisfied former employee and charged him with violating his obligations to privacy. Sheridan responded with a suit, which is pending, and he was not interviewed for this book. The legal battle was destined to drag on for months and the issue quickly left the headlines.

In St. Louis, the assembly line was slowly firing up. It was an agonizing process, beginning with a single P-Zero vehicle moving, snail-like, in isolation along the vast line. The first minivan to make the trip in early October had ended in the scrap yard. At one point in the tracking system, the body shell was carried too close to the ceiling and its roof was peeled away by a low-hanging girder like the lid of a sardine can. The first P-Zero to be completed on October 19 — which was driven in triumph to the airport to pick up Ted Cunningham as he arrived for an inspection tour — would not initially start and was discovered to be lacking brake fluid. These glitches were part of any mass-production startup of an automobile assembly line and were quickly corrected. Other equally vexing problems would arise in their wake, all of which were customary components of such a complex enterprise.

As the holidays approached, a bit of good news buoyed the team. The corporation was preparing to announce record profits of $3.7 billion, which would mean bonuses of about $7,500 each for the sixty thousand hourly workers. But concern centered around the reality that the NS project remained $23.4 million "out of bed," in Frank Sanders's phrasing. Clarification of the situation would come six days before Christmas, when Eaton, Lutz, and a cadre of senior management flew to Phoenix for one final ride-and-drive before volume production commenced.

The brace of Gulfstreams once again roared into Deer Valley Airport with Eaton's G4 N800CC leading the way. The splendid sixteen-passenger jet, with its leather captain's chairs with the doe-skin inserts, had barely rolled to a stop when Lutz's slightly smaller and older G2 N807CC hit the runway and the pilots braked hard, its twin engines in full reverse. Theodore and his team of engineers and sales types greeted the Detroit contingent in the lobby, while Tom Persons tended the four freshly built NSs that he and his crew had driven out from St. Louis three days earlier. The trip thankfully had been trouble-free and the vehicles — a Town & Country loaded with options and the 3.8-liter V6, a pair of short-wheelbase versions (one Dodge, one Plymouth) with new 2.4-liter four-cylinder engines, and a long-wheelbase Dodge, heavily optioned, with the 3.3-liter V6, were positioned in the parking lot. With them for comparison purposes were a pair of current AS Voyagers and a Windstar and a Mercury Villager.

Following a briefing in an upstairs conference room, the group drifted into the harsh Arizona sunlight and climbed aboard the waiting fleet. As Jim Donlan, the corporation's chief financial officer, drove the Windstar into traffic, he noted the length of the exhaust pipe on the NS Town & Country in front of him. "That pipe looks a little long," he mused. "Imagine how much money we could save if we trimmed an inch off each one." "Is that all you bean counters ever think about — saving money?" came a voice from the backseat.

The plan was to head northwest out of metro Phoenix with a lunch stop at the Wickenburg Inn prior to a 120-mile mountain drive toward Bagdad, nestled 4,100 feet up in the shadow of Blue Mountain. The roads would be fast and open, giving the expert drivers among senior management like Eaton, Lutz, and Castaing the chance to wring out the vehicles. The climb to the 5,000-foot summit of the twisty Yarnell grade was a route much favored and offered an excellent measure of handling and power. The run was not without its hazards. The local police were well aware that auto companies used area roads and kept a lookout for strange vehicles being driven at unseemly speeds. Bud Liebler was nabbed for running 75 mph in a 45 mph zone, but was released with a warning by a cop more interested in the new NS than in writing tickets.

At the Bagdad turnaround, Lutz was effusive not only about the improved handling of the NSs — which he had once denounced as worse than an aged Buick — but also about his newly acquired C3 Cunningham coupe with a muscle-bound Chrysler V8. Lutz lived surrounded by motorcycles, helicopters, vintage race cars, and his latest toy, an ex–Warsaw Pact, Czech-built Aero L39 Albatross military jet trainer. He had retained a former Russian fighter pilot to teach him to fly it. Lutz grinned widely as Theodore noted that the short-wheelbase Dodge minivan with its 2.4-liter, 150 hp four-cylinder was indicating 115 mph on a level stretch in the Peeples Valley, confirming that the base engine offered excellent performance for the price.

Talk inevitably turned to comparisons with Ford's Windstar, the biggest roadblock to the NS's dominance. Theodore noted that the short-wheelbase NS was, according to the team's measurements, only 1 percent smaller in interior capacity than the Windstar. He commented that Ford was continuing to scramble to get a sliding left-side door in its product mix. Early newspaper and magazine stories, now beginning to appear in volume thanks to Kowaleski's ongoing series of "backgrounders," all celebrated the Chrysler option. This was apparently forcing some radical redesigning in Dearborn. "Now my spies tell me they've given up on a full left-side slider as too expensive and are going to a larger driver's door that will provide access to the rear seat. We rejected that setup almost from the start. People hate big, heavy, cumbersome doors, which is exactly what they'll get with that kind of compromise," Theodore said with a certain air of satisfaction.

The little convoy made its way back to Phoenix's Pointe Resort at Tapatico Cliffs, where the session would end with a debriefing, followed by cocktails and dinner. Eaton was generally enthusiastic, although he understood Theodore's continued concerns about poor headliner fit and with the paneling around the front door interior handles. There was still too much shake at the rear of the vehicle, and engine idle with the 2.4 liter was objectionably rough and noisy. Despite the headway that had been made, Theodore estimated that no less than 300 MITS issues remained. Most of them were minuscule details that would in the past have been ignored in the name of maintaining the schedule. But this time every effort would be made to correct them before volume production began to "ramp up" in early February. Sanders's $20 million-plus deficit remained a source of concern. Considering the magnitude of the project, it was considered small change. But team pride, if nothing else, demanded that the savings be found and the budget met to the penny. As the meeting adjourned, Bernie Swanson smiled broadly and said, "Hey, Frank, maybe we ought to take a run up Vulture Mine Road. Who knows, maybe with a little digging we can find your missing twenty million." Sanders smiled lamely and moved on.

Cocktails were served on a terrace overlooking the lights of downtown Phoenix. Still dressed in his casual khakis, Eaton slipped into his engineer's mode as he nursed a scotch and began to discuss the nuances of the NS's suspension. No one could recall in the recent history of the automobile business when the chairman of a major US car-maker was conversant with the arcana of suspensions. By tradition they were "numbers guys," "beanies," finance experts who left the nuts and bolts of the business to others. Company presidents like Lutz often had engineering backgrounds, but CEOs in the modern era, almost never. "To be frank," said Eaton, "if I had my druthers, I'd set up a minivan with the stock suspension but with a larger sway bar to add roll stiffness." Sway bars, roll stiffness, shock valving, spring rates, camber angles; all were familiar subjects to this former engineer, this unlikely car mogul, this quiet man who was leading Chrysler out of its dark age into what appeared to be a bright new future.

Later that evening, following dinner, Bob Lutz — the man conventional wisdom predicted would be Eaton's enemy and who had turned out to be his closest ally — took the NS out for a night drive to evaluate the improved headlights. He would pass them, yet another example of how the two men at the very pinnacle of the company were intensely interested in the *product* as opposed to the dollars generated by the product.

The December ride-and-drive was a bright spot. Then matters turned rapidly bleak for Chrysler. Lee Iacocca was back in the headlines as his short-lived marriage to Darrien ended in acrimony and lurid demands for alimony. An Ohio man announced that he was suing Chrysler and seat-maker Atoma for $40 million, claiming they infringed on his patent for an ingenious integrated child-seat the corporation had been using on its minivans and sedans since 1991. Chrysler's lawyers dismissed the claim as a "fiction of gigantic proportion." Still, there was the impression that once again a major corporation was beating up on a little guy.

But that promised to be a tempest in a teapot compared to a bombshell from the National Highway Traffic Safety Administration. In November they had announced they were investigating charges that the rear latches of the AS and T-115 minivans were failing in certain crash situations and spilling passengers out of the vehicle. The story had first risen up in March, when NHTSA had revealed that it had received reports of thirteen minivans being involved in crashes that had taken eight lives. Now, nine months later, the reported incidents had exploded to fifty-one crashes involving no less than seventy-four passengers being ejected through ruptured lift-gates. Twenty-five deaths were said to have resulted. Many of the accidents and several of the fatalities involved children, adding potential drama and poignancy to a story the press was sure to cover with relish.

This was potential catastrophe. All remembered the openly outrageous *60 Minutes* treatment of the Audi 5000 and the shibboleth of "unintended acceleration." Try as it might, the much-honored German automaker could not convince the press and public that the charge against it had been openly rigged and that an automobile engine overpowering the braking system in the situations described was an engineering impossibility. The company was nearly driven out of business in the United States during the ensuing hysteria and had still not fully recovered. The same had happened to Ford's subcompact Pinto, which had been cleared in several high-visibility court trials in the 1970s of having a flawed fuel tank design that incinerated passengers in certain crash situations. But consumers remembered the claim, not Ford's vindication. The most egregious violation of the public trust and the most vicious attack on the industry had come a year earlier when NBC's *Dateline* had been discovered by GM investigators to have rigged a pickup with blasting caps to "enhance" the chance of fire in a filmed side-impact sequence. The ruckus centered around a jury award of over $100 million given to the Georgia family of a young driver after he had been burned to death in a full-sized Chevrolet pickup. The award was made based on a contention that the GM side-mounted fuel tanks were unsafe, although they met all current government standards and were capable of passing even upcoming 1997 standards of being able to withstand side impacts of 33.5 mph. General Motors tests indicated that the pickups could absorb impact of 50-plus mph but it did no good. The safety lobby, led by the hysterical Center for Auto Safety (which had titled its so-called investigation "Campaign GM Firebomb"), Ralph Nader, and others, forced Transportation Secretary Frederic Peña to threaten a recall of all 9 million–plus GM C/K series pickups. This was despite the fact that over the twenty-one-year span that the vehicles had been on the road data indicated that only one *in 40,000* side-impact collisions with the vehicles involved a fatal fire.

General Motors, after threatening a vigorous legal battle, had settled the pickup issue with a token fine and avoided a costly recall. A large staff at NBC, including the head of its news department, had been fired following the *Dateline* scandal.

Chrysler executives were hardly naive enough to believe that their contention that their minivans were statistically among the safest vehicles on the road would call off the wolves. They were facing formidable foes in the government, within the safety lobby — which was heavily funded by the American Trial Lawyers Association — and within an essentially antibusiness, antiautomobile national media. It was understood that NHTSA and the Center for Auto Safety were aching for a fight. They needed an issue. Passionate, headline-grabbing issues like children being dumped into traffic by a failed minivan door were rare in an environment where auto safety was rapidly losing importance among public issues. Vehicle design was radically better. Restraint systems — seat belts, air bags, interior padding, etc. — were vastly improved, as were roads, tires, headlights, brakes, and suspensions. Better yet, drunk driving seemed to be on the decline. Auto deaths — including those inflicted on pedestrians, farm-implement drivers, and motorcyclists, had dipped below forty thousand per year, meaning that fewer than two people died in America per 100 million miles driven.

But if the latch situation was handled improperly, Chrysler could end up stereotyped as a typically arrogant mega-corporation with no regard for the welfare of its customers. "We know the vehicles are safe. Our families ride in them every day. But if one person is killed, especially a child, we have to treat it as a big deal," said Tom Edson.

He was right. It was a major deal, with NHTSA threatening a recall of the more than 4 million T-115 and AS minivans on the road for a retrofit of the rear lift-gate latch. Worse yet, that would open an avalanche of product liability suits from litigants lawyers had formed up. Several groups of aggrieved survivors had been organized to counter Chrysler's contention that their minivans were not only safer than most passenger cars but that many of the crash victims had fallen out because they had failed to wear their seat belts. Theodore was infuriated. He told the *Wall Street Journal* that "product liability lawyers are trying to create as much adverse publicity as possible to serve their own interests." While public cynicism about the money-grubbing motives of lawyers was on the rise, the vision of innocent children being flung onto the road through a door with a latch that had been specifically underdesigned to save money was potential dynamite. And the lawyers had such a case. They possessed a 1990 internal Chrysler memo from engineer H. G. Hook to then–platform team manager John Nemeth indicating that for tooling costs of $125,000 the corporation could have upgraded its lift-gate latch on the upcoming AS redesign to meet the federal side-door pressure standards of 2,000 to 2,500 pounds. There being no federal standards for lift-gates, the minivan door with a single latch and a designed pressure standard of 750 pounds was left in place. The corporation's justification centered on the contention that the minivan lift-gate was a cargo door not intended for passenger egress or exit. This made sense, although it was admitted that the NS was to be equipped with a double latch and much greater strength.

"I took a deep dive into the NHTSA data," said Theodore. "I knew that the minivan was among the five safest passenger vehicles on the road — statistically — and that our ejection rate for passengers was better than the competition. NHTSA took a swing. We swung back."

But the government was playing dirty pool. As Chrysler fed data to NHTSA, it was being leaked out the back door to various safety and legal advocacy groups. Included in the confidential material was the Hook memo and a series of videotapes that purported to show latch failure during barrier crashes conducted by the company. Theodore and others explained that the tapes meant nothing because in all cases shown the latches on the prototype machines were either *removed* or *taped* shut and were therefore unrelated to real-world performance. But the damage was done. The adversary groups had more than enough ammunition to make a passionate, seemingly altruistic case against Chrysler through an unthinking or latently sympathetic media.

A tragedy in early December worsened the situation for Chrysler. A family of six, including five children (all without seat belts) was killed in Broward County, Florida. Their minivan was hit broadside by, ironically, another Chrysler minivan, during a rainstorm. A Florida highway patrol investigator told the Associated Press that he believed the rear latch on the fatal vehicle failed under impact and hurled the rear seat riders out of the opening. Clearly, hundreds of product-liability class-action lawsuits could follow and, worse yet, the mark of Cain could be placed on a vehicle that had become an American icon and symbol of the American family. "It's like somebody discovered Barney was a child molester," groaned one platform team member.

The latch fiasco was the centerpiece of an avalanche of bad press that hectored the corporation during the Christmas holidays and threatened to blight plans for the NS introduction at the Detroit automobile show a few weeks hence. As the NS program turned the last corner before 1995's rollout, huge concerns arose. Rising interest rates, an expected decline in the market, and resulting profits in the first quarters of 1995; an aging boomer population who might not embrace minivans; the nagging issue of poor quality control; the specter of more and better competition; the apparent restlessness of Kirk Kerkorian and his potential for mischief, all preyed on the chairman and the president. Nineteen ninety-five would be a showdown year that would determine if the nearly $3 billion dice roll with the NS would pay off or go down in history as Chrysler's Edsel.

12

In the Trenches

THE GREAT unwashed, the quirky, querulous, unpredictable public, were at last to get their first look at the NS. It would come at home, in Detroit, at the North American International Automobile Show, which was to open on January 7, 1995. There the tire-kickers would poke through the small fleet of P-Zero and C-One prototypes that had been buffed and polished for initial public display. A vast area in the center of the main gallery of Cobo Hall, perched on the edge of the Detroit River in the shadow of downtown, had been reserved. It would be staged with the precision of a Broadway musical. A team of professional female models — veterans of the Detroit auto show circuit — had been scripted and rehearsed with spiels to hawk the various models of the NS, ranging from low-line Plymouths to pricey Town & Countrys. It would be standard auto show fare; brightly painted cars and flashy women planted on small stages, surrounded by the gaping vox populi, whose curiosity was to be at best sated in brief spurts amidst the din of microphones and music from nearby competing displays and the restless murmur of the milling throngs.

It would begin in earnest on Saturday, the opening day of the show, but the great exploding supernova of publicity was to come three days earlier, during a special press introduction designed solely to score with the network news shows and the morning chat sessions, and to be rebroadcast worldwide. The presentation was to be purely visual, a gimmicky bit of show-biz trickery that would, in a thirty-second sound bite, make its way into tens of millions of living rooms. It was the job of Tom Kowaleski and his public relations staff to devise a quick-hitting *moment* like the classic window-crash that had been employed so effectively with the Grand Cherokee a few months earlier in Paris. It had to be shocking, outrageous, and sufficiently simpleminded to attract the attention of local television station news directors and to persuade them to air a brief clip on their prime-time newscasts.

The game had been played a hundred times before by every automaker in the business. Cars had been introduced amidst clouds of fake smoke and fire, planted on mountaintops and on the decks of aircraft carriers, dropped from ceilings, run through walls and off cliffs, fired out of cannons, launched from airplanes, inflated in computer simulations like rubber life rafts, floated through outer space, hung on walls of museums and hustled by celebrities, haunted by wild animals and harangued by the best hucksters in the business, all in worshipful supplication at the altar of the great god Sound Bite. Some, like the assault through the window, had been widely successful; others — most of them, in fact — had been quickly forgotten or totally ignored.

Kowaleski and his twenty-person team were sufficiently anchored in reality to understand that a spectacular auto show launch would at best produce a short burst of publicity and in the long run would mean little to the success or failure of the NS. Still, the pride factor — the raw pleasure in upstaging the competition on home turf — offered special incentives. It was known that on the day before Ford was planning the introduction of its new Taurus and Sable sedans, while General Motors would debut the updated Chevrolet Cavalier and Pontiac Sunbird compacts as well as a flashy new Blazer sport-utility that was sure to butt heads in the marketplace with the Grand Cherokee.

As planning progressed, a mood of corporate angst descended on the public relations operatives. They had become intimately involved with the minivan over the past three years. Every interior feature, every subtle sweep of the bodywork, was ingrained in their consciousness. Now came the dread. Was the NS going to live up to expectations? Was it radical enough? Would the public understand the nuances of its multiple features? Was it too similar to Ford's Windstar styling? Were minivans passé, too nerdy in a 1990s world where boomers seemed to be threatening to desert the once-favored minivans in favor of the flashier sport-utilities now flooding the market?

To counter any potential erosions of interest or sales, it had been decided to give the minivan a major launch at the auto show — a spectacular party-crash that would produce a sensation within the invited press and generate the desired news clips on television. Such an effort would cost time and money and would expose the corporation — and the public relations staff — to ridicule if the show flopped. Kowaleski was aware of prior efforts within the industry that had been poorly produced and had been lampooned by the press. This must not happen to the minivan, especially when rumors were filtering in that Ford was planning a spectacular of some kind to preview their totally redesigned Taurus and Sable. The NS would have to arrive on the scene in such a way as to outshine Ford, if for no other reason than to take a bite out of a rival that was openly bragging that it planned to displace Chrysler as the number-one producer of minivans in the world. Ford was to be the target while, ironically, General Motors, still the largest and most powerful automaker in the world, was essentially ignored.

The message had to be transmitted that Chrysler was about to leapfrog the competition in the minivan market. The challenge was to develop a visual demonstration of a leapfrog — if such a thing was possible. "We wanted 'leapfrog' to gain life of its own," said Kowaleski. "After we developed the concept in early 1994, we worked to create a major photo opportunity, especially for the networks." To do so meant the creation of a stage set at the auto show that would rivet the audience as well as expand the theme for use — on a limited basis — at subsequent shows scheduled for Los Angeles, Chicago, Geneva, New York, Frankfurt, and Tokyo. Moreover, intracorporate rivalries had to be served. While the minivan platform team had maintained no particular loyalty to either the Dodge or Chrysler/Plymouth, the two divisions' sales and marketing groups offered a whole new set of complications. At the street level of the business — the trench warfare involved in the actual selling of automobiles — there was no love lost between the two organizations. The Dodge and Chrysler/Plymouth corporate operatives, not to mention their dealer organizations, operated in separate orbits. Each fought the other for sales. While Chrysler/Plymouth was considered the flagship division of the corporation, Dodge's Caravan minivan consistently outsold the Voyager and the Town & Country (and also, for no good reason, tended to outrank the others in various consumer surveys although the vehicles were built on the same assembly line with identical components). This rift had to addressed to insure that both egos and pocketbooks would not be damaged.

Because Cobo Hall had no space available for a special theatrical showing, it was decided that the square footage reserved for the Dodge exhibit would be converted for the minivan introduction. This meant that specially designed stagecraft would have to be dismantled and the normal Dodge display would have to be erected within the two days between the introduction and the opening of the auto show. The job of designing and building the "leapfrog" theatrics was given to Don Schmidt of the Corporate Merchandising Group, who in turn contracted with the Dearborn firm of Exhibition Productions, Inc. to build a special counterweighted lever that would literally "leapfrog" a Chrysler Town & Country minivan across the stage. Ross Roy, the venerable Detroit promotion and marketing firm that had worked with Chrysler for years on such ventures, was retained to create a stage setting that was to resemble a swamp — complete with frog sounds in the background — and a large video screen at stage right upon which a puppeteer dressed suspiciously like Kermit the Frog was to carry on a running dialogue with Eaton and Lutz during the show. Bob Abele, who had produced the Iacocca Las Vegas extravaganza, was once again assigned the task of creating a cohesive and compelling act. "We like Bob's sense of theater," said Kowaleski. "He's got a very 'Broadway-like' concept of show business, which is what we were looking for."

Ross Roy writers, working closely with the public relations staff, scripted a lengthy nursery rhyme, beginning with the traditional "Once upon a time, long ago and far away" prelude. It was designed as a litany of minivan features, in labored verse, to be read by Eaton and Lutz as they exchanged humorous asides with the crypto-Kermit. At the conclusion of the reading, a red NS Town & Country was to soar across the stage, to be joined by a Dodge and a Plymouth version driven into view by key members of the mini-van team.

Kowaleski sent out three thousand elaborately produced four-color "teaser invitations" to the introductions although the event was scheduled for the pre-opening "press day" at Cobo and anyone on the premises was invited. Seats for eight hundred were set up, with a spillover area planned for another eight hundred. He made a special effort to be sure that his "A-List" press members were on hand or fully apprised of the event. This included twenty-five to thirty key publications and financial people: the editors of the four major enthusiast monthlies, *Car and Driver, Road & Track, Automobile,* and *Motor Trend;* the so-called daily deadline people like the *Washington Post's* Warren Brown and the *Chicago Tribune's* Jim Mateja, as well as beat reporters from *USA Today,* the *Wall Street Journal,* and Detroit's two dailies; financial reporters from *Forbes, Fortune,* and *Business Week;* trade media writers from *Automotive News, Ward's Reports, Auto Industry News;* and key Wall Street analysts led by the widely respected Maryann Keller, Auto Pacific's Chris Cedegren, and Lehman Brothers' Joseph Phillipi.

But the key to a mass audience was television, and the event would be considered a failure unless it was carried on the three network news shows and newscasts around the world. To reach such a vast crowd, Kowaleski and the team bought time on two satellites to offer a live, worldwide feed. A pair of local television production houses developed a three-camera shoot (actually four cameras, including an on-board "frogcam" that recorded the minivan's "leap onto the stage"). "This was to be a photo opportunity, pure and simple," said Kowaleski. "TV people want a pretty picture. You've got to give them something that's visual, quick, and very much to the point. That was the intent of the 'leapfrog.' It's always a gamble. You either get it or you don't."

As luck would have it, Kowaleski was about to get more television coverage than he asked for. Also lurking in the background were the noted proponents of yellow journalism from *Inside Edition* who had been hectoring the corporation on the issue of the allegedly failed lift-gate latches. Most of the national media had stepped back from the story until firmer documentation could be established (recalling the debacle of the NBC's *Dateline* attempted assassination of GM's pickup trucks). But *Inside* was hanging on, airing Chrysler's own pirated videotape ostensibly showing the failed latch crash test accompanied by tearstained interviews with victims involved in minivan accidents. At the same time Ralph Hoar, the Arlington, Virginia, "safety consultant" who was among the first to identify the problem, continued to call for a major recall of all minivans dating back to those first produced in 1984.

In the midst of the auto show preparation, Chris Theodore had become totally distracted with the lift-gate issue. While his primary emphasis ought to have been directed to the start-up of volume production at St. Louis by the end of the month, his days were consumed gathering data to defend the minivan against what he believed to be an egregious injustice and a blatant misrepresentation of fact. The deeper he probed into the approximately twenty-five deaths connected to the rear latch opening, the more he became convinced the entire story was a tempest in a teapot. Not only did the data indicate that the four million–plus Chrysler minivans enjoyed a safety record above the industry average, but the majority of the fatalities involved *unbelted* passengers. Twenty-five deaths in four million vehicles was a microscopic percentage. Moreover, as an engineer he understood that no vehicle or any component thereof could be entirely crashproof. Surely, the lift-gate latch could rupture under extreme conditions, and surely its design could be improved upon (as it had been on the NS), but he was convinced that the government's eighteen-month study of the issue had been a witch-hunt and that no compelling evidence could be produced to justify a recall and a refitting of the latch. Theodore was ready for a fight.

But cooler heads were counseling a more prudent response. Bud Liebler, the corporate boss of public relations, advocated a discreet swallowing of pride and a quick settlement of the issue. He had been subjected to an ambush interview by *Inside Edition* at a private New York function and understood the potential for mischief. A lurid case could be made that Chrysler was stonewalling a problem that was killing babies — the most heinous of corporate crimes. Tabloid television was more than capable of making such a case, and he believed the best way to counter the potential slander was to announce a fix and "get on with it."

"We weren't General Motors dealing with a pickup truck driven by contractors and farmers," he said. "This is a family vehicle. While I knew that Eaton and Lutz could defend our position in all of the fifty-one accidents that were supposed to have involved latch failure, winning legally and in the court of public opinion are two different things entirely. Here we were, the industry leader in mini-vans, about to introduce a new model, sold in part for its safety features to American families, with this cloud hanging over us. The entire issue centered on pride. We believed we were right. Chris had the data to defend ourselves in court and against government recall, but do you defend the principle in a lingering legal battle that keeps the issue in front of the public or do you swallow your pride and move ahead? We knew we could afford the recall. Money wasn't the issue, but we were faced with research from our minivan customers that indicated confidence in the company and product. They seemed to be saying, 'Chrysler cares about us,' and a protracted public battle might put that level of confidence at risk."

If the rear-latch battle wasn't enough for him, Theodore was getting bad news from St. Louis. Les Wolfe and his team were reporting endless slowdowns that threatened to push the volume production even farther behind than the acknowledged five-week delay caused by the body jig problem. Nightmarish, niggling glitches were rising up. Some of the windshields being supplied by Chrysler's McGraw Glass division were being rejected because of waviness — a faint distortion that arose during the curing process of what was the largest, most complex piece of glass the division had yet produced. Added to the trouble was a squeak in the front doors, traceable to the bonding between the paint and door seal molding. Numerous patchwork fixes were being tried, including the insertion of a length of tape between the two surfaces, all of which infuriated Theodore. The problem had been known about for months, yet the attempted corrections had been compromises, as opposed to a major headlong assault that would have involved a significant redesign. "It's the goddam 99 percent syndrome again," he groused. "We should have fixed this months ago, but we kept pecking at it with compromises." (Volume production would actually begin with small strips of tape installed to prevent the squeaking until new molding material could be designed.)

But these were mere irritations compared to the potentially massive problem centered around the aluminum cross-member that formed the spine of the entire front suspension. This was Theodore's baby. He had advocated its use, despite its extra cost and complexity, based on its weight savings and its precise dimensions that made suspension alignment not only simpler but more exact during manufacture. The cracking problems encountered earlier had long since been corrected, but the outside supplier, CMI Precision Moldings, Inc., of Southfield, Michigan, was encountering major obstacles in reaching volume production at their Bristol, Indiana, factory. A well-respected firm privately owned by Michigan industrialist Ray Witt, CMI had taken to the complex task of molding and machining the 26-pound hunk of aluminum at the projected rate of 3,050 units per day (the ultimate target to supply St. Louis, Windsor, and Graz with sufficient inventory). Initially the production rate would be 1,150 a day for St. Louis, but based on information arriving from Bristol, that goal was simply unreachable in the short term.

It was hardly expected that the assembly line would be cranked up instantly to spit out vehicles at maximum volume. Following the start of V-One or volume production, seventy-five days would be consumed to "ramp up" to full capacity on the line. The time would be required to fine-tune the assembly process and the complex stream of parts being sourced from outside suppliers. But the casting problems in Indiana threatened the entire process and embodied a problem that could put the NS months behind schedule.

Bernie Swanson, whose suspension group was responsible for the part, had long since seen danger signals flying. While CMI was experienced in aluminum molding for the automobile industry, the cross-member was to be the largest and most complex piece they had ever tackled — and the largest ever intended for volume automotive production. CMI's Bristol operation normally employed about 170 workers, but the Chrysler contract required an expansion of the facility and increasing the workforce to 500 hourly workers. The process involved the molding and machining of the aluminum through a series of automated stages. The aluminum ingots, weighing 85 pounds, were cast on circular "dial machines" resembling giant lazy susans, then were plucked off by robotic arms and transported by a conveyor system through a complex sequence of curing, a 14-hour heat-treating process, and precision trimming operations that would slice nearly 60 pounds of waste (recyclable aluminum) off the part before it was finished and shipped. Much of the CMI equipment, including the conveyors and an immense trimming machine intended to make the initial slice of slag from the molded part, was built by a so-called third-tier supplier, this created the potential for a fatal weak link in the industrial food chain.

The big trimming machine was designed and built by a tiny shop in Toledo — a father-and-son operation with a workforce of sixteen. The immense device — the first of two scheduled for Bristol — was to be delivered and set up by October, but word reached the platform team that a delay at least until Christmas was a probability. This generated a flurry of legal jousting between CMI and their supplier, while Theodore and Swanson fretted. Suddenly the entire production schedule for St. Louis was threatened. Without the trimming machine from Toledo, the cross-member could not be fabricated, which would neutralize the entire NS program.

"This is the weakness of the system wherein you depend on outside suppliers, especially second- and third-tier operations," lamented Swanson. "In the automobile industry we build mules, prototypes, and pre-production units that go through endless testing cycles. But with a lot of suppliers — especially the small ones — it's strictly 'eyeballing it in.' They don't have the time or the money to do a proper job of design and development, so they sometimes rush into a job. And when you become totally dependent on a single supplier, as we did with CMI, who in turn is relying on sixteen guys in Toledo, everything is a risk."

In theory Chrysler's policy of employing outside suppliers for 70 percent of its parts made sense. Enormous savings were realized by having first-tier companies design, develop, and manufacture the pieces, but what was often forgotten was that the first-tier operations in turn depended on tiny facilities that could affect both volume and high quality.

As CMI began its start-up, dozens of other glitches appeared. Not only was the big trimming machine malfunctioning, but the robots lifting the still-hot ingots out of the lazy susan molds were sometimes damaging the pieces. The conveyor belts were not working properly and some of the precise final drilling, trimming, and machining systems were flawed. A crisis was building in Indiana, and a team of engineers led by Swanson was dispatched. This could be a career-breaker for Theodore. By being a firm advocate of the big aluminum cross-member as opposed to a more conventional steel fabrication, he was pushing the envelope. The aluminum design was clearly superior, *if* it could be produced in volume. CMI's engineers assured him that the problems would be solved, but as the turmoil of the Detroit auto show unfolded around him, the confusion at Bristol was escalating, not subsiding.

The St. Louis assembly line was fitfully burping out C-One preproduction vehicles to a point where Tom Persons and three of his staff were able to drive the four minivans intended for the auto show to Detroit. Happily, they made the trip without incident. The other display vehicles were regussied prototypes fitted with production interiors and trim. To the general public they appeared exactly like the minivans that would arrive in showrooms three months hence — provided the St. Louis and Bristol production delays could be solved.

The televised "leapfrog" introduction was scheduled for 1:30 P.M. on Wednesday, January 4. Kowaleski had reasoned that a session immediately following lunch would create a "buzz" among the throngs of journalists in attendance. The Ford introduction of the Taurus and Sable had been well received, if a bit conventional with its standard fare of fake smoke and strobe lights, but Kowaleski was gambling that the flying minivan would produce his desired "photo op" and successfully upstage the competition. The crowd of fifteen hundred journalists, a large number of them European, jammed the Dodge area as Eaton and Lutz, dressed, "daddy"-like, in vee-necked sweaters, sat on stage and began their reading. A few asides, inserted by the public relations crew into the Ross Roy rhyming, joked about how the ever-vigilant Jim Dunne had failed to snap a spy photo of the NS, giving an insider's spin to the verses. As the text ended, the canned music rose to a crescendo, the lights dimmed and the Town & Country swooped, albeit jerkily, across the stage and landed with a small, realistic splash. The crowd clapped as two more minivans hustled on stage. The journalists surged forward for interviews and a closer examination of the three vehicles. It had worked. The network news shows aired the leap, the dailies covered the minivan story in depth, and research indicated that the worldwide satellite feed had created 125 million "impressions." Within hours after the introduction, work crews were dismantling Don Schmidt's complex launching system and erecting the Dodge display that had to be in place by the time the black-tie charity event formally opened the show the following Friday evening.

In a business where fame, or even simple notoriety, can be measured in hours, if not minutes, the minivan launch was deemed a major success. If the "leapfrog" gimmick was being sneered at by some of the more cynical journalists as cornball, the vehicles it showcased were not. The NSs were being universally well received, not only by writers seeing them for the first time, but by veteran members of the press who had been privy to their development through the series of "backgrounders" the public relations staff had been organizing for over a year. The following afternoon, when Cobo Hall was quiet, save for the work crews finishing up the displays and the various teams of models and announcers rehearsing their spiels, Bob Eaton was seen touring the vast building, examining the wares of the competition. He was alone. No retinue of public relations spokesmen, marketing types, vice presidents, or bodyguards that often attend corporate princes in public, but alone. An interested automobile man quietly scouting his rivals. Spotting someone he knew, Eaton approached with a broad smile. "Isn't this great?" he effused. "A European journalist just came up to me and said, 'Based on what's going on here, one would think Chrysler is the largest automobile company in the world!'"

His solo tour seemed a perfect example of not only his management style, but of the generally open atmosphere he had created within the corporation. It was in part attributable to the recent sales successes and the confidence they had generated. But the ambience was different than at, say, General Motors and Ford, where decades of profit and domination of the marketplace had produced only paranoia and defensiveness. Perhaps it was Chrysler's smaller size, or its incessant brushes with bankruptcy, but there was no question that the new culture, led by Eaton and Lutz, had generated an attitude of accessibility and quiet confidence unique to Detroit.

The following evening, during the charity party that opened the auto show for the industry royalty and their couriers, Eaton was scheduled to do a twenty-minute live interview with Larry King, who had brought his CNN talk show to Detroit. It was initially planned that Eaton would participate in a one-hour roundtable with GM boss Jack Smith and Ford chief Alex Trotman. This idea was accepted by Eaton and Smith, but became bogged down within the byzantine politics at Ford, where Trotman's handlers rejected the plan. The three men could not appear together, said the Ford men. Trotman would speak to King one-on-one, but not in the presence of Eaton and Smith. "This is a classic example of the protectionism that pervades the industry," mused one senior Chrysler manager. "Here's Trotman afraid to appear on Larry King — who throws foozballs, for God's sake! You have to wonder, what are they afraid of?"

If there was anyone to fear in the media, it was hardly King or for that matter the legions of journalists who generally covered the automobile beat. To be sure, some were hopelessly unqualified and manifestly ignorant of the business. The automotive press corps included a former fashion editor of a woman's magazine, while one top financial journal had a female who, according to Bud Liebler, "wouldn't know an automobile if it ran over her." A major nationwide daily had a staffer assigned to the car beat who had come from a small midwestern paper with no automotive experience. He had become notorious throughout the industry as both ignorant and arrogant — a buffoon who had to be treated with deference, not only because of his printed observations — generally involving a fussiness about cup-holders — but for his atrocious driving skills. But these individuals were minor distractions compared to the mischief that could be caused by the television tabloids who perpetually poked through the detritus of society seeking sensation and sleaze. *Inside Edition* was back in town, cameras rolling in search of more "news" about the minivan latches. The producers requested an interview, and after considerable internal discussion, Kowaleski relented, with the proviso that the corporation provide a background session to explain its case. This had been scheduled three weeks prior to the planned interview with Dale Dawkins, the Chrysler chief of safety research.

The producers accepted the plan and appeared for an intense two-hour briefing on the latch issue. They departed with Kowaleski, believing a logical explanation had been provided that justified the corporate position of nonculpability. "We were naive," he would later lament. The taping crew, led by on-camera interviewer Steve Wilson, appeared on Friday afternoon as planned and was led to a fourth-floor conference room at CTC for the Dawkins interview. As was the case with all such sessions, Chrysler appeared with its own cameraman and a lawyer to keep things honest.

"I should have known this was guerrilla television when I noticed the two *Inside Edition* cameramen were working off battery power," recalled Kowaleski. "That gave them total mobility, meaning they could chase us all over the building if we let them. When Wilson started his interview with Dawkins, all our background information, all our safety data, all our statistics, went out the window. Poor Dale was trying to field questions about dead babies while Wilson bored in for the kill." The whole thing was suddenly out of control. Kowaleski put his hand over the camera and left the room seeking a security guard to have Wilson and his crew escorted out of the building.

Wilson and one of the cameramen rushed after him, elbowing their way down a narrow hall as the interview descended into chaos. Terri Hautman, an associate of Kowaleski's on the public relations staff, followed along with the company cameraman. Suddenly in the jumble of bodies, a phone pager and a box of 3/4-inch videotape tumbled to the floor. As Hautman bent to pick them up, Wilson and his cameraman wheeled on her and snatched at the box of tape. "How low can you stoop?" he screamed on camera, "That's *our* tape!" The implication was clear — and a brilliant piece of attack television. Wilson was apparently attempting to create the impression that Hautman was pirating a valuable — and by inference, incriminating — *Inside Edition* tape. He began wrestling with Hautman, a petite blonde, as the camera rolled. She angrily resisted him until the brief mismatch ceased. At that point tempers cooled and Wilson apologized. Threatened with legal action by Chrysler, the encounter was never aired by the producers, although an artfully edited interview with Dawkins, including Kowaleski's hand blinding the camera, was broadcast repeatedly — each time eroding any Chrysler claim of innocence. The issue was to percolate within Highland Park for another two months.

They came by the thousands to the black-tie opening of the show as a blanket of wet snow pelted the city. Elegantly coifed women glided among the shimmering automobiles in company with what appeared to be attendees at the world's largest maître d' convention. (It was claimed to be the largest — nearly 15,000 guests — black-tie affair in the nation.) The Chrysler and Dodge exhibits were jammed as senior members of the platform team sipped champagne and basked in the glow of their labors. On a nearby platform rotated a glistening golden show car called the Atlantic, a retro-styled coupe done by Tom Gale and the design studio that called forth the glamour and panache of such 1930s machines as the Bugatti Type 57 coupe and a sensuous Talbot Lago grand tourer. Thanks to the Atlantic and the adjacent minivans, Chrysler Corporation did indeed seem to be the largest automobile company on earth. At least for that glittering moment in Detroit.

13

Return of the Mogul

IN THE WARM afterglow of the Detroit show, Chrysler — at least publicly — seemed to be enjoying a winning streak. The minivan had indeed "leapfrogged" into the living rooms of America. CARMA International (Computer Aided Research and Media Analysis) reported that among 116 stories appearing in 63 major media outlets including 100-market newspapers, news weeklies, television reports, and financial publications, 91 percent of the reports on the minivan were favorable. Only 3 percent were judged to be negative, and a number of those were simple slights, as opposed to overt criticism. The frog act had worked, at least in terms of grabbing attention at the show, but a vast chasm stood between accolades from the press and planting half a million new NSs in America's driveways.

In St. Louis the start-up of production was sluggish at best. The nearby Holiday Inn remained packed with team members, who shuttled into town in search of solutions to thousands of problems, large and small. The few minivans that were dribbling off the line at the rate of 100 to 200 a day were excellent examples. The inspection demerits issued for production flaws averaged below forty, which might have been a vast improvement over the old standard one hundred, which often served as an acceptable benchmark for Chrysler's K-car offerings, but it was still far too high for Chris Theodore's goals. The patchwork addition of a polyurethane strip to the door frames in order to cure a persistent squeak was hardly Theodore's idea of high quality, nor was the bottleneck at CMI's Bristol, Indiana, plant, where the aluminum cross-member was still far from perfect. In desperation, Theodore sent Bernie Swanson and a team of engineers to the plant on a permanent assignment until the problems could be solved. Swanson found a rat's nest of trouble. Not only was CMI grappling with capacity demands far beyond anything it had attempted before, but rapid expansion had forced the management to employ many Asian and Hispanic workers who couldn't speak English. "The guys were good workers," recalled Swanson, "but here we were trying to explain how to mold and trim and machine a high-tech piece of aluminum with hand signals!"

As Swanson and others battled the slow ramp-up toward full-volume production — which now might be months away — they could not ignore the bright news spilling forth from their cross-town rivals at Ford. Their new Taurus, daringly styled, was about to go into full production at the company's vast assembly plant in suburban Atlanta. Ford officials bragged — justifiably — that the transition from building old Tauruses to new would be accomplished without a break in production. Not one hour of assembly time would be lost in the changeover. This feat had been accomplished by the Japanese on repeated occasions, but the Taurus would mark a first for the American industry and would contrast vividly with the fitful start-up in St. Louis.

Beyond the erratic production volumes lurked the issue of the rear lift-gate latch. Pressure was building from the bureaucrats at NHTSA to force a total recall of all 4 million T-115s and ASs that had been produced. A wrestling match was developing between the corporation and the government, with a mass of litigants poised to leap into the fray. Chrysler appeared to be girding for battle. In documents prepared for NHTSA by Theodore and the corporate legal staff, Chrysler maintained that the government lacked legal grounds and therefore could not ask Chrysler to "voluntarily" make the recall — as demanded by a group of consumer groups. Suzanne Clark of Winston Salem, North Carolina, the founder of an organization called Chrysler Van Owners Concerned About Latches, was meeting with William Boehly, NHTSA's assistant administrator of enforcement, and openly calling for an instant recall.

During a half-dozen Washington meetings with Boehly and his staff, Theodore contended that the government was using flawed data, especially in terms of comparing the Chrysler minivans only to other minivans. All station wagons and hatchback sedans that employed rear lift-gates and were theoretically as prone to accidental opening in crashes ought to be included. He also maintained that the special crash test conducted by the government was rigged to cause the rear latch on the subject AS to fail, which skewed the results in favor of complainants.

As angry and truculent as the corporation appeared in public, the tone inside Highland Park's executive suite was more conciliatory. Bud Liebler understood too well the power of the press and the so-called consumer advocates. The scuffle with *Inside Edtion* was only the opening volley in a dispute that was sure to dominate the headlines for months to come and to blur the impact of the NS. The entire issue was beginning to spin out of control. Ralph Hoar, the Virginia "safety consultant" who was leading the attack in the latch battle, was charging that Chrysler had instigated a "secret recall," wherein some owners of AS-model minivans were having their lift-gate latches repaired if they made a formal complaint. The corporation denied the claim (with good reason — there was no secret recall), but Hoar's accusation only amplified the suspicion that the corporation was trying to hide the flaw.

Ironically, the lift-gate story was having little impact on minivan sales or warranty claims. Chrysler dealers around the nation reported minimal feedback from consumers. District and zone service representatives were receiving but a handful of requests to change the lift-gate latches. Still, Liebler and other veterans of public relations wars believed it was time to cut losses and yank the story out of the headlines by negotiating a "voluntary recall" with the government. Chrysler could thereby avoid the implied censure of a mandated government recall, which would mean that every existing 1984–1995 minivan might have to be repaired. The voluntary alternative would permit the corporation to fix the latches for any minivan owner who sought the repair. Those who counseled this settlement reminded the hard-liners about the Alliance and

Encore debacle that still cursed the corporation. Following the purchase of American Motors, Chrysler had been forced to continue
the tedious recall of two notably mediocre sedans produced by
AMC in the early 1980s. Both the Alliance and the Encore were Renault designs, with large quantities of French-built components.
Among them was a heater core that tended to leak, first steaming
the windshield and then pouring boiling water on the feet of front
seat passengers. According to the Department of Transportation recall order number 541, every one of the 120,000-odd Alliances and
Encores sold in the United States had to be repaired. Chrysler
opted to fit each with a new heater box. As the argument over the
latches dragged on in Detroit, nearly one hundred men scattered
along the corporation's twenty-five zones were still assigned to
changing the Renault heater cores, although the vehicles had been
off the market for *ten years*. The corporate mandate was explicit:
Locate every Encore or Alliance and fit it with a replacement core.
Chrysler men were poring through motor vehicle records, scouring
junkyards, and touring back country roads in search of the cars. If,
for example, one was found in a scrap yard, ready for the crusher,
the rules were the same: Remove the old core and leave a $120 re-
placement on the seat! If the Alliance or Encore was located in a
farmer's field, its wheels off and rusting into dust, a flatbed trailer
was brought to the scene and the wreck was dragged to a Chrysler
dealership where the heater core change was made. The vehicle
was then returned to its final resting place while the baffled owner
was given $150 for his trouble. This example of insane overregula-
tion had cost millions of dollars and uncounted man-hours. No one
had any idea how long the rest of the search would take. Many of
the little French nightmares had simply disappeared. Most wreck-
ing yards kept no record of the vehicles they scrapped. Hundreds of
lost cars were rotting away in rural woodlots or in city garages and
would never be located. Only a tiny percentage of the vehicles were
still registered and being driven. But the search went on in a weird
dance among the red tape.

    If, argued the peacemakers, a decade or more was required to
locate 120,000 Alliances and Encores, how long and how much
money would it take to find 3.9 million Caravans, Voyagers, and

Town & Countrys? How many millions — even billions — would be consumed in the search if NHTSA demanded that every van ever built be fitted with a new latch?

Theodore, Eaton, and Lutz still resisted what they considered to be capitulation in a winnable battle. After all, they argued, their data confirmed that at least sixty-three other car, van, and sport-utility models currently on American highways had worse safety records than the minivan — among them Ford's rival Aerostar. Any compromise would be an admission of culpability and might open the floodgates to hundreds of lawsuits. But others argued that the gamble was too great; that if Boehly and his NHTSA cohorts decided to mandate a formal recall, the minivan's reputation would be permanently damaged and the costs would multiply a hundred-fold. Moreover, Liebler had word that ABC's high-rated, prime-time news show *20/20* was preparing a segment on the lift-gate issue. This was potential dynamite. The assaults from the syndi-cated sensationalists at *Inside Edition* were mere pinpricks com-pared to the big guns being loaded at ABC. Liebler understood that it was exposure on *60 Minutes* that murdered the Audi 5000, and that the same level of damage could be inflicted by a biased report on *20/20*. An interview with a tearstained mother who had acci-dentally killed her little boy under the wheels of her Audi 5000 had been devastating — if manifestly distorted — television, and Liebler knew full well that similar heart-wrenching tales could be dredged up from among the minivan crash victims. It was time to fly the white flag.

As the struggle over the lift-gate issue bounced around the Highland Park executive suite, Tom Kowaleski and his public rela-tions team were putting the finishing touches to an elaborate "long-lead preview" for the NS. These events were standard fare in the industry: a two- or three-day outing at some scenic location where selected members of the press and the financial community would be given the opportunity to drive production versions of the auto-mobile. Because the deadlines of monthly magazines differed from those of newspapers and weeklies, an embargo was normally set whereby everybody would have an equal chance to break the story during late April and early May.

The plan involved a major, double-header public relations dog-and-pony act. It took place over a hectic one-week span, February 21–28, and involved nearly two hundred journalists, divided into four groups. The venues were the spectacular Napa Valley and the dizzying scenery of Big Sur. The trip was organized so that a pair of new products — the repowered JA Stratus and the NS minivan — could be introduced in tandem. Airfares and all expenses were paid to those whose publications permitted such largess. (Many major newspapers forbade their employees from accepting such freebies in the name of editorial independence. Other magazines accepted such corporate hospitality but did not hesitate to criticize their hosts and their products once they returned home.)

The attendees flew to San Francisco, where they gathered at a nearby Hyatt Regency and drove a fleet of Dodge Stratus sedans fitted with new 16-valve 2-liter and 2.4-liter engines northward to the elegant Auberge du Soleil hotel in Sonoma. Following a dinner and press briefing, the journalists (and spouse or other guest) spent the night on Chrysler's tab before driving to Sears Point Raceway for some handling demonstrations. Following a carefully planned format, including detailed route instructions (and even a prepaid ticket for the Golden Gate Bridge), the group drove back to the Hyatt for another briefing dealing with the NS minivans. That led to an afternoon drive in a gaggle of thirty-one PVPs and ten C-Ones southward through Monterey to the lavish and stupefyingly expensive ($600 a day) Post Ranch at Big Sur. There, Chrysler hosted yet another dinner and cocktail party as well as breakfast the following morning. The day was spent with free-form driving that included a trip to the Hearst Castle, sixty miles south along the spectacular Coast Highway.

Kowaleski and his crew had organized dozens of such long-leads. Many had involved gimmick road rallys, racetrack handling tests, celebrity guests, and other diversions. But this time the NS was to be the star. No added entertainments were needed. After a full day of driving and sightseeing, the journalists returned with overwhelmingly favorable impressions. But Kowaleski also knew the proof would come in print. Comments to the host over cocktails might be deceivingly polite and positive. Final judgment would have to wait until the gathered throng made their good-byes and sat down at their word processors and typewriters. Only then would he know if the NS had passed muster. Only then would he know if the nearly $500,000 spent on the long-lead would produce real value.

At the same time, Lee Iacocca kept blundering into the head-lines thanks to his nasty divorce battle with third wife Darrien Earle Iacocca. The pair were sparring over support payments, which the former Mrs. Iacocca claimed should total $25,000 a month plus $175,000 a year for upkeep of their Bel Air, California, home. Also demanded: $100,000 for her lawyer, and $3,200 a month for her mortgage payments on a California home she had owned prior to the marriage. She argued that an earlier agreement for a piddling $10,000 a month had been made under coercion while her brain was addled on Prozac and Halcion. The gossip columnists and tabloids were having a romp with the story, joy-ously quoting Darrien as sneering, "The only time I saw Lee happy was when his Chrysler stock was at sixty. We thought he was on Prozac." Iacocca countered by charging her with calling up his sec-ond wife, Peggy, to determine his weak points in their divorce ne-gotiations. He also grumped that Darrien was renting out their Aspen ski lodge and pocketing the fees. The entire affair had de-scended into a street fight between a pair of rich, spoiled ex-mates while the public stood by in amused witness. But to the old friends of Iacocca at Chrysler, it seemed as if the chairman was losing the last vestige of his dignity. Sadly, it was just the beginning.

With the CMI situation still critical, production at St. Louis con-tinued to be sporadic at best. Some of the minivans being manu-factured were being allotted to Chrysler's rental car companies in Florida, where consumers would get a first peek at the products while serving as the most unforgiving and creative car-wreckers in the world. Millions of miles of proving ground miles in the hands of professionals wouldn't reveal flaws that normal civilians could dis-cover in a matter of hours. Other NSs were being employed as training vehicles in the various zones and districts around the na-tion. Dealership technicians were getting hands-on exposure to the mechanical nuances of the new machine. In April, a series of formal dealer previews would be held in major cities. There, the corporation's 4,500-odd dealers would be given the full technical and marketing background on the vehicles.

By mid-March, Liebler and the advocates of compromise on the latch issue won their case. Eaton, Lutz, and others conceded that a protracted battle over the question would further harm the introduction of the NS and potentially cost the company uncounted millions in legal damages and in damage to its fragile reputation for quality. A pivotal reason for their change of position was the indication that the latches were an apparent nonissue with minivan owners. An 800 hotline (1-800-MINIVAN) had been created to take customer calls regarding the problem, and the response was amazing. Ninety-eight percent of the customers were indicating they were perfectly satisfied with their vans and expressed little or no concern about the potentially flawed latches. The same intelligence was filtering in from zone and district service representatives — men and women who were on the front lines whenever a warranty problem arose. If this was the case, the corporation might ease out of the situation with minimal financial outlay and little or no damage to its image.

A deal was finalized with Boehly and his NHTSA operatives that permitted a "voluntary recall" without penalty or sanctions, thereby avoiding any implication of federal penalty or culpability. The deal was simple: Any owner of a 1984 to 1989 T-115 model could drive to his or her dealership and get a stronger modified liftgate latch installed free of charge. Owners of 1990 to 1994 AS models would receive the same deal, except that their vehicles would be fitted with the newer, stronger NS latch system. If the owners of every one of the entire 3.9 million minivans that had been built responded (an impossibility, because perhaps half the vehicles had long since been wrecked, scrapped, or were out of service), the campaign might have cost billions. But based on the measurements of public concern over the hotline and through dealer sources, it appeared that no more than 100,000 to 200,000 owners might request the change. With the total cost — the part and labor — estimated to be about $20–$40 (depending on whether it was a manual or power release), it appeared that Chrysler could escape the issue for figuratively nickels and dimes — including an advertising and communication campaign to notify all owners of the offer.

The details would have to be worked out with the dealers, who generally received a 40 percent markup on all warranty parts. It was known that some dealers would eagerly partici- pate in the change, which was scheduled to begin in the fall. Some were planning giant tent-sales, wherein owners would be invited in for a Jiffy-Lube-like quick change. While their latch was being replaced, they would be fed and entertained and pitched with new Chrysler products. Other dealers complained about the extra work and demanded up-front compensation. As usual, the dealers were operating as diffuse, recalcitrant, and un- predictable independent representatives in the field. But the broad-brush policy had been set and the major issue of a costly and embarrassing recall had been defused, at least in the short term.

The deal was announced on March 27, gaining banner headline coverage in *USA Today* and other major dailies. Liebler was the point man, quoted repeatedly as maintaining that no data sup- ported any contention that the minivans were uniquely unsafe or worthy of government action. He also added, "But it does no good for owners if Chrysler complains about unfairness, questionable sources, accuracy of data."

To the general public, the issue appeared dead. But safety advo- cates like Ralph Hoar valiantly tried to keep the controversy alive. "Neither Chrysler or NHTSA is providing adequate warning to parents of the risk they expose their children to until these latches are upgraded," he warned — choosing to conveniently ignore two realities: one, that most state laws require all children either to be in car seats or to be belted nowhere near the lift-gate; and second, that the lift-gate was not designed for use as a door. Boehly was also not prepared to let go. He was to demand that all half-million 1995 AS minivans be included in the recall and finally, a month later, to require upgrading the solenoid on the power-remote re- placement latch to prevent an accidental opening by pressing a switch on the instrument panel. Boehly also noted that NHTSA would continue to monitor the issue and grumbled to *USA Today*, "We weren't going away."

This was hardly an idle threat. Chrysler was not walking away from the issue unscathed. Boehly's implication was clear: The corporation was under the gun to repair a sufficient number of latches on its own (an unstated total) or face the threat of a mandated recall. The lack of consumer response was more a problem than initially realized. The very lack of concern by minivan owners implied they might ignore the recall notices, imperiling the "voluntary agreement." "If they don't show up at the dealers, we're in trouble," said Theodore. That could mean a mandate of the Alliance/Encore magnitude that could potentially flatten the corporation's profits for years to come. How an essentially contented consumer body could be attracted to the dealerships remained a mystery.

As the headlines decreased in size, it was learned that ABC was canceling its *20/20* segment and that various consumer groups were retreating on their threats of massive class-action lawsuits. But Liebler understood full well that image repair was an endless challenge. On the same day that the latch repair issue made the news, *Consumer Reports*, the nannyish but widely respected product-evaluation monthly, placed its annual automobile test issue on the newsstands. Chrysler took a major hit. The editors denounced the entire product line as offering worse-than-average reliability and singled out the wildly successful new Ram pickup and the Jeep Wrangler as having the worst quality within their market segment. General Motors was also slammed, while Ford was praised for maintaining the best quality among the domestics, although still well behind the best of the Japanese like Toyota and Honda. This, coupled with the magazine's earlier removal of the LH sedans from its recommended list, was disastrous news. Tom Kowaleski fought back by trying to explain that the data came from 1993/94 models and that most of the problems had been solved. "The overall quality is high and reliability should be judged by the car starting every morning," he gamely told *Automotive News*. To be sure, the data *Consumer Reports* used was based on older models, but the result was current and instantly damaging. The public relations staff worked hard to counter the news by trumpeting the fact that the NS would be sold at the same prices as the current AS — and be generally cheaper than comparable Windstars. They also butted heads with Ford over which van had the most cargo capacity. During the Detroit show, Chrysler had bragged that the NS had more room than the Windstar and had openly mused about the Ford product's inability to carry a 4x8 sheet of plywood. Ford was furious. Mary Ellen Heyde, a Ford minivan executive, complained that Chrysler was employing an outdated SAE (Society of Automotive Engineers) standard for determining interior space and that her Windstar was in fact roomier. Chrysler countered by announcing that the short-wheelbase NS had nearly as much interior room as the longer Windstar, and that the long-wheelbase NS had 18 percent more cargo space. Ford argued the difference was no more than 5 percent. The entire dispute raged within the industry and meant little to the public, but Chrysler kept hammering at the fact that the Windstar did not have room for the plywood sheet and was not equipped with five mph bumpers. Finally Ford let the issue drop. Later magazine tests with normal bundles of luggage — odd-sized bags, strollers, coolers, etc. — would prove that the NS did in fact have larger capacity.

As Liebler and company readied themselves for a March trip to New York and a series of speeches by Eaton and Lutz at the annual New York Automobile Show scheduled for the Javits Center, he believed that the latch issue was for all intents and purposes under control, at least for the short term. He was prepared to field questions about the *Consumer Reports* bombshell and about the production delays. Liebler already had learned that the first quarter sales and financial reports, due in a few days, were not good. A slump was in the offing and surely the press would want to know why profits had dropped 37 percent during the first quarter of 1995. The final quarter of 1994 had generated earnings of $938 million, or $2.55 per share. The opening three months of 1995 would see that total drop to $538 million and per share profits dip to $1.55. Controller Jim Donlon was preparing a statement that would predict the trend to continue, with reduced earnings for the second quarter as well, due to a decline in domestic car sales and the slow ramp-up of minivan production. Donlon would cite other factors in the decline besides a sagging market. They included a $100 million tax write-off to launch the NS; a generous $115 million write-off to make the latch repairs; an estimated 4 percent jump in the prices of plastic, rubber, steel, and aluminum, and an overstock of low-line, low-profit AS models that would dilute the market until the higher-priced NSs began to arrive in volume. Donlon was also prepared to predict that the rebate wars would accelerate in order to counter Ford's aggressive showroom tactics. Rebates and leases were already costing the corporation $590 per vehicle and were edging toward $750 — a number that would adversely affect the bottom line as Chrysler struggled to maintain its 15 percent share of the domestic market and a 2 percentage-point lead in minivan sales over a surging Ford.

Surely the issue of finance would surface, although as he and the executive staff boarded the corporate jets for the quick ride to La Guardia's executive terminal, Liebler had little idea that it and the other subjects of discussion would be swept away in a tide of ink and videotape as Kirk Kerkorian barged back into the boardroom.

The auto show was to start routinely. Eaton planned to give the keynote address to a breakfast meeting of the locally based International Motor Press Association in one of the Javits's giant conference rooms. After returning to the corporation's Waldorf Towers suite following a financial briefing with the leaders of Morgan Stanley, Eaton received a cryptic three-minute phone call from Kerkorian informing him that in the morning a formal statement would be issued claiming that his wholly-owned Tracinda Corporation was seeking to take over Chrysler. Eaton, who knew Kerkorian only "on a cordial basis" as the corporation's largest single stockholder, dazedly hung up the phone. "I was shocked," he would recall later. He had been informed by his office that a call from Kerkorian was expected, but the expectation of a takeover bid was never considered. Liebler's first indication of trouble came via a phone call during dinner later the same evening. It was from associate Steve Harris back in Detroit. He told him that Kerkorian was planning to issue a statement at nine o'clock Eastern Time the following morning regarding his plans for a hostile takeover.

Liebler had hardly discounted such a move, based on Kerkorian's grumbling about the stock dividend the previous autumn, but if Harris's call was right, it meant that precious little time remained to issue a response prior to Eaton's breakfast speech. For openers, his prepared text would have to be tossed away. Liebler convened with Eaton and speechwriter Mike Morrison and financial public affairs specialist Sam Messina at the Waldorf Towers suite early the following morning to await the Kerkorian statement. Eaton already knew the essential details of the takeover attempt but had to wait until 8:50 for formal confirmation. It was then that he received a call from Kerkorian's Las Vegas headquarters confirming the details. It was instantly decided that Eaton would return to Detroit with Morrison while Liebler would fill in at the IMPA breakfast — the first public utterance in the hottest big-business story to break in Detroit in decades.

As Eaton headed off to La Guardia, Liebler taxied to the Javits Center, where five hundred IMPA members and their guests were finishing up their eggs and coffee and settling in for what they expected to be an enthusiastic Eaton extolling the virtues of the new minivan planted on the stage behind him. As the introduction began for the absent chairman, Liebler was on the phone, awaiting a fax of the formal Kerkorian statement. Finally, at 9:20 A.M., the text spewed out of the machine and Liebler rushed to the podium.

Making quick apologies for his boss's absence, the corporate public relations chief — one of the most urbane and poised in the business — began reading the fax. "Here I was, in front of five hundred people, reading the Kerkorian document for the first time — a document that could determine the fate of Chrysler for years to come. My hands were shaking as I said, 'Until ten minutes ago, the minivan behind me was the most exciting thing in my corporate life.' Then I started to read the salient parts — a $20.8 billion offer for Chrysler stock at $55 a share, etc., etc. It wasn't until the third page that I saw Lee's name. I thought, *'Oh shit! he is involved!'* I was stunned. I'd been Iacocca's friend and his public relations man for five years. We'd traveled together, hung out together, laughed together, and fought corporate battles together. I considered him to be a great man, a corporate giant. But he had retired, left honorably, and now he was back, and I couldn't understand why."

Stunned by the enormity of the Kerkorian-Iacocca intrusion, Liebler read the statement and then left the stage without taking comments from the now-agitated press. "I got into a cab and rode around the city for twenty minutes to gather my thoughts. I just couldn't wing it on an issue this important." After speaking to Eaton again by phone Liebler returned to the press room and made a brief statement saying that Chrysler would issue a response later in the day following an emergency teleconference meeting of the board of directors. But, off the record, he knew full well what Bob Eaton would say publicly later in the day, "The company is not for sale."

The news exploded on Wall Street, sending Chrysler common stock soaring 9 1/2 points on the first day of trading. It closed at 48 3/4, after selling as high as 52 1/2 earlier in the session.

It was obvious that Iacocca's involvement was already paying big dividends. Not only did his name lend enormous headline value to the story, but there was little doubt that his inside contacts made him privy to Donlon's expected gloomy financial report. By announcing his bid twenty-four hours before Chrysler admitted to a 37 percent drop in quarterly earnings, Kerkorian's parlay gained enormous impact. But as the news swirled through the industry, the media, and the world financial markets, the endlessly repeated question was "Why?"

The obvious answer was Kerkorian's demands for higher return from a corporation he considered to be undervalued and poorly run. But why would a seventy-seven-year-old man estimated to be worth $2.7 billion launch into a debilitating, pressure-laden campaign to obtain Chrysler? Surely it was the heady warfare available only to those who play high-stakes financial games. When somebody posed the question to Chris Theodore, he mused, "Why would a guy with nearly three billion bucks want more at age seventy-seven? Hell, why would a guy at twenty-four want more than that? When you get to that point the numbers are meaningless." As for Iacocca, the motivations seemed obvious: Raw ego was his driving force.

At seventy years of age and out of the headlines and out of the business that had brought him riches and fame over the span of nearly half a century, Iacocca clearly missed the action. In an interview with the *Los Angeles Times* he said, "A lot of people can't understand why these two old guys would do it all. We don't need the money and so on. But Kirk likes these things. It helps keep him young." Surely Iacocca was speaking for himself as much as his partner.

The former chairman maintained repeatedly that he had no interest in running the company if their takeover bid succeeded. To some, that possessed the same level of logic as Adolf Hitler pleading that he invaded France only to obtain a lifetime pass to the Louvre. "Of course he wants to run things again," said a senior Chrysler official who knew Iacocca personally. "He got shoved out the door. He wanted to stay. He saw these new guys, Lutz, Eaton, Castaing, and Gale, getting all the credit. He hated that, especially Lutz, who he shot down to succeed him. You talk about greed and boredom. Throw in revenge as well."

As word of the takeover bid ricocheted through the platform team, the reaction was more disappointment than apprehension. Most of them understood that Eaton and Lutz wouldn't give way without a fight and it would be business as usual at least over the short term. But the presence of Iacocca puzzled them.

To many it seemed a betrayal. After all, they had stood with him during the dark days of the early 1980s. They had cheered his rallying cries, risen to his incantations about loyalty and devotion to duty. Now he was back, seemingly marching with the enemy. "Doesn't the old son-of-a-bitch ever know when to shut up?" growled a member of the platform team who had fought side-by-side with him. "He's like your drunken uncle who's always the last to leave a party," grumbled another. "Go home, Lido, and stay home." Greed and egomania seemed the obvious reason for his alliance with Kerkorian, but to others who knew him, the answer seemed more complex. "Think about this. Among his pals in Las Vegas and Los Angeles Lee Iacocca is a poor man," said one senior executive. "Sure, he's got millions, most of which are tied up in Chrysler stock. But compared to guys like Kerkorian and

Alan Paulson [the man who sold Chrysler Gulfstream and a former member of the board of directors] Lee's a piker. These guys count their millions by the hundreds and thousands. Lee wants to be a big guy, a real *player*, Vegas style. That's why he's in this game."

Some recalled that it was Iacocca who strengthened Chrysler's so-called poison-pill policy in 1990 — whereby stockholders could rebuff a hostile takeover by buying back stock at deep discounts. It was enacted to fend off an expected assault by his future pal Kirk Kerkorian. The "pill" would be activated when a takeover artist's share reached 15 percent and remained in place as a significant barrier to the pair's plans, although Iacocca's view of the policy had ironically reversed itself. So too, apparently, had his sentiments about corporate raiders. In his second bestselling book, *Talking Straight*, published in 1988, he lashed out at them as "schoolyard bullies" and "robber barons." He described a typical target as a "company with a solid asset base, low debt, consistent profits and a few bucks in the bank to help get through the next downturn. When I went to school we called that good management. Today we call it fair game." He could also call it "Chrysler." While denouncing greenmail as "blackmail in a pinstriped suit," he noted, "I won't do an unfriendly merger. That's a mindset of mine."

Following his terse initial statement claiming that the company was not for sale, Eaton convened the board in an emergency meeting and produced a lengthier and more defiant denouncement of the Kerkorian proposal. It was prepared with the knowledge that the raiders were trying their high-wire act without a net; that the financing of their bid was, as one senior Wall Street analyst said privately, "singly the most half-assed takeover attempt in the history of high finance." He had a point. Kerkorian and Iacocca appeared to lack one critical ingredient in their proposal: money. Their plan, as outlined by Tracinda employee and Kerkorian aide-de-camp Alex Yemenidjian, involved the use of $5 billion in investor equity (Kerkorian's 10 percent and about $50 million from Iacocca); another $5.5 billion in Chrysler cash reserves (the irony that Chrysler would use its own funds to buy itself out); and the acquisition of $12.3 billion from unnamed additional sources. The investment house of Bear Stearns was mentioned publicly as aligned with the pair to arrange the financing. Yemenidjian, who was acting as the spokesman for Kerkorian, insisted this was not a leveraged buyout and that the corporation would not be required to pledge assets in order to pay down debt. According to him, when the dust settled Chrysler would enjoy a strong financial condition. He also noted that the present management would stay in place and no layoffs were being considered.

While Kerkorian remained silent and elusive as the press headlined his bid as the largest corporate takeover attempt since the sensational battle by Kohlberg Kravis Roberts in their $25 billion blitzkrieg of RJR Nabisco in 1989, Iacocca leapt back into center stage. Operating from Tracinda's Las Vegas headquarters, and from his estate at Indian Wells, California, he gave repeated telephone interviews, including one to *USA Today*'s Micheline Maynard in which he took direct aim at Bob Eaton. "I hired him to do quality improvements; he's addressing it although more slowly than he could have. He'd be the guy to have to prove he can do it. If he doesn't do that, he will not fulfill why he was hired. So now you're on the spot, Bob. You'd better get on with it and get your act together. Ford is improving and so is GM. The track is fast."

It was classic Iacocca. Tough, terse, quotable. He went on to tell Maynard that he wouldn't think of removing Eaton from the chairmanship and that he had no plans to involve himself in direct management, but added, "Of course if they got in a jam I'd be there in twenty minutes." A Chrysler man, reading this, joked, "Yeah, and if Lee gets involved, we'll be in a jam in twenty minutes!"

Liebler was now in the uncomfortable position of rebutting his old boss. He responded icily to the slam against Eaton by saying, "We're shocked and disappointed that Mr. Iacocca has chosen to engage in such an attack."

But Eaton had an attack of his own in mind. It was more mannerly and restrained, but hit the raiders head on. Speaking for the board following the emergency meeting, Eaton produced a hard-edged letter to Kerkorian that totally rejected the bid. He was operating from serious strength. He knew that Bear Stearns had backed out of the deal, fearing that its existing business with Chrysler would disappear. No other financial house appeared ready to ally itself with the raiders, although Chrysler had lined up Salomon Bros. and CS First Boston on its defensive team. Moreover, the UAW, the Chrysler dealer council, and the numerous other large stockholders were standing firm with the management. While automakers like Volkswagen, Mitsubishi, Honda, Fiat, Peugeot-Citroën and even Ford had been bandied about in the press as possible purchasers of Chrysler, Eaton knew full well this was nonsensical hearsay. No other major automaker was in the game. Some believed Kerkorian and Iacocca might be attempting a major bluff, perhaps only with the simple goal of driving up the stock price and thereby raising their equity position. Even this was not working. As the deal appeared to be increasingly hollow, Chrysler's stock prices receded, down $3 on the day Bear Stearns publicly dropped out to sit only a few dollars higher than the low-$40s price it maintained prior to the Kerkorian opening gambit.

The options were clear. If Kerkorian and Iacocca were able to mount a concerted attack, Eaton's carefully marshaled rainy-day account of $7.5 billion would surely be consumed in the struggle. Already credit rating agencies were having another look at the corporation's fragile debt situation and were mumbling about a possible downgrade if the bid materialized. Eaton's announced plans to invest $23 billion in new product development over the next five years would surely be canceled. An Iacocca return to the corporation in any capacity appeared certain to trigger chaos in the management suite. Lutz was known to be openly disdainful of the former chairman's automotive acumen and would surely leave. Eaton, because of Iacocca's intemperate public criticism, might also be a casualty as would Francois Castaing, who was a firm ally of Lutz.

There appeared to be no upside to the bid, no positive aspects to the takeover of a corporation that seemed capable of generating profits of $3–4 billion a year for the foreseeable future; a company being celebrated for excellent management with a long-range vision and the highest per-vehicle profit (estimated at $1,300 versus $650 for Ford and $247 for General Motors) in the American industry. The old Bert Lance homily came to mind: "If it ain't broke, don't fix it."

If there was one sticky point that seemed to justify Kerkorian's intrusion, it was the modest stock price and low $1.60 dividend. While some analysts insisted Chrysler's stock was worth as much as $100 a share, the price was mired at less than half that. Some Wall Streeters fretted that Chrysler's board was too distracted with a cash reserve buildup at the expense of stockholders. If that situation could be corrected, surely any remaining stockholder discomfort would be eliminated and even more of Kerkorian's support — the little that remained — would be diffused. Finally the curious, reclusive billionaire spoke. The son of an immigrant American fruit farmer, and an eighth-grade dropout, he seldom gave interviews and only now responded to the press because he apparently realized his position both financially and personally was about to be totally discredited. On April 26, less than a week following his opening volley, Kerkorian released the text of a cryptic letter he had faxed to Eaton the night before (and which Eaton quickly rejected). He noted that Eaton represented less than 1 percent of the stockholders within the confines of the board of directors. "Many of these people are not even employees," he charged. "We [Tracinda] have been the largest shareholder of the company much longer than you have been CEO. Accordingly, we challenge you and your Board of Directors to permit the shareholders of the company to vote on the following." Kerkorian outlined two demands: Permit a shareholder vote on the sale of the company at $55 a share while answering the question: Do the shareholders alternatively favor an increase in the annual dividend to $5 a share? Kerkorian also noted, "As you know, we never intended this transaction to be hostile. You [Eaton] turned it into a hostile transaction." Kerkorian also responded to the Chrysler charge that he lacked sufficient financing for the takeover. "Chrysler has openly intimidated commercial and investment banks into refusing to discuss the transaction with us. I find it hypocritical on your part when you say you have grave doubts that such financing is feasible." Kerkorian also dismissed Eaton's proposal for increased dividends or share repurchase to boost the price of the stock as "hopelessly vague and noncommittal."

In the letter Kerkorian admitted that he was having trouble obtaining financial backing and conceded that if the shareholders failed to back his proposals, he would withdraw his bid to buy the company. How the shareholders would be polled was unclear. It was too late to place the question before the annual meeting set for May 18 at St. Louis and appeared a hollow gesture. Clearly the man who had made billions in high-dollar Las Vegas real estate and in the motion picture business was overmatched against Chrysler. His play was being covered in Highland Park and now it appeared to be a matter of saving face, rather than redecorating the CEO's office for his pal. In fact, Iacocca was about to undergo a "de-Stalinization" that would have done the old politburo proud. Before the Kerkorian struggle ensued, it was planned that the new fifteen-story executive building being completed adjacent to the CTC would be named for Lee Iacocca. His bronze bust would stand in the lobby. Now word was passed to the press that his name would be excised from the building and his bust relegated to a storage room deep in the basement. He now had no more chance of being honored on future corporate edifices than Benedict Arnold did of appearing on a commemorative postage stamp. The payback of what was considered his betrayal was quick and decisive.

Iacocca's response to all this appeared to be bafflement. Here was a man who less than a decade earlier was among the most recognized and revered Americans. A possible presidential candidate. An earthy immigrant's son who represented the highest aspirations of the American dream. Now, suddenly he was being denounced in hundreds of editorial pages and in countless magazine stories across the nation. He was described as a greedy crackpot who seemed prepared to destroy his former company in the name of raw ego gratification. His popularity plunged and in shocked silence he disappeared from the headlines as quickly as he had reappeared.

While columnists, editorialists, and financial experts argued over whether the entire episode was a game of stock manipulation, overt greenmailing, clever arbitrageur tactics, or a ham-fisted hostile takeover by two addled septuagenarians, Chrysler was also gaining headlines on a variety of other fronts, none of them exactly the kind of stuff Liebler & Co. were dreaming up in the public relations departments.

Automotive News, followed by the *Wall Street Journal* finally sniffed out the reason for the production delays in St. Louis, identifying CMI International and its aluminum castings as the source of trouble. Both publications, soon followed by others, noted that the delays could cost thousands of NSs expected for delivery in the second quarter. Chris Theodore manfully told the *Wall Street Journal* that the difficulties were about resolved. "We're in sync now," he said, all the while maintaining daily contact with Bernie Swanson and his squad of harried trouble-shooters as they hand-signaled their way toward a solution. Production rose in fits and starts toward six hundred units a day, about three hundred off the targeted "ramp-up" pace planned and far from the maximum daily output of 1,150 minivans.

Despite Theodore's brave public statements, the production glitches were beginning to escalate into a major crisis. The March date — extended from the original January startup of volume production — was now past. Swanson's crew was on the verge of a solution, but the unfilled pipeline of dealer inventory was now a problem. With a massive advertising campaign about to break in May, dealer stock would not be adequate to meet demand. Hordes of eager customers surging into showrooms, only to find salesmen desperately hawking outdated ASs with none of the new models in sight, would be a marketing disaster. While it was clear that volume production would finally begin in June, it was impossible to build up minimal dealer stock by May, and a decision was made to postpone the advertising blitz until the fall, when the corporation had already precontracted for hours of prime-time programming and had major positions in both the National Football League and big league baseball schedules.

As Eaton and the board of directors strengthened their defenses, it became apparent by the end of April that Kerkorian's assault had failed — at least in the short term. To be sure, Eaton would reach out to stockholders with more liberal dividends and a more aggressive effort to boost stock prices beyond the mid-40s range where they had languished since the brief Kerkorian/Iacocca sendup. Per-

haps the greatest damage had been inflicted in terms of sheer distraction away from more pressing problems facing the corporation:
the slow launch of the NS, the impending slowdown in the American automobile market after three solid years, the continued attack
by Ford on their precious minivan market, and a potential war
with the United Auto Workers over continued outsourcing of critical parts (triggered in part, by the proposed sale of its McGraw
Glass Division and the rumored divestiture of its Huntsville, Alabama, electronics operation).

Eaton would have to deal directly with the stockholders and
perhaps with Kerkorian face-to-face at the St. Louis annual meeting in mid-May, but until then the takeover challenge seemed to re-
cede. Kerkorian fell silent, as did Iacocca. Clearly shocked over his
public pillorying he disappeared from view, granting no interviews
and surely puzzling over how to resuscitate his ruined image.

In the meantime the minivan had to be brought to market, and
quickly. Swanson and the engineers at CMI were steadily sorting
out the production problems with the aluminum cross-member,
while the master-cylinder O-ring failure (from a fourth-tier outside
supplier) had been solved. Overall, the assembly line at St. Louis
was working reasonably well, with the products pouring off the line
representing the finest quality vehicles ever produced by Chrysler
Corporation. At one point a brutal thunderstorm bombarded the
plant with enormous hailstones, damaging nearly two thousand
new vans parked in the marshaling yards, but beyond the vagaries
of Mother Nature, the minivan seemed a solid bet. The traditional
early summer minivan buying season would be lost. While the paltry supply of NSs were being scooped up as soon as they reached
the dealerships, the volume sales that had been expected — perhaps as many as 300,000 units in a mad binge of hot-weather buying fever — would not happen. Surely this would adversely affect
Chrysler's bottom line for 1995 and would increase criticism of the
management by Kerkorian and his small chorus of allies.

Initial tests and stories about the NS produced rave reviews. Its
smoothness, low wind noise, and vast interior space were celebrated, as were its easily removed seats, its fourth sliding door, and
its tight turning circle. Its superb visibility, its masses of storage

area, its high-output rear air-conditioner, and its slick, carlike handling all received plaudits. *Car and Driver*, noted for its hard-eyed comparison tests, evaluated the NS head-to-head with a Windstar and declared it a clear winner.

In the marketplace, customers crowded showrooms for a first look and paid premium prices for the few thousand that were available. But until more came to market, the dealers and the Chrysler sales experts were more concerned about cleaning out the inventory of aged ASs that still cluttered their lots. Aggressive rebate and leasing programs were instituted, while the massive television campaign remained on hold.

Slowly the legendary AS drifted into oblivion. Production had ceased at St. Louis on February 10, while the last one slipped off the Windsor line on May 18. The final AS/T-115 minivan — the little box that had saved Chrysler — was built at Graz, Austria, on August 11, 1995. It was the 5,147,522nd motor vehicle in a line that would go down in history as one of the most significant of all time.

With the minivans in such scarce supply, individual vehicles were carefully allotted. Major urban dealers' outlets received two each. Smaller dealers got one to employ as a traffic builder and for demonstration rides. Chrysler's so-called turn and earn program — a supply policy that pegged allotments of hot-selling models to the selling rate of each dealership, i.e., the more sold, the more received — would not apply to the NSs until volumes increased. With St. Louis expected to reach maximum volume of 1,100 per day by mid-June and Windsor's conversion going smoother than expected, the NS would become readily available in the late summer. This would be over four months late, despite the cheery statements issuing from Highland Park, but company officials had no choice but to remain optimistic that America's ardor for minivans would not dampen and that the new competition coming from Ford, GM, and the Japanese would still remain off target.

Despite the decline in the auto market and a drop in profits for the first two quarters, Eaton appeared at the annual stockholders meeting a clear winner. He was applauded for his quiet but unyielding stance against Kerkorian and Iacocca (who did not appear). The wisdom of his $7.5 billion rainy-day fund seemed perfect for the moment, amplified by the sluggish market for which it had been created.

He assured the gathering that dividends would be increased to two dollars a share as soon as possible. He was also preparing to announce the establishment of an $8 billion line of credit that would further thwart any takeover bids by Kerkorian and Iacocca. Under the new credit agreement established with a consortium of sixty-one banks led by Chemical Banking, Inc., Chrysler would be barred from raiding any of the $3.3 billion in assets of its own Chrysler Financial Corp. subsidiary in the event any shareholder obtained over 50 percent of its common stock or gained control of its board of directors. It was an artful move to reinforce the "poison pill" takeover defense by a chairman who had risen to his post without major credentials on Wall Street. Fifteen years earlier, Iacocca had employed his legendary charisma to woo suitors in the financial community and in Washington. Now the tables were being turned on him by a quiet man who relied not on showmanship and bluster but deliberate, calculated tactics with the long-range welfare of his company a singular priority.

Eaton was quoted as saying, "I want to be the first chairman in the history of this company who will *not* preside over a 'recovery.'" The reference was clear: Lee Iacocca had bragged that he had led two such comebacks. Eaton was rejecting such roller-coaster tactics in the name of steady, deliberate growth. The contrast between the man and the aged patriarch who had hired him became clearer by the day. Lee Iacocca was the last of the moguls; Eaton was the first of the legitimate "car guys" to lead Chrysler. His successor had wrapped himself in the same mantra for nearly five decades, but it was now revealed as a hopeless charade. Lee Iacocca, in the final tragic days on the public stage, had appeared in the emperor's clothes. In the end he revealed himself as a self-aggrandizing huckster who happened to end up in the automobile business.

Yes, he claimed stewardship of the minivan. Yes, his personal dynamism had saved the corporation in the early 1980s. Yes, he had acquired American Motors — and unwittingly infused his company with new blood and new thinking, which he for the most part rejected. Yes, he had built the elegant Chrysler Technology Center, perhaps in the now-blighted hope that it would become his permanent monument.

But he had resisted changes in management style to the more streamlined and agile platform teams. He had spent flagrant amounts of money on nonautomotive properties and diffused the company's elemental business goal — to sell world-class automobiles. He had governed in the end like a mad king, watching dozens of top executives flee his court as he sought more personal power and glory. Surely Eaton, a soft-spoken Kansan, whose claim to a common grassroots American birthright was as legitimate as Iacocca's endless bleat about his immigrant Italian background, solidified his position as chairman. He could no doubt recall the early days; the grand finale at Las Vegas when the great man — the last mogul — stepped regally off his throne. It had been pomp and artifice of the first order. A perfect moment of corporate theatrics for industry's greatest performer.

The irony that Iacocca had chosen to attempt a comeback at the very moment the new minivan was coming to market was inescapable. While Chrysler was once again reinventing itself — this time hopefully with a sense of permanency — Iacocca had attempted the same thing. It had worked before, but now the act was tired and shabbily self-serving. Circumstances had been sufficiently altered within Chrysler — and the world of big business — to a point where flashy, shoot-the-moon high-rollers like Iacocca and his pal Kerkorian bordered on the irrelevant and the faintly ludicrous. The king was dead, this time for good.

There was peace in the valley, at least for a short term. Much in the way of challenges lay ahead. Three to four million NSs would have to be sold over the next six years. Other new models would have to be designed. Corporate quality levels demanded more improvement. Development time had to be reduced. The corporation's financial reputation needed more polishing. Young lions like Theodore and Edson would wrestle for power as their claim of bringing the NS to market essentially on time and more importantly on budget would be measured against their rivals on other teams, building other models. Kerkorian would no doubt be heard from again, if for no other reason than to save face, and Ford would remain relentless and resolute in their bid to become number one in the world of minivans. There was no beginning and no end in the automobile business, only blurred transitions from one perilous adventure to another. In the case of the NS, the wondrous little box that formed the cornerstone of Chrysler, it had at least opened with a hopeful first act. That was all that could be expected in the biggest, wildest business of them all.

14

The End of the Beginning

B Y AUTO mogul standards, Chairman Robert Eaton's office was little more than a large, bare room. As the first clouds of autumn 1995 began to scud across Detroit's skies, he greeted a visitor in his corner office on the fifth floor of the aged K. T. Keller Building and bemusedly pointed out a large crack in one of the beige-painted walls. If not a symbol of Eaton's spare, no-nonsense administrative style, the crack at least represented imminent change and high hopes for the corporation he headed.

Come January 1996, he and his entire staff were scheduled to move en masse to the new fifteen-story executive office building in Auburn Hills — now renamed Chrysler World Headquarters following the exorcism of Lee Iacocca's name from above the door. The Keller Building, once the headquarters of long-forgotten Maxwell and Chalmers, but two of the nearly five thousand American-made automobile brands that had died early deaths over the last century, was soon to be torn down along with most of the Highland Park structures that once served as Chrysler's home base. Only the Walter P. Chrysler Building and the company's extensive dynamometer facility were to avoid the wrecker's ball, leaving the city with yet more vacant acreage as a monument to a downsized automobile industry. Eaton was in an expansive mood. In the broad scheme of things, the future looked bright for Chrysler. He was pleased with the launch of the minivan, despite the delay. "It was one of our smoothest launches yet," he said, fully aware that projects of such complexity never work exactly as planned. He evidenced no concern, often expressed by some auto analysts, that the

public fascination with minivans had waned in favor of the booming sport-utility market. "Chrysler has traditionally been the most
cyclical company in the most cyclical industry," he said, vowing to
maintain a steady course and not chase trends. "We think the minivan market will grow and we'll seek niches in the overall market,
perhaps with smaller versions, perhaps higher-performance models. This is a value-conscious decade. The weakness in the luxury
car market is an indication of that. Minivans embody tremendous
value, especially now that they are being accepted in all market
segments."

He had reason to be optimistic. FMR Corporation, the parent of
giant Fidelity Investments, had recently nearly doubled its stake in
Chrysler to 48.3 million shares, making it the second-largest single
stockholder, next to Kirk Kerkorian. Fidelity's share was now 13
percent of the common stock, a few million short of Kerkorian's
13.6 percent and was greeted with open arms by Eaton and his
board, who viewed the purchase as yet another roadblock to the
Las Vegas threat. Clearly Eaton considered Fidelity as an ally
against any further mischief Kerkorian had in mind. And what of
the reclusive billionaire?

"He's an enigma. A one-man band. He moves his people around
and you seldom deal with the same person twice. We know one
thing: The game isn't over. If this was a baseball game, I'd consider
us in the fourth inning," he said, his expression darkening. He
spoke little of the man who had hired him and who he replaced
in the CEO's office. "I'm not sure what [Iacocca's] game is. He and
Kerkorian probably reinforced each other in the beginning. He was
in town recently, talking about converting the old Hudson Building into a gambling casino," Eaton said, shaking his head in
bafflement.

The general sense of optimism rose from a number of sources,
despite the corporation's sag in earnings during the first half of
1995 ($727 million, down $1.1 billion from the boom year of
1994). The losses were attributable to a number of factors, including the cost of the NS launch and higher incentives and promotion
to unload the remaining ASs. But in general the financial community remained bullish about Chrysler, predicting that its stock

prices would rise to the $60 range in 1996, based on the impend-
ing success of the minivan.

The delay in the May advertising launch was a blessing in disguise. Now the brands could be introduced during the NFL football
games and in pre-contracted evening prime time network shows
when the viewership was vastly larger than in the spring. Bozell
would remain true to its original Plymouth concept and its tagline
("The Next Generation of Minivan"). BBD&O's plan for Dodge
("As Original as the Original") was unchanged as well, although a
heavier emphasis would be placed on print than for Chrysler and
Plymouth. As intended, sticker prices remained at the same level as
the AS. *Automotive News* estimated that prices were up an average
of $144, or only 0.72 percent.

The St. Louis assembly line was completely up to speed, as was
that in Windsor. Both were punching out over a thousand minivans
per day, with a smaller-than-expected level of demerits. Quality
seemed high, although a "Fast Feedback" tracking system, using
inputs from the vans placed in the Dollar Rent-A-Car fleet in
Florida and from early customers revealed wind noise around the
fourth door and some loose interior trim items. Also looming in the
background was the unending saga of the AS and T-115 lift-gate
latches. Chrysler was rushing to have redesigned latches in the
hands of the public by October as the government increased the
pressure, threatening a full recall, while members of the safety
community demanded release of NHTSA video tapes that purported to prove the existing latches failed in crash tests. It was an
issue that, like a chronic toothache, refused to go away.

Inevitably, it became a lawyers' game. Seven major class-action
suits (six in California, one federal) were filed as Chrysler faced two
dilemmas: customer indifference and supplier problems. It was apparent that the latches were a nonissue with a majority of minivan
owners. Yet Chrysler had agreed to replace 60 percent — or about
2.5 million — latches to conform to the government agreement.
That meant inducing, cajoling, bamboozling, or otherwise attracting the owners into the dealerships for the free parts replacement.
Moreover, Dura Automotive Systems, the firm contracted to manufacture the electric rear latch, was laboring to get up to speed with

production. "It took us fifteen years to build four million minivans, now it was up to us to match that number with a warranty program in less than a year," said a company service representative. "It was a nearly impossible assignment."

On December 8, the corporation reached a U.S. District Court settlement in San Francisco that Chrysler would do its best during calendar year 1996 to replace the required 60 percent of the latches or spend $14 million on consumer awareness programs to improve the rate of replacement. Chrysler instructed its dealers to, if necessary, replace the electric latches with manual versions temporarily and then make a second switch when the electrics became available.

The Center for Auto Safety and other Washington-based consumer safety pressure groups, most of whom were closely aligned with the American Trial Lawyers Association, screamed foul and threatened an appeal. The lawyers representing the class-action plaintiffs were soothed with a $5 million payoff and were comforted by the court ruling that Chrysler was still liable for claims of personal injury or wrongful death. In all, there was little question that the issue of the minivan latches would linger in the American legal system for years to come.

Eaton was only too aware of these threats: the latch and the government, the continued Kerkorian assault, the new competition from other companies seeking his minivan market, the nagging need to increase quality, plus a mass of unseen challenges that were sure to rise up. "I have a saying that I think is true," he said. "Whoever has the most problems and *solves them*, wins."

A few doors down from Eaton's along the hushed hall of Mahogany Row, Bob Lutz held court, a foot-long cigar in hand. The chromed cylinder head of the straight-8 Atlantic show car that dazzled the audiences from coast to coast lay on the carpeted floor, next to his prized Lamborghini engine. He spoke expansively about his newest toys, an Italian-bodied 1950s-vintage Cunningham coupe with a Chrysler V8 that he drove in vintage sports car events and his Czech-built Aero L-39C Albatross jet fighter trainer. "I keep it at Willow Run. After work I jump in it and do some aerobatics, then a few touch-and-goes, and put it away. It's a great way to relax."

He too was pleased with the minivan launch, and discounted the delay as part of the business. "The amazing thing is we're selling nearly 100 percent four-doors. People want the extra door, just as we expected. As I said, when was the last time you saw a three-door sedan? Better yet, we're attracting a whole new breed of minivan customer, younger, more affluent, better educated, with household incomes over one hundred thousand dollars. The old AS was an appliance. The NS is fun to drive while being sensible. The whole minivan concept is going to enjoy a steady expansion in the market."

When asked about the threat to Chrysler's share of the market by Ford and General Motors, among others, Lutz's square jaw firmed up and his expression darkened. "We're looking for sales, not shares," he said. "We want to sell our 600,000 minivans and not worry about what share of the market that encompasses. We'll be very happy if demand exceeds supply, which is the opposite of the thinking in this town. I can remember when Lee would say, 'We're within a couple of points of beating Ford's Explorer with Grand Cherokee so let's throw a thousand-dollar rebate out there and catch 'em.' We'd give away a thousand bucks on each vehicle that was selling perfectly well for nothing but management glory. No more. No more incentives simply to increase volume for market share."

An early supporter of platform teams, Lutz remained committed to the concept. He talked expansively of the company's quickened pace in developing new products, its advanced computer programming, its improved crash simulations, its target of producing all-new vehicles in under thirty months. He discounted concerns about the platform teams ossifying into horizontal chimneys. "We'll move people around, it's that simple. Francois's [Castaing] Tech Clubs, which bring together engineers from all the teams and permit them to maintain a constant flow of information, will prevent that. The platform teams work and they're here to stay. We want that cross-breeding, even as the company slowly shifts half our volume to trucks, including the minivans. In the future we'll continue to have three truck platform teams and two car teams. That's where this company is headed."

While the leaders of the corporation could begin to breath easier about the entire NS project, Chris Theodore and his team at CTC remained hard at it; heads-down and totally occupied with the project. He had moved into a newer home with Tracy and had changed radio stations on his morning drive. All of Michigan had been plunged into mourning when the much-loved J. P. McCarthy had died suddenly, in early August from a rare blood disease. Otherwise little had changed at CTC, where the early warranty claims and feedback from new owners confirmed the wind noises and squeaks around the fourth door and inconsistent fit on both interior and exterior trim. These flaws demanded correction if any progress was to be made in the poor J. D. Power ratings that besieged the company. The government's latch issue, which Theodore still believed was a bum rap, would not go away, and while the NS was being celebrated in showrooms and in the press as the best minivan in the world, there was no time to ease up at the CTC.

The accolades were widespread and overtly enthusiastic. In addition to literally hundreds of positive road tests and reviews in daily papers and in major monthly magazines, the NS was awarded *Motor Trend*'s "Car of the Year" — the most visible and coveted of the various year-end trophies offered to the industry. *Car and Driver* countered by including the minivan in its "10 Best" listing, while *Automobile* and *Road & Track* offered it unstinting praise. Both *Popular Science* and *Popular Mechanics* singled out the minivan for recognition as well. In the marketplace, the vehicles were gobbled up at a furious rate, with the public's demand for the fourth door surprising even the most optimistic of the team members. Dick Winter, the team's chief product planner and a major supporter of the extra door, was amazed to discover that more than 90 percent of the NS customers were demanding the left-side door as well as seeking the higher-priced (and higher-profit) Caravans, Voyagers, and in particular the luxurious Chrysler Town & Country. Demand for the fourth door was so strong, in fact, that senior management decided to shift production to 100 percent fourth-door models. Three-door models would be sold on a special-order basis, but the overwhelming — and somewhat shocking — acceptance of the fourth door doomed the older configuration. It further amplified the major tactical error committed by Ford and its three-door Windstar. But there was little time for celebration. General Motors was known to be readying its 1997 minivan, complete with a fourth door and what was expected to be interior space and convenience elements that would rival the NS. So too for Toyota and Nissan, both of whom would surely come to market with better versions than their past efforts. Overall, the industry was acknowledging that Chrysler's box was perfectly sized and that attempts to reinvent the minivan were doomed to failure. Imitation being the sincerest form of flattery was only superficially comforting to Theodore's team. They fully understood that the days of the free ride were over and that minivan clones were on the way from a number of quarters that were bound to steal sales. As the market share for NS zoomed upward toward 48 percent by the end of 1995, the team at Auburn Hills knew fully well that there was precious little time to savor their victory and that the battle would soon begin again with even more intensity.

Tom Edson had already accelerated the meetings of his Fab Five Committee, now assigned to long-range planning for the next permutations of the NS. There being no stability in the automobile business, no opportunity to sit back and wait for a given product to mature before beginning a new model, the "Fab Five" (actually six) — Edson, Frank Sanders, Tom Norman (who had replaced Peter Rosenfeld, who had been promoted to international operations and reported directly to Francois Castaing), Eurostar's Chip Sestok, planner Dennis Malecki, and manufacturing specialist Les Wolfe were meeting regularly to discuss feasibility for new variations on the NS theme. Thanks to the more than $2 billion the corporation had committed to new engines and transmissions in the immediate future, they were able to consider lighter, more powerful, more fuel efficient powertrains as areas for improvement. New materials were on their wish list. Chrysler was, like the rest of the industry, on a weight saving campaign, with aluminum and numerous types of plastics ready to replace steel in the basic body structures. Later models of the NS would be lighter, quieter, faster, more nimble, and more laden with convenience items — provided the intended designs passed Sanders's hard-eyed evaluations regarding cost containment.

Bernie Swanson's suspension group was hard at work on an all-wheel-drive version of the NS, which had initially been tabled because of cost considerations. The connection of the rear wheels to the drive-train to enhance traction was a tricky and expensive undertaking to reach a limited market. But in keeping with the team's philosophy to offer an NS model for virtually every application, Swanson's team moved ahead with the design. Undue rear-end noise was discovered that would slow progress, but plans remained in place to offer AWD as an option during the 1997 model year.

The original members remained essentially in place, save for Rosenfeld's promotion and electrical engineer Cindy Hess's transfer to the large car team — a move prompted by the ongoing policy to maintain an interchange of top engineers between the various teams. Rich Schaum, who had headed the powertrain team, had earlier been promoted to head the Jeep/Truck platform team, but otherwise most of the key players were unchanged. Surely other promotions — and demotions — lay in the future, based on individual successes and failures in the NS program.

It was too early to tell, long-term, who had won and who had lost in the management performance evaluations that determined individual fates. On the surface, it appeared as if they had all done yeoman duty, but surely some had failed to live up to expectations and would fall by the wayside. Others — seemingly including the key operatives like Theodore, Edson, Rushwin, Sanders, and Winter — had been stalwarts. They had plunged into the project and worked together as Castaing and the creators of the cross-functional teams had envisioned. They had endured long hours, enormous pressure, and the constant specter of disaster on a variety of fronts. In the short term, at least, success was theirs.

In early September 1995, the wily Kerkorian played another card — an ace. He hired ex-Chrysler chief financial officer Jerome "Jerry" York away from IBM (where he had enjoyed success in a similar role) and positioned him as the point man to marshal support within the financial community to continue his takeover bid. The strategy was clear. York was respected as a hard-nosed numbers man who had brought IBM back to fiscal solvency after leaving Chrysler in 1993. It had been York who, during Chrysler's last major crisis in 1989/90, had created a consortium of major banks to continue a line of credit to the corporation's dealer body. A West Pointer, York espoused military bearing and a no-nonsense approach to business. It was apparent that he might be able to establish an alliance between Kerkorian, Fidelity, and other major shareholders to seize control of the company. It seemed a foregone conclusion that Kerkorian would seek a seat for York on the Chrysler board of directors, giving him a man in court with enormous clout and experience.

Should York succeed in establishing a foothold large enough to permit Kerkorian and his financial allies to take over Chrysler, the portent was obvious: The "car guys," the Eatons and Lutzes, the Gales, Castaings, and Theodores, would be driven from power. Yet another industrial giant would tumble into the hands of people who cared more about the bottom line than about what makes a proper automobile and why people buy them. For too many years the Yorks had dominated the Detroit industry and had brought it to the very brink of oblivion while its great rivals in Japan and Germany had concentrated on *product*, before *profit*. Such a change of course for Chrysler, just now shedding its reputation for shoddy products, would doom it to fall back into the pit. Surely Kerkorian would drive up the numbers short-term: The dividends, the profits, the stock prices, and the Wall Street celebration would be lusty — and brief. As the drive for the bottom line accelerated, costs would be slashed — especially if York succeeded in replacing Eaton as CEO. Both product development and quality would surely suffer.

York had increased profits at IBM without being conversant with the computer industry. Said a longtime IBM veteran who had left the company in the early 1980s to become a multimillionaire manufacturer of computer components on a worldwide basis, "York gutted IBM's research and development and new product programs. Wall Street loves him now, but when IBM comes up short in the future in terms of new product, his image will change. These money guys never learn." The memory of Alfred P. Sloan, the legendary CEO of General Motors, lingered. Sloan was the quintessential finance expert in the automobile industry. It was he who had observed in the 1930s, "General Motors is not in the business of making automobiles. It is in the business of making money." This theme had driven Detroit's Big Three until the late 1980s, and if there was a primary lesson to be learned from the Chrysler experience — and in a more limited way from a revived Ford — it was that men with hard knowledge about product were the key to success in the new world market. Men like Eaton and Lutz represented the future; Jerome York and the narrow-band, profit-at-all-cost Wall Street money manager's philosophy represented the mustiest of anachronisms.

The dispute shifted slightly in Chrysler's favor when in September the board of directors doubled the stock buyback program to $2 billion, pumping the price of common stock to nearly $58 a share. A Kerkorian spokesman grumped publicly that the move was a "tiny step in the right direction" while the *Wall Street Journal* reported that Kerkorian had lured York away from IBM with a cash payment of $25 million and further incentives that could total more millions based on Chrysler's stock performance. It was during the same meeting that the Chrysler board continued its revenge against Lee Iacocca by rejecting his bid to exercise his stock options of $44.4 million. This would trigger a lawsuit by the former chairman, which Chrysler countered with litigation accusing Iacocca of transferring confidential and proprietary corporate intelligence to Kerkorian as early as 1989. This firefight only amplified the total disintegration of the relationship between Iacocca and his former associates and promised to drag on in a mire of legal maneuvering for years to come.

Lee Iacocca steadily faded from the front lines in the Tracinda attack as Jerry York took up the vanguard. He began sniping in the press that the board of directors was hoarding too much cash and thereby shortchanging the stockholders. He demanded Tracinda representation on the board of directors. Eaton fought back, noting that "I don't want a Las Vegas gambler running Chrysler." When asked if he thought York was qualified to run the company, he answered with a sharp "no." In a speech to major Wall Street investors, Eaton described Kerkorian as a "big negative" who was not good for either the company or its stockholders. He noted that since the battle for control had begun, Chrysler's stock had risen only 12 percent while GM's had jumped by 29 percent. This position was reinforced publicly in a series of national print ads that warned that Chrysler's "momentum might be threatened" by continued interference of Tracinda and its agents.

The struggle escalated in November 1995 when Joseph Antonini, the recently deposed CEO of Kmart, resigned from Chrysler's board. As expected, Kerkorian demanded that he be replaced by Jerry York. Kerkorian outlined four demands: (1) York on the board, (2) the addition of two extra seats on the board, (3) raising the poison pill antitakeover from 15^d to 20 percent of common stock (thereby opening the door for Kerkorian to take an overwhelming shareholder position), and (4) an independent committee to review the corporate finances, presumably to support the Tracinda demand for a $2 billion annual buyback of stock to enhance shareholder value. While Eaton made no public response, it was clear that he would resist the demands although it might be impossible to keep York from banging on the door forever. With a proxy fight possible, Kerkorian and his raiders seemed destined to remain in the game for the foreseeable future.

In the meantime, beyond the sniping between Las Vegas and Highland Park, the NS was booming. Its November share of market soared to 48 percent of all minivans sold, while Windstar sales plummeted 21 percent over the year before. Supplies of the Ford product ballooned to 100 days (60 days of inventory is considered satisfactory; anything beyond that become surplus). The Oakville, Ontario, plant was idled periodically to let demand catch up with supply. It was obvious that Ford had committed a major strategic blunder by omitting the fourth door. Ed Hagenlocker, the president of Ford Automotive Operations, defended the decision by noting that their buyer surveys indicated only one-third of their prospective customers had expressed a desire for a left-side opening. He then admitted, "But clearly there's a market."

With all three NS assembly plants now running full tilt — Graz had come on line without problems in late September and was expected to produce its budgeted 55,000 units annually — the

NS seemed to have a clear road ahead. Then in November the corporation announced that it was recalling 20,000 units from Windsor to replace rear seat-mounting bolts. A supplier mix-up had permitted bolts of lower strength than specified to be installed. Rather than risk breakage in a collision, the vehicles were recalled to install proper capacity bolts. A month later a fuel leak was identified. It had been discovered that an NS, its tank topped up with gasoline and parked on an incline, might leak. This was corrected with a new gasket for the fuel filter neck and a grounding strap to prevent static electricity from causing a fire. The corporation notified all dealers to hold any unsold vans until the fixes could be made. The dealers were reimbursed for losses in floor-planning (the interest paid on inventory) until the repairs were completed.

The two recalls had little or no effect on sales. As the year ended, 249,310 NS minivans had been sold (in addition to 214,257 of the now departed AS). Demand remained brisk, especially for the fourth door, well-optioned Dodge and Plymouth brands. Better yet, the luxurious Chrysler Town & Country was a major success, surprising even its most ardent supporters with its acceptance among upscale purchasers. Problems centered not on demand, but on supply of specific models. It was apparent early in the production cycle that the low-line, short-wheelbase, three-door models generated little interest. The midline Dodge and Plymouth models — priced in the $22,000 range and equipped with the fourth door, rear twin buckets (called "quad seating"), and other options were clearly the volume sellers. But they remained in short supply, as did rear air-conditioning. As stocks of the three-door models piled up in dealers' lots, the dealers began screaming about shortages of the hot-selling four-door models. Many complained that the corporation was slow to recognize this major shift in the market and therefore lost considerable volume during the late summer and fall selling season. Those complaints were corrected in the relatively short term, although the fevered demand for the fourth door shocked even its most ardent supporters. Fears that the NS might falter in the face of a baby-boomer abandonment to sport-utility vehicles were unfounded.

So too were rumors that swirled throughout the industry that Chrysler would ally itself with Volvo or Mercedes-Benz in a defensive move to fend off Kerkorian. Eaton and his board would stand alone, ready to wage the ongoing car wars with a solid product lineup and conservative fiscal policies. He understood that the seesaw world of the international car business would not change. The winners of today were the potential losers of tomorrow. Auto men like Eaton and Lutz understood history. They remembered the 1980s, when the Japanese appeared superhuman and destined to dominate the industry. They too recalled Ford's being celebrated as a superpower as recently as 1993 — before its Contour, Windstar, and, most recently, its flashy new Taurus, received tepid receptions from the public. They knew that the current success of the NS offered no assurances for the future. The reality was ever shifting. The tastes of the public were impossible to divine. Nothing was guaranteed other than more surprises, more challenges, more crises.

Already revitalized and more pugnacious United Auto Workers leadership was speaking of Chrysler as a new target. The union had given concessions to the company during its years of difficulties, but now was eyeing Eaton's $7.5 billion kitty with the same lust as Kerkorian and York. It was time, said the union, for payback for the sacrifices the workers made over the last decade. The threat of a future strike was openly suggested. The irony was palpable; Eaton had tried to protect his shareholders and his workforce from external threats like recession, market shifts, and natural disasters. But now the very same groups he hoped to insulate from trouble were seeking to raid their own safety net. The annual report, issued on January 20, 1996, left the issue unresolved. Thanks to strong fourth-quarter earnings of $1.04 billion — boosted by minivan sales that were up 26 percent over the year before — Chrysler's yearly net earnings were $2.03 billion on gross sales of $53.2 billion. Stockholders made $5.30 a share, well beyond Wall Street's expectations but a figure surely to raise more protests for revenue sharing from the Tracinda crowd and additional cries for higher wages from the United Auto Workers.

Almost simultaneously General Motors released details of its new minivan, first to be introduced in Europe as the Opel Sintra and later in the United States as the Chevrolet Venture, Pontiac Trans Sport, and Oldsmobile Silhouette. As expected, the new vehicles would ape the NS by offering both an optional left-side door and long- and short-wheelbase models. They were acknowledged by Theodore and the team as legitimate contenders.

Still, the corporation appeared to be in solid shape within the minivan market for some time to come. The product was unequaled and there was enormous name recognition among the general public and a feverishly loyal owner body.

Despite Chrysler's income drop, 1995 was its third best year in history. It remained a highly profitable and well run company. Some analysts maintained that it held as much as $500 per vehicle profit advantage over Ford and General Motors, in the main because over 60 percent of its production was concentrated on trucks and minivans, which in general enjoyed higher margins than comparable passenger cars. The good news only increased the demand from Kerkorian and the UAW to split the pot.

The union issue would have to wait until the end of the current contract later in 1996, but the Kerkorian toothache would not go away. The two sides butted heads publicly through the New Year's holiday with little sign of a compromise. Kerkorian and York continued to threaten a proxy fight at the annual meeting in May 1996 unless York was given a seat on the board of directors. Moreover, the Tracinda directors demanded the creation of an outside committee to review the corporation's cash management policies (with the specific mission of handing over more money to the shareholders) and raising the so-called poison pill trigger from 15 to 20 percent for any given takeover threat. None of this was acceptable to Eaton, who was adamant that the divisive and combative York be kept off the board.

Clearly the situation had to be resolved. Wall Street was becoming restless and the long-term stability of the corporation was being threatened. Quiet, private negotiations began in Beverly Hills in late December when Eaton and Kerkorian sat down for the first time to personally deal with the problem. Further meetings, headed by Chrysler vice chairman Tom Denomme and Tracinda's York, were held in New York. There seemed to be little room for compromise. York continued his public criticism aimed at Chrysler's slumping car sales — but ignoring its tremendous strength in minivans, trucks, and sport-utilities, which were the fastest growing market segments — while Tracinda made formal moves toward a proxy fight. Eaton on the other hand remained adamant that York would not sit on his board.

In the end it was the two leaders who settled the issue. During a series of phone calls in mid-January 1996, Eaton and Kerkorian reached a deal. It was, in a broad-brush sense, tit-for-tat: Chrysler would buy additional shares in return for an end to the proxy fight. The details, announced on February 9, stated that Kerkorian would agree to a five-year standdown in any dealings with Chrysler. This meant no proxy fight, no takeover bids, and no increase in his shares of stock. In return, Chrysler agreed to add Tracinda executive James Aljian (but not York) to the board of directors and to begin an immediate $2 billion stock buyback with an additional $1 billion set for 1997.

As a footnote to the deal, another board member was added: financial manager John Neff, who had controlled Windsor and Gemini Mutual Funds' 14.8 million Chrysler shares. And Lee Iacocca was to receive his held-up retirement money. Chrysler would pay him $23 million while Tracinda agreed to add another $32 million to settle all claims and suits. Iacocca in turn consented to quit as a Tracinda consultant. Adding insult to injury, the Chrysler board announced that it was waiving the mandatory sixty-five-year-old retirement policy in the case of Bob Lutz, permitting him to remain on board for at least another four years. This had to be particularly rankling to Iacocca. Not only had he been literally shoved out the door on his sixty-fifth birthday, but he had served as the primary roadblock for Lutz to succeed him. Surely this was the final blow in the destruction of the Iacocca image at Chrysler.

As the meanest, coldest winter in decades continued to lash the nation, Chrysler announced $500 discounts on its entire lineup of vehicles except for the minivan and the low-selling Viper sports car.

The exclusion of the minivan from the pump-priming tactic so common in the industry was a major affirmation of the vehicle's appeal.

If one truth had been revealed by the turmoil and expense of the NS program, it was the viability of the cross-functional platform team. Chris Theodore and his little cadre had done it right. Left to their own devices, relying on their own instincts, they had brought the NS to market essentially on time and within budget. Better yet, they had created a quality vehicle that met the needs of its consumers. But as the sales escalated and the awards poured in (The North American Car of the Year, awarded at the 1996 North American International Automobile Show), no one stopped to celebrate. There was no time.

As sales of the NS soared, Chris Theodore was transferred to run the small-car platform team, which had produced the Neon and was now locked in a struggle with GM's Cavalier, Ford's Escort, and a fleet of Japanese rivals for a share of the intensely competitive economy car market. Theodore was to be joined by old NS teammates Tom Edson and Ernie Laginess as he moved to the fourth floor of the CTC and a major new challenge. Theodore was also given the assignment to continue development of the Viper sports car.

There were other changes. Jack Kerby and Herm Greif, both thirty-year veterans at Chrysler, retired with honors. At the top level Ted Cunningham, the vice president who had served as "Godfather" for the minivan team, was reassigned as the executive in charge of the corporation's Mexico operation — a move some industry insiders considered as punishment for the less-than-perfect launch of the NS. He was to be replaced by supply chief Tom Stallcamp, while engineer Gordon Renschauer, transferred from the large-car platform team, where he had been a powertrain specialist, took Theodore's place as NS team leader. Other personnel moves, some up, some down, some inconclusively lateral, continued. There was no stasis, no stability, no status quo in the everchanging battlefield called the automobile industry. New men, new machines, new customers, new surprises would arrive with the inevitability of Michigan's vivid four seasons. Only the most astute, the most nimble, and perhaps the most lucky would survive. As the new year began, Chrysler Corporation appeared to be among the anointed. How long the blessing would remain was beyond guesswork.

The war continued.

Index